Following the theoretical perspective of his earlier book, *Ceramic theory and cultural process* (1985), Dean Arnold's ethnoarchaeological study explores the relationships of ceramic production to society and its environment in the Peruvian Andes. The book traces these contemporary linkages through the production, decoration and use of pottery and relates them to the analysis and interpretation of ancient ceramic production. Utilizing an ecological approach within a single community, Arnold expands the scope of previous ceramic theory by focusing on the population as the unit of analysis in production and decoration.

Ecology and ceramic production in an Andean community

NEW STUDIES IN ARCHAEOLOGY

Series editors

Colin Renfrew, *University of Cambridge*
Jeremy Sabloff, *University of Pittsburgh*

DEAN E. ARNOLD *Wheaton College, Wheaton, Illinois*

Ecology and ceramic production in an Andean community

CAMBRIDGE
UNIVERSITY PRESS

Published by the Press Syndicate of the University of Cambridge
The Pitt Building, Trumpington Street, Cambridge CB2 1RP
40 West 20th Street, New York, NY 10011–4211, USA
10 Stamford Road, Oakleigh, Victoria 3166, Australia

First published 1993

Printed in Great Britain at the University Press, Cambridge

A catalogue record for this book is available from the British Library

Library of Congress cataloguing in publication data

Arnold, Dean E., 1942–
Ecology and ceramic production in an Andean community /
Dean E. Arnold
     p.   cm. – (New studies in archaeology)
Includes bibliographical references.
ISBN 0 521 43289 8 (hardback)
1. Indians of South America – Peru – Quinua (Huamanga) – Pottery.
2. Indians of South America – Peru – Ayacucho (Dept.) – Antiquities.
3. Ayacucho (Peru: Dept.) – Antiquities. 4. Man – Influence of
environment – Peru – Quinua (Huamanga). 5. Peru – Antiquities.
I. Title. II. Series.
F3429.1Q85A76 1993
985'.292 – dc20   92–34658   CIP

ISBN 0 521 43289 8 hardback

WD

To my daughters,
Michelle and Andrea,
who with my wife are the loves of my life

CONTENTS

FIGURES

TABLES

ACKNOWLEDGEMENTS

Field work in Quinua was supported by an NDFL Title VI Fellowship and the Department of Anthropology of the University of Illinois, Urbana. I am grateful to the United States Office of Education for permitting me to use the Fellowship in Peru even though it was not normally awarded for research abroad. Mamerto Sanchez C. provided gracious hospitality in Quinua. To him and other Quinua potters (such as Victor Sanchez and Juan Rojas), I express my appreciation for their cooperation and kindness. William P. Mitchell generously shared his facilities with me in Quinua and has been especially helpful and generous with data that have made this book possible. B. F. Bohor of the Illinois State Geological Survey ran the X-ray diffraction analyses of the ceramic raw materials and interpreted the results of these analyses. I am also grateful to R. T. Zuidema and especially the late D. W. Lathrap for their guidance, encouragement and support which made the field work possible. Rich Nickel, Michael Anderson, Delores Ralph Yaccino, and Dawn Stultz produced many of the drawings. Melinda Korell, Pauline Roelofs and Delores Ralph Yaccino provided typing and editing assistance, and Alva Steffler and Rose Graham made some of the high contrast photostats used for publication. My research assistants over the years, Prudence Rice, Ruth Ann O'Connell, Laura Montgomery, Dan Gross, Delores Ralph Yaccino, Lori Hughey and Charles Shrack, worked on some of the data at various stages of the analysis and provided bibliographic assistance. The late Gary Vescelius lent an aerial photograph produced by Fotoservicio Aereofotográfico Nacional, Lima. Margaret Hardin, Dorothy Washburn and James Vreeland provided encouragement for the development of the design portion of this work. Michael O. Dillon of the Field Museum provided botanical names for some of the wild plants used to fire pottery by narrowing the list of botanical names found in Towle (1961) and Soukup (1970).

The Research Office of the College of Liberal Arts of the Pennsylvania State University provided funds for preparing some of the illustrations for publication. The Department of Sociology and Anthropology of Wheaton College, the Wheaton College Faculty Development Fund, the Wheaton College Aldeen Fund and the Wheaton College Alumni Association all provided support for the preparation of the present manuscript. I also wish to express my appreciation to the Governing Body of Clare Hall, Cambridge, for a Visiting Fellowship there during the first six months of 1985 in order to continue work on this manuscript. Ian Hodder and the Department of Archaeology in Cambridge provided much intellectual stimulation and a quiet place to work. A return to Cambridge in 1992 brought this work to conclusion and I am grateful to the Governing Body of Clare Hall, Sander Van der Leeuw, Ian Hodder and Paul Mellars for their hospitality. Warren DeBoer, David Browman, Brian Bauer, William P. Mitchell, Charles C. Kolb, Tim Murray, Sander Van der Leeuw, Bill Sillar and two anonymous reviewers provided helpful criticism that improved the final form of this work considerably. My parents, Mr. and Mrs. Eldon E. Arnold, have provided constant concern, support and encouragement for me. Finally, my wife, more than anyone, has provided editorial assistance and helped me see this project to its completion.

I also thank the Anthropos Institut, the Institute of Archaeology of UCLA and the editor of *Current Anthropology* for permission to reproduce previously copyrighted material. Figures 5.27 and 2.14 were originally published as figure 2, p. 863, and as plate f between pp. 864–865 in "Native pottery making in Quinua, Peru" by Dean E. Arnold, *Anthropos*, 67 (1972). Figures 7.15(a)–(c) were originally published as figure 6, pp. 151–153 in "Social interaction and ceramic design: community-wide correlates in Quinua, Peru" by Dean E. Arnold in Prudence Rice (ed.), *Pots and Potters: Current approaches in ceramic archaeology*, pp. 133–161, Monograph XXIV, Institute of Archaeology, University of California, Los Angeles, 1984. Figures 2.7, 2.8, and 4.2 were originally published as figure 3, p. 185, figure 4, p. 186 and figure 6, p. 189 in "Ceramic Ecology in the Ayacucho Basin, Peru: implications for prehistory" by Dean E. Arnold in *Current Anthropology*, 16: 2 (1975). R. T. Zuidema provided photocopies of two historical documents about Quinua which are found in the National Archives of Peru.

Ann Kraft, Michelle Shannon, Sara Czarnecki, Lori Hughey, Charles Shrack, Pat Popuvac, Tracy Smith and Amy Jo Inniger helped prepare the index.

PREFACE

The field work for this book occurred between February and July, 1967 when I lived in the village of Quinua, Department of Ayacucho, Peru. I went to Peru to work with Dr. R. T. Zuidema who had been newly appointed to the faculty of the Department of Anthropology at the University of Illinois, Urbana. Dr. Zuidema was then teaching at the University of Huamanga in Ayacucho and supervised graduate students who were doing research in the Ayacucho area during his last semester there. Several graduate students were involved in this program, but each had his/her own research project in cultural anthropology and/or archaeology.

My original purpose in going to Ayacucho was to obtain comparative data for my ethnographic research in Yucatan which I had carried out in 1965 and 1966. Just before I left for Peru, I had completed a master's thesis relating the selection and use of ceramic raw materials in Mexico to Maya Blue, a unique blue pigment used by the ancient Maya. Blue was the color of sacrifice for the ancient Maya and was used on figurines and ceramic offering vessels. Human sacrificial victims were also painted blue before their beating hearts were ripped out on the sacrificial altar at the Temple of the Warriors at Chichén Itzá. The composition of this blue pigment had been a mystery until the late 1960s when it was identified as a clay-organic complex of indigo and the rare clay mineral attapulgite (now called palygorskite). Attapulgite had been identified from Yucatan, but in 1965, my ethnographic work revealed that Ticul potters were using attapulgite and were aware of its unique properties. Ultimately, I was able to suggest two ancient sites where the Maya may have obtained this rare clay mineral for use in Maya Blue.[1]

The connection between my research and Maya Blue had been stimulated by the discovery that the contemporary potters of Ticul possessed a sophisticated knowledge of their raw materials. The linguistic categories of these materials denoted certain contrasting attributes. Furthermore, raw material selection and use indicated that potters' practical knowledge was based upon characteristics which corresponded to the physical properties of the minerals present in these substances. This correspondence led me to suspect that if Maya categories of ceramic raw materials could be related to physical and/or mineralogical characteristics in a living community, it might be possible to identify communities of potters in ancient ceramics based on the study of paste. Comparative ethnographic data from the Andes would provide cross-cultural support for such an hypothesis and hopefully would show its validity outside of Yucatan. To operationalize this hypothesis in

Peru, I had planned to survey the pottery-making communities in the Ayacucho Valley and collect samples of ceramic raw materials, analyze them using X-ray diffraction, and ascertain whether different communities used mineralogically different materials. If successful, this research would be an important ethnographic test for identifying the source communities of ancient ceramics.

After I arrived in Ayacucho, however, I was not able to implement my original research design. First, I learned that ceramic production in the community of Quinua was so complex and distinct from that of other communities that it merited its own intensive study. Quinua potters utilized a variety of decorative techniques to produce a diversity of vessel shapes which were used for utilitarian and ritual purposes. Other pottery-making communities in the Ayacucho Valley produced only utility wares which were most often undecorated. The unusual character of Quinua pottery was underscored by the fact that it was exported all over the world as an ethnic or third world craft. This market was graphically illustrated to me soon after I arrived in Peru when I remembered having seen a display of Quinua pottery in a department store (Carson, Pirie, Scott and Company) in downtown Chicago a year-and-a-half earlier.

A second factor that influenced the decision to change my research design was the unique character of the culture history of the region. Besides having such unusual and complex ceramics, the village of Quinua was only a few kilometers from the ancient site of Huari, a massive urban settlement which was the capital of one of the largest pre-Inca states in ancient Peru. Huari had been the source of several polychrome styles which were among the most complex in the central Andes and some of the modern Quinua potters live directly across a canyon from the site. The uniqueness of Quinua pottery in the Ayacucho Valley and the closeness of its potters to Huari suggested that there may be an important link between the modern potters of Quinua and the ancient potters of Huari that was not shared by other potters in the valley.

A final reason for changing my original research design was more practical. Another anthropologist (William P. Mitchell) was working in Quinua on a very different project[2] and he offered me a corner of his room to put my sleeping bag. Mitchell ate his meals with a local family headed by a potter and he suggested that I might be able to eat with them as well. The prospect of having my need for food, shelter and informants met so easily was too good to refuse.

With my research site and research topic radically changed, I set about studying pottery production in Quinua. Basic description seemed like a good place to begin, but much to my frustration, I soon discovered that most, if not all, potters were not making pottery. I had arrived in the midst of the rainy season (mid-February). Travel was difficult because of the rain and mud. Rain fell almost every day turning streets into a sea of mud which stuck to my boots like glue and made walking along narrow mountain paths an experience comparable only to mud wrestling. Slipping and sliding my way through the community was a frustrating experience. There was little sunshine; fog and mist often blanketed the area during the day making the climate depressing. The rain also caused frequent landslides, cutting Quinua off from bus and truck traffic to and from the city of Ayacucho and complicating trips to obtain supplies and mail.

I took some comfort from the fact that the Spanish conquerors had also found the rainy season miserable in Quinua. After founding the first Spanish settlement in the valley on or near the present site of Quinua in January of 1539 (Rivera Serna 1966), they abandoned it in favor of a lower and warmer location across the valley, citing the disagreeable climate as a reason.

Fortunately, Mitchell's host and principal informant at the time was a potter. Unlike most potters who were also agriculturalists and made pots only in the dry season, Mitchell's informant worked in the government-run artisan center for most of the year, but during the summer vacation (the rainy season of January–March), he made pottery in order to make extra money. He was not able to make much pottery during this time. But, even with the pottery he *did* produce, he still had to wait until April to completely dry and fire his vessels. Visits to households of other active potters during this time did not yield much data until late March and early April and even then, few potters were practicing their craft. Furthermore, most Quinua potters were also peasant farmers and needed to work in the fields during the rainy season. Most did not begin making pottery until the harvest was completed in late June which was just before I was scheduled to leave the field.

The early part of my research in Quinua was thus a time of great frustration. Few observations of pottery making were made. For years afterward I felt that much of my field work was a failure because of my inability to gather abundant data on pottery manufacture. These lingering frustrations and disappointments are one of the reasons for the long delay in the publication of this research.

Years after my field work in Quinua I began to evaluate my experiences more objectively. I was preparing some material for publication (Arnold 1972a, 1972b, 1975a, 1975b) and began to reflect on my data and the frustrating experiences of trying to observe pottery making during the rainy season. I began to realize that my research in Quinua had been colored by my field work two years earlier in Mexico which had also occurred during the rainy season. In Yucatan, the mornings were most often bright and sunny with rain falling almost every afternoon. Potters took great precautions to avoid drying and firing their pottery during rainfall. When it rained during firing (and it did frequently), potters also employed safeguards to keep their fuel dry and their kiln hot. Pottery production was thus still possible during the rainy season. Rainy weather did not prevent production, but just complicated it by delaying and/or extending the period necessary for drying and firing.

Pottery production in Quinua, however, was different. While heavy rains only prevented pottery production for relatively brief periods in Yucatan, fog and cool temperatures were the factors which precluded pottery production in Quinua. It was not the amount nor the intensity of the rainfall that was important, but rather the number of daylight hours with rain, cool temperatures and fog. The moisture from fog and rainfall drove the relative humidity so high that pottery and clay could not dry adequately. Cloudiness prevented the radiant energy from the sun from drying the pottery. Pottery that was made during the rainy season risked damage from leaky roofs and prolonged drying. The climate thus made pottery making extremely difficult, if not impossible, and few ceramics were made during the rainy season. Any vessels that *were* made could not be fired.

Much to my surprise, I discovered that my inability to observe pottery production during the rainy season in Quinua was itself a very important observation. Weather and climate had a significant effect on pottery production. Further, the scheduling of subsistence activities (like agriculture) could preclude ceramic production among part-time household potters who were also farmers. Weather and climate patterns were thus important limiting factors which prevented the development of full-time ceramic specialization in Quinua and were probably important variables in limiting production in areas with a heavy rainy season elsewhere in the Andes as well. These insights changed my view of ceramic production as I saw that what was important was not just production itself, but rather how it was tied to the environment and subsistence. These reflections and the events that stimulated them were pivotal in my thinking at the time and were one of the most significant factors that led to the development of *Ceramic theory and cultural process* (Arnold 1985).

My experience with the unpleasant rainy weather during the first two months of my field work in Quinua was confirmed by data from the weather station in the city of Ayacucho some 15 kilometers to the southwest (Rivera 1971). Ayacucho is lower in altitude and drier than Quinua, but the Ayacucho weather data do provide some indication of the precipitation patterns in Quinua. My perception that it rained almost every day during the first two months of my stay in Quinua was borne out by the meteorological data. During each of the months of February and March of 1967, there were only *two days* without rain in the lower and drier valley to the west (Rivera 1971: 41).

In retrospect, the rainy weather of February and March, 1967 proved to be atypically high for the nine-year period 1962–70 (Rivera 1971).[3] Precipitation for these months was also atypically high for the ten-year period 1961–70.[4] Again, these data came from the city of Ayacucho which was lower and drier than Quinua, but they did reveal an abnormally wet period *even in Ayacucho* during February and March, 1967! My experience with pottery production in Quinua thus could not be generalized to every year, but it *was* clear that weather and climate did affect ceramic production depending on the days with cloudiness, rain, fog, and high humidity.

The significance of the limiting effect of weather and climate on pottery production was reinforced even more during field work in Yucatan during the summer and fall of 1984. During the rainy season (June–September), potters dried their vessels in the sun in the morning. As the sky clouded up in the early afternoon, however, and the first drops hit the roof of the potter's house, family members quickly removed green pots and drying clay from outside the house. Sometimes they arrived too late and pots were destroyed by the rain. At other times, vessels were damaged by movement in and out of the house.

As the rains tapered off in the fall, another problem loomed: hurricanes. During the late summer and fall of every year, low pressure areas arise out of the Caribbean and western Atlantic and head west and north. Few of these ever bring severely destructive winds and rains to Yucatan like those which occurred with Hurricane Gilbert in September, 1988, but these low pressure cells include massive cyclonic bands of heavy clouds which are hundreds of miles in diameter. These cloud bands often extend over the northern Yucatan Peninsula bringing cool temperatures and heavy cloudiness. One may not see the sun for days on end. Often this cloud cover may be accompanied by constant rainfall over a period of several days.

These weather patterns completely disrupt the pottery-making process and eliminate a week or more of production time. In the fall of 1984, Yucatan experienced a week of cool, rainy weather associated with the periphery of a tropical low pressure area. Household pottery production in Ticul largely stopped during this time. If this weather pattern strikes at an inopportune time in the production sequence, the potter can lose two to three weeks of economically productive time. Normally, potters are on a two-week cycle from the time they obtain the clay until they receive payment for their fired vessels. If these massive tropical depressions occur when the potter needs clay, he must first wait until miners can dig the clay. Since clay is extracted in deep subterranean mines which are subject to the collapse of overburden, clay mining is dangerous during unpredictably rainy weather, and occurs only after the persistent rainy weather passes. The potter must wait until the miners make their weekly clay delivery. He must then dry his clay in the sun for two days even before he can begin making pots. Finally, he faces the problem of drying newly formed vessels in the sun.

For those household potters of Ticul who depend on their craft to make a living, adverse weather is a factor contributing to their poverty. For those on a regular salary who are only inconvenienced by bad weather, it is hard to understand the devastating effect of such delays on a household that requires regular ceramic production to maintain the minimum subsistence level. When potters live on the edge of poverty with no accumulated capital for such low periods, the loss of two weeks of economically productive time can be crippling to a family with several mouths to feed. This problem can only be mitigated by the investment in larger houses, workshops and drying sheds or by being hired as a wage laborer in a workshop that has these facilities.

In Quinua, the weather and climate thus radically affected my research strategy for describing ceramic production. The frustration with the climate in Quinua and the relative dearth of production data collected in the early weeks of my field work led me away from a focus on ceramic production. Early in my research it became clear that Quinua pottery was unique in the valley primarily because it was elaborately decorated. Observation revealed that it was painted in three different decorative schemes and was used locally to celebrate local rituals and to store and carry food, water and other liquids.

In the late 1960s, the archaeological community in the United States had been excited by the work of Longacre (1964) and Deetz (1965) who had tried to demonstrate that designs on ancient pottery could reveal ancient patterns of social organization. Realizing that the link between design and social organization needed to be tested ethnographically, I began to collect design data on every vessel that I saw in use in Quinua. During the early weeks of my field work, Mitchell told me that land tended to be inherited patrilineally and post-nuptial residence patterns tended to be virilocal. Furthermore, men were potters and learned to make their designs from their father (Mitchell 1991a: 62). Both men and women, however, painted the pottery, but men controlled the content of the designs painted by their wives. Since potters could recognize the author of a pot by its painted style, my residence in Quinua provided a natural opportunity to test the hypothesis that patterns of learning and post-nuptial residence were expressed in the design of the pottery. To adequately test this hypothesis, however, it was necessary to collect provenance information on the potter who made the vessel, how he learned the craft and the location of his residence as well as data on the pottery design itself. Although some of this type of data were collected, it was impossible to collect the same kind of data for every vessel observed. Some vessels were in use and their producer was unknown. Furthermore, given the limitations of climate on ceramic production and the subsequent scheduling conflicts of pottery making with agriculture, the sample size for well-provenanced vessels was too small for analysis. My lack of facility in Quechua further complicated these problems. Informants had said on occasion that each subsection of the community had its own ceramic style, but I was never able to obtain enough design data from known potters in these different subsections to verify such statements empirically.

Nevertheless, the Deetz/Longacre hypothesis was far more complex than just the learning of specific designs by potters who followed a particular inheritance and post-nuptial residence pattern. The Quinua design data indicated that ceramic design was more complex than simple counts of design elements (Longacre 1970; Hill 1970). Moreover, decoration was not limited to a single design zone on a pot (e.g. Deetz 1965). While the pioneering efforts of Deetz, Longacre and Hill have enlarged the horizons of the kinds of inferences that could be made from ceramic analyses, the assumptions about the nature of ceramic design in these works were still untested in 1967. The organization of the Quinua designs revealed that the design structure on ceramic vessels was complex and required attention to a greater variety of variables (like vessel shape, design fields, design zones and symmetry patterns) than just the design elements. When the analysis took these variables into account, important ethnographic insights emerged about the relationship of the designs to the community.

During my research in Quinua, there were about forty households of potters in the community. This number was compiled from my own list of potters, Mitchell's list and from a survey of pottery-making households in the community conducted by the Quinua artisan center. I visited nineteen of these households and my research consisted primarily of questioning potters and observing their work. Most of the interviews and observations took place in the rural *pagos* of Llamahuilca and Lurinsayuq. Few households were visited in the *pago* of Muya. Some observations of pottery making were also made at the artisan center in the village of Quinua. Since the potters at the center utilize several innovations not shared by other Quinua potters, this book describes the technology of the artisan center potters separately from that of the rest of the potters in the community. Besides observations of pottery production, I collected samples of raw materials from potters. Sources of clay, temper, and paint were also visited and samples were collected from these locations. Many visits were made to the Quinua and Ayacucho markets, observing especially the kinds of pottery present and the nature of the transactions used for selling pottery. I also visited the markets in Huanta and Huamanguilla for the same purpose and these visits (as well as those to the Quinua and Ayacucho markets) enabled me to observe those vessels fabricated and marketed exclusively for local consumption. These observations helped me to see which shapes were actually the most useful and popular with the local populations, and to ascertain the designs that potters used on these vessels. This approach aided me in limiting the focus of my analysis largely to the decorated utilitarian pottery made in Quinua rather than describing all of the pottery produced there. I also visited the pottery-making areas near Luricocha, the pottery-making *barrio* in the city of Ayacucho and collected as much information as I could about pottery-making communities outside of Quinua.

I also recorded the designs of many of the vessels which were being sold in the local stores of Quinua. Most of this pottery did not include the shapes described in this work, but some shapes in these stores were identical to those sold in markets elsewhere in the valley. Hence, vessels from these stores provided information on design supplementary to information obtained from potters or from pottery observed in the local markets.

When I returned to Urbana in 1967, I submitted my samples of ceramic raw materials to Dr. B. F. Bohor of the Illinois Geological Survey (now at the United States Geological Survey in Denver) for analysis by X-ray diffraction. This technique had been used on the ceramic raw materials I collected in Yucatan and had confirmed a relationship between the potter's knowledge of his raw materials and their mineralogical composition. Since the samples from Quinua were collected by potters using their own selection criteria, I was interested to see if the Quinua potter's knowledge of his raw materials corresponded to the mineralogy of these substances. In addition to the X-ray diffraction studies, I also separated plastics from non-plastic materials physically by using a 44 micron screen and then examined the larger fraction using a binocular microscope.

An incomplete analysis of the design data served as the basis for my dissertation (Arnold 1970), which contains the raw data. A more thorough analysis began around 1975, was largely completed in 1979 and then reanalyzed in the 1980s. The raw data used for the design analysis in this work can thus be found in my dissertation (Arnold 1970).

It was always tempting to postulate a cultural historical relationship between the modern and ancient potters of the valley. The close proximity of Quinua to Huari and the unique character of Quinua ceramics seemed to make historical continuity between the two communities probable. It was equally tempting to relate the modern pattern of ceramic technology to the Inca conquest of the region. During my research in Quinua, I learned that Tom Zuidema had discovered that the Incas had placed colonists in the Quinua region from the town of Acos located southeast of the Inca capital of Cuzco. Since none of the other pottery-making communities in the Valley were known to be colonists from Acos, Zuidema thought that the Acos Indians may have brought knowledge of pottery production with them to Quinua. Thinking that the modern Quinua ceramic production may thus have its origin in Acos rather than the ancient site of Huari, I decided, upon the urging of Dr. Zuidema, to visit Acos. I wanted to find out if the people of Acos made pottery and, if so, whether there was any similarity of the Acos pottery to the contemporary pottery of Quinua. Could the origin of Quinua ceramic production be found in Acos?

The journey to Acos was a great lesson in Andean ecology and the difficulties that the Incas must have faced in moving their colonists over some of the world's most difficult terrain. Even with modern transportation, the 250 km from Quinua to Acos was an arduous five-day journey. I traveled overland to Andahuaylas (thirteen hours), then to Abancay (about six more hours), and finally to Cuzco (six additional hours). Another day was required to travel from Cuzco to Acomayo and part of another day from Acomayo to Acos. During the first leg of the trip to Andahuaylas, the bus zigzagged up and down mountains from snowstorms to subtropical river valleys with xerophytic vegetation and groves of bananas and oranges. During the next leg of the trip from Andahuaylas to Abancay, the lights of Abancay twinkled in the valley below hours before we arrived by road. The only part of the journey which was not characterized by up and down travel was the relatively short hour-long trip across the flat Plain of Anta and through the Urubamba/Vilcanota Valley near Cuzco. Not included in the difficulties of such a lengthy trip were the problems with the accoutrements of industrial civilization: a punctured gas tank, an overheated radiator and two flat tires (one with no spare).

After a difficult five-day trip from Ayacucho, I arrived in Acos one afternoon in early June, 1967. Unfortunately, there were no potters in Acos nor in the surrounding area, but there were several archaeological sites nearby. So, I spent three days in the community doing a brief archaeological reconnaissance and collected small surface samples of ceramics.

I have abandoned the possibility of ever finding a direct culture historical link between Quinua potters, on the one hand, and Acos and/or Huari potters, on the other. Nevertheless, the close proximity of Quinua and Huari suggest that much could be learned about the ancient ceramic production of the Valley by means of a detailed study of the modern ceramics of Quinua.

I returned to Quinua for a very brief visit in June, 1978 and in April, 1979. I had always wanted to return to Quinua and obtain the provenance data for decorated vessels along with kinship diagrams and residence information that were necessary to adequately test the Deetz/Longacre hypothesis. After the analysis of my 1967 data, the prospect of obtaining adequate data to accomplish this task looked very promising. The aim of the 1978 trip was to briefly assess the situation in Quinua and lay the ground work to return in the future and collect the data necessary to test the relationship of ceramic design to patterns of learning, residence and descent.

Unfortunately, about a year after my 1979 visit, the political situation deteriorated in the Department of Ayacucho because of the activity by the "Shining Path" guerrilla movement (the *Sendero Luminoso*). A number of attacks were made on villages in the Ayacucho region killing peasants and village officials. These attacks continued for the next several years.[5] Mitchell reported that Quinua itself had been attacked once and a policeman killed.[6] In August of 1984, there was a news report of a mass grave discovered in the town of Huanta 10 km from Quinua (France Presse 1984). Missionary reports listed other massacres not covered by the secular press.[7] Ayacucho has been under a state of emergency for much of this time and further visits to Ayacucho have been very dangerous. Serious ethnographic work has been out of the question. Since this writing project began (about 1982), the situation in Ayacucho (as well as in Peru) has deteriorated and does not look as if it will improve in the near future. Any return to Quinua to complete the work begun in 1967 is extremely unlikely. Therefore, I consider my research in Quinua finished and provide this work as a general summary of my results.

There is a bit of irony for me in the recent guerrilla activity in the Ayacucho area. In early May, 1967, I visited the market in the village of Huamanguilla, about a two-hour walk from the village of Quinua. I had wanted to go to Huamanguilla to observe the pottery sold there and learn about the possible locations of other pottery-making areas outside of Quinua. I had only spent a few minutes in the market and had just begun my observations when a member of *Guardia Civil* (the police force in these rural areas) told me that the commander of the police post wanted to see me. I complied and he escorted me to the police station. Inside, the commander promptly asked me why I was in Huamanguilla. I explained my work, but unfortunately I had forgotten to bring my passport and my letter of introduction from the *Casa de la Cultura* in Lima which introduced me as a student researcher under the supervision of Professor Zuidema at the University in nearby Ayacucho. Because guerrilla activity had occurred in the region two years previously, the commander was concerned that I might be a guerrilla. After emptying my pockets and camera bag at his request, he asked one of his officers whether a jail cell was ready. He deliberated with another subordinate about telegraphing the police in Quinua to verify my claims, but after questioning me further and forbidding me to take photographs, he allowed me to leave. I suspect the absence of automatic weapons in my camera bag and hand grenades in my pockets were the most convincing evidence that I was not a guerrilla, but I shall never forget the lesson I learned: always carry some identification and letters of introduction with you when doing field work in an area where you are not known and then check with the local authorities before proceeding.

This incident has a double irony for me because it is now well documented that the "Shining Path" guerrilla movement had its beginning at the University of Huamanga in Ayacucho.[8] Since I often interacted with University students there, I have occasionally wondered whether any of the students and faculty I knew are now members of the infamous terrorist group. The cautious acts of the Huamanguilla police were perhaps understandable, if not prophetic. The frightening potential of this situation for foreign ethnographers is borne out by the detention and imprisonment of a North American anthropologist, Cynthia McNamara, in Ayacucho in 1987 (Lopez 1988).

The field research for this monograph was thus done in the pioneering years of ethnoarchaeology before many of the works cited in this volume were published. In 1967, there was a need for ethnographic studies of pottery production since very little of this kind of work had been done. This was before the word "ethnoarchaeology" had been rediscovered[9] and before the current popularity of the subject. The great irony of this work is that although the research was done in 1967, it is more relevant today than it was twenty-five years ago. There is far more interest in ceramic ethnoarchaeology now than there was then. Nevertheless, if I were to study Quinua ceramic production today, I would approach it differently.

It was a struggle to find how best to represent the native words in an ethnography of which the readers may know neither the language nor the culture. In this work, I could have used a Spanish orthography which represents the dominant colonial culture of the Andes. Rather, I have chosen (with a few minor exceptions) to use an orthography that expresses the integrity of the highland people of Peru, the Andean Quechua. The orthography utilized for Quechua words in this work thus corresponds to published orthographies of Ayacucho Quechua that use three vowels rather than the five vowels used in Spanish (Parker 1965; Soto 1976). The "ll" used in Soto's orthography, however, replaces Parker's lambda for simplicity of transcription. When Spanish loan words are used, however, the text uses a Spanish orthography.

The field research upon which this book was based was my first experience in the Andes, and like many ethnographic experiences, it changed my life and left unforgettable memories. Through it, I learned much about the Andes and even more about anthropology. There was no greater teacher of Andean ecology than the experience of being there. I shall never forget the azure skies and emerald green fields that I could see from the balcony of my house after the end of the rainy season. Exhausting hikes in the high altitude (sometimes as high as 4,000 meters) and countless vistas of staggeringly beautiful Andean scenery remain a vivid memory. Visits to countless colorful Andean markets and rubbing my body down with DDT powder to keep off the fleas will be etched in my memory forever. The diurnal oscillation of temperature was no more graphically portrayed than when, after waking early one morning to wash and shave, I discovered that the water left outside the night before was frozen solid. And, then, three hours later, I wore only a sweater as I trekked along Andean roads and trails.

Most of all, my experience in Quinua taught me about the holism of anthropology. I learned the importance of refusing to be satisfied with reductionistic and narrow interpretations. Understanding another culture (even though that understanding may be very incomplete) best comes from immersion in a culture through the time-honored and classic ethnographic technique known as participant-observation. This kind of experience combined with an understanding of the environment, history and prehistory of an area provide a holistic perspective that is unique in the social sciences and creates special insight into human behavior.

Finally, this work represents a slice of life in Quinua that no longer exists. Cultural evolution, guerrilla activities, population growth, migration, religious change and a cash economy have changed Quinua irreversibly (Mitchell 1991a). Nevertheless, this work has much to say about the relationship of ceramics to environment and society which has relevance beyond Quinua, Ayacucho or Peru.

1

Introduction

Since the invention of fired clay vessels about 10,000 B.C., pottery has become one of the most abundant artifacts left behind by ancient humans. While written records are restricted to a relatively small number of societies in the last 6,000 years and largely represent the work of political, social, and/or religious elites, ceramics provide information about how ordinary people actually lived, not just the literate. Ceramic artifacts are thus the products of the actual behavior of ancient peoples, and inferences of the past based on pottery can extend understanding of ancient societies beyond the verbal accounts of the learned, the wealthy, the privileged and the influential.

What do the ancient ceramics tell archaeologists about the societies that made them? Traditionally, archaeologists have used ceramics for formulating chronologies, for tracing political and economic relationships and for reconstructing ancient lifeways (see Sinopoli 1991 for a review). Ceramics, however, do not speak for themselves, but like all data, they must be interpreted (e.g. Anderson 1984).

In recent years, the study of contemporary, pre-industrial ceramic production has become an important tool for interpreting ancient ceramics. Archaeologists have long recognized the value of using contemporary societies to understand ancient ones where the two were linked in a direct historical way. But, more recently, they have asked fundamental questions about the relationships of artifacts and society and have turned to the study of the material culture in the ethnographic present. With few exceptions, however, answers to their questions were not found in the ethnographic literature. Archaeologists thus began studying contemporary societies themselves and this approach became known as "ethnoarchaeology," a term first used by Jesse W. Fewkes in 1900.[1]

While anthropologists have described pottery making among traditional societies for decades, ethnoarchaeology addresses questions that are specific to archaeology: How are artifacts and behavior related? Is social organization reflected in ceramic design? Can the different use-lives of pots affect interpretations of ancient pottery? How do patterns of discard and site-formation affect the interpretations of ancient ceramics? Since its beginnings in the 1960s, this "ethnography" of ceramic production, use and discard[2] has grown tremendously with research focusing on those parts of the world where pre-industrial potters still remain.[3]

Despite the enthusiasm for ethnoarchaeology, some archaeologists have cautioned their colleagues about utilizing ethnographic data to interpret the past. Hodder (1982a, 1982b) has warned against using contemporary societies uncritically to reconstruct ancient societies, while others have argued that the present differs so fundamentally from the past that ethnoarchaeology has limited use in archaeological interpretation (e.g. Rice 1987: 466–468). For those who argue that ancient and modern societies share similar cultural processes, Gould (1980, 1983) retorts that uniformitarian principles are inappropriate to interpret the past. He believes that ethnographic data should only be used to choose between competing inferences. Still others, however, argue that ethnographic work among contemporary peoples is essential for the development of a middle range theory relating material culture to its behavioral causes.[4] They argue that it is not the ethnoarchaeological *data* which should be applied to the past. Rather, they believe that a *theory* should be derived from the ethnoarchaeological data and then be used to interpret the artifacts of ancient societies.

If ethnoarchaeological data are so relevant to archaeological interpretation, how should one approach the study of a contemporary material culture? How should one study ceramic production, for example, in order to provide a useful theory for interpreting ancient ceramics? Certainly, great differences exist between the modern and ancient potters, but similarities exist as well. If ethnoarchaeology is to be used effectively in archaeological interpretation, it is essential to focus on the similarities in order to develop a theory for making inferences from ancient ceramics. A previous work (Arnold 1985) argued that there are widespread processual similarities in pre-industrial ceramic production between the present and the past and that these similarities consist of common adaptive processes that link ceramics, the environment and society. Describing these adaptive processes provides the foundation for developing a cross-cultural theory of ceramic production which can be used both in the present and in antiquity. Without such a cross-cultural approach to theory formulation, the application of ethnoarchaeological studies to archaeology is hopelessly tied to direct historical analogies and ethnographic homologies or mired in a slough of relativistic cautionary tales.

This book takes the ecological approach of an earlier work (Arnold 1985) one step further by using an ecological perspective to describe ceramic production in a single community. The purpose of the book is to elucidate the relationships linking ceramics, culture and the environment in one society at a single point of time. At the end of the book, these relationships are then applied to ancient ceramic production in the same region. This approach to the past is not based on homologies with modern ceramic production, or direct historical continuity, but rather on the adaptive processes that are common both to ancient and modern societies. Such processes occur in the Ayacucho Valley and in a variety of societies around the world (see Arnold 1985). The book is thus part of a continuing attempt to work out a theory relating contemporary ceramics to culture and the environment in a way that can be applied to ceramic production in antiquity.

Conceptual approach of the book

If archaeology has learned anything from the philosophy of science, it is the importance of theory formulation prior to the presentation of data. No matter how "objective" data may seem, these data are already theory-laden having been collected with certain *a priori* conceptual frameworks in mind (Hanson 1958; Kuhn 1962). No scientific undertaking is liberated from the personal, paradigmatic, theoretical, and interpretive presuppositions that affect data selection, collection and interpretation. The task of scientific investigators, then, is not to eliminate all bias in scientific description, but rather to be sure that one's interpretive, paradigmatic and theoretical biases are explicit. The personal background, interpretation and experience affecting this study have already been carefully described in the preface of this book. So, attention will turn now to its paradigmatic and theoretical underpinnings.

One of the most fruitful paradigms for developing a theory of ceramic production comes from cultural ecology. Originally pioneered by Julian Steward (1955) and now encompassed by cultural materialism,[5] cultural ecology seeks to generalize about cultural similarities and differences by analyzing the relationships of a culture's environment to its technology and social organization. A cultural ecological approach takes the position that the environment permits a range of choices that human beings can use for survival. By understanding the relationship of the environment and the technology of a society, it is possible to understand those forces that have selected the technological patterns that are necessary for a culture's survival. In some cultures, there may be a wide range of possible choices, whereas in others, the range of choices may be very small. In any case, cultural ecology is concerned with adaptation and the contribution that a culture's environment makes to its technology, social organization and beliefs. The ecological approach thus gives methodological priority to working out the relationships of the environment and the "exploitative or productive technology" (Steward 1955: 40), or, as Steward says, "the material culture of a society."[6]

Since ceramics are one kind of material culture and are part of the "exploitative technology," the study of ceramics fits well within the paradigm of cultural ecology. Applying this paradigm to ceramics means that one should first analyze the relationships of ceramics with the environment. Once such relationships are understood, one can then examine how ceramic production articulates with the rest of the technological subsystem of a culture and then with its social structural and ideological subsystems. By studying ceramic production as an adaptive phenomenon and seeing its relationship to the environment and to the society, it is possible to develop theoretical explanations that can be tested against the data from other societies and then be applied to the past as well. This approach thus creates cross-cultural explanatory generalizations which can help explain ceramic production in the past as well as in the present.

The attempt to develop such a theory is often attacked by those who argue: "My data from the BugaBuga (or the Fulano site) does not support this explanation, therefore it is false." Few archaeologists would want to argue, as this objection implies, that adaptive processes are so relativistic that they change from society to society and from one point in time to the next. Scientific explanations are probabilities. In the physical sciences, the probabilities of such explanations accounting for natural phenomena are much higher than in the social sciences, but they are still probabilities. "Law-like generalizations" of human behavior that approach the probabilities of the physical sciences are not possible. Explanatory theories of patterns, events and processes are never certainties and there are always data that do not fit the pattern. In the science of humanity, the probabilities of an explanation occurring are never 100 percent certain, seldom occur in more than 60 percent of the cases and in some cases may occur less than 50 percent of the time. No explanation fits all cases. But, to reject all theorizing because it does not account for all cases is to embrace a highly relativistic view of the past in which there are never any cross-cultural patterns of regularity. To the contrary, patterns of convergence and divergence in cultural evolution suggest that such general adaptive processes do exist.

An ecological approach to ceramic production

Ceramics can be approached by several methodologies at several levels of analysis. This work uses a cultural ecological paradigm and methodology to understand contemporary ceramic production. The application of cultural ecology to ceramics was first suggested by F. R. Matson who wanted to redirect ceramic studies away from the specifics of pots and potsherds towards the humans who made them. Matson thus coined the term "ceramic ecology" to express this concern and defined it as "one facet of cultural ecology . . . which attempts to relate the raw materials and technologies that the local potter has available to the functions in his culture of the products he fashions" (Matson 1965a; 1965b: 203).

The concern with "raw materials," "technologies," and "products" in Matson's definition, however, implies a heavy emphasis on ceramics as objects with limited recognition of the relationships that exist between ceramic production and society, on the one hand, and between ceramics and the environment, on the other. The preoccupation with ceramics as "objects" is understandable given the concrete and tangible data of archaeology, but if archaeologists want to infer patterns and processes of ancient societies, they must move beyond the ceramics themselves and focus on their relationships to the sociocultural system as a whole. *Relationships* should be the subject matter of ecology – whether ceramic or cultural. If one embraces an ecological approach to ceramic production, one would expect a wider range of relationships between ceramics, society, and the environment than just the "functions" of the ceramic product in the society that Matson suggested. Nevertheless, the concern with "relationships" in Matson's "ceramic ecology" was pioneering and does imply a broader relational paradigm even though it was not explicit. Matson's "ceramic ecology" thus represents an important conceptual change in the way that archaeologists have viewed ceramics. Understood more broadly, then, an ecological approach to ceramic production should focus on the relationships of the ceramics, *their production, use and discard* with the rest of the sociocultural system and the broader ecosystem.[7]

Since the formulation of "ceramic ecology" in 1965, Matson's ideas have inspired a number of studies[8] and the development of several volumes.[9] Kolb[10] broadened

Matson's ecological viewpoint and provided a conceptual and methodological guide for ceramic analysis using an ecological approach. Arnold (1985) refined the ceramic ecological perspective to include a systems paradigm and provided cross-cultural data for a number of widespread relationships between ceramic production and the sociocultural system, on the one hand, and the environment, on the other.

The application of cultural ecology to ceramics thus reflects a paradigm which emphasizes the relationships of ceramics to the environment and to the socio-cultural system. This focus assumes that culture can be usefully described as an open subsystem of the larger ecosystem and that all parts of it, including material culture, have relationships with other parts such that changes in one part produce changes in others (see Sharp 1952). This view of culture goes back to functionalism in anthropology, but is conceptually rooted in the organismic model of society from nineteenth-century social thought.

Applied to archaeology, the use of the systems paradigm means that there is a relationship of material culture to the intangible aspects of culture, and that the archaeologist can potentially infer ancient behavior of a society by studying the material culture of that society. Giving assent to this notion, however, does not mean that material culture can tell archaeologists everything they want to know about a society. Nor does invoking it mean that *all* of the aspects of a society are reflected in the material culture. Indeed, ceramics probably encode far less social and environmental information than archaeologists would like to believe they do. Rather, the point of using a systemic paradigm is far more basic. In a system, ceramics, like all parts of culture, have relationships with other parts of culture. But, the crucial component of this paradigm concerns the focus of research: the relationships between ceramics and social and environmental phenomena should be the focus of study rather than the ceramics themselves.

The systemic view of culture thus provides an important theoretical framework congruent with an ecological approach. The point is a simple one. Ecology focuses on interrelationships, but in order to study these relationships, an ecological approach to ceramics must assume that relationships exist between ceramics and the environment, on the one hand, and between the ceramics and the rest of culture, on the other. In an ecological approach, ceramics are not studied for their own sake. Rather, it is the linkages of the ceramics with social behavior and environmental conditions which should be the focus of research.

Unfortunately, these relationships cannot be inferred from the ceramics themselves. They cannot be discovered by analyzing the ceramics using scientific techniques like trace element or mineralogical analyses. Rather, these relationships must be brought to the process of interpretation from a theoretical understanding of the relationship of ceramics to environment and society in a broad range of societies. There is nothing inherent in the ceramics that can provide this information. Archaeologists thus have a problem; they must infer these relationships with little help from the analysis of the ceramics themselves. It is thus the task of the ethnoarchaeologist to discover those relationships between ceramics, the environment, and the society which actually exist and those which do not, and to test assumptions in the interpretation of ancient ceramics using ethnographic data.

In addition to the congruency of a systems view of culture with an ecological approach, a systems paradigm is also congruent with a set of formal properties which is characteristic of systems. This congruency enables cross-cultural comparison of the relationships between ceramics, environment and culture. Systems have a wide variety of characteristics which are isomorphic (that is share the same basic form) and these can be applied to any number of disciplines. All systems (whether living or non-living), for example, can be viewed as being characterized by goal-directed behavior and the processes of control and communication (Boulanger 1969). The first of these characteristics, goal-directed behavior, consists of the desired end-point of the system. This goal, however, does not need to be a conscious, human-directed goal, but may be a mechanical, inanimate goal. Human cultural systems, however, have the goal of survival which may be mediated by the preservation of the internal order of the society, and the production and transfer of information, matter and energy which foster that survival. Ceramic production is an alternative subsistence technique where the links to obtaining food are more complex than subsistence agriculture in which the technology provides food directly to a family. Potters must produce pottery successfully if they want to survive and obtain food for survival. A second characteristic shared by all systems consists of the processes of control and communication that permit the system to achieve its goal. These processes collect information about the difference between the desired goal and the actual performance of the system and then work to reduce that difference.[11] These processes are called feedback mechanisms and are viewed as mutual causal relationships in which the output of the system affects the input.

There are two types of feedback mechanisms: regulatory (or negative) feedback and deviation amplifying (or positive) feedback. Regulatory or deviation counteracting feedback promotes equilibrium and counteracts deviations from stable situations over long periods of time. This process of control prevents divergence from a prescribed set of boundaries. Deviation amplifying feedback, on the other hand, promotes or amplifies deviations as the result of some external input into the system (called "kicks") which the system cannot regulate. This mechanism causes the system to expand and reach stability at new, more complex levels (Maruyama 1963) when the inputs causing the expansion eventually become regulated and create new parameters for the system. Deviation amplifying mechanisms are thus the means by which the system gains new information and cause disequilibrium and change within it. In some situations, feedback may be both change-inhibiting (deviation counteracting) and change-inducing (deviation amplifying).[12]

The isomorphous relationships between ceramic production, the environment and the sociocultural system thus consist of basic feedback mechanisms which stimulate (deviation amplifying) and/or limit (deviation counteracting) ceramic production in a culture-environmental system. An earlier work (Arnold 1985) argued that these mechanisms are based on certain chemical and physical phenomena that underlie the nature of pottery itself, are adaptive processes and are tied to some of the fundamental processes involved in ceramic production. They are broadly classed into categories which include resources, weather and climate, degree of sedentariness, scheduling, demand, people-land relationships and innovations (Arnold 1985). They possess isomorphous (but not identical) relationships found in a broad range of societies throughout the world. The mechanisms thus have relevance to many different societies and can be applied to diverse societies in the present and the past as either stimulating or hindering the initial development of the craft and its growth and development into a full-time specialty. It is thus possible to partially explain the development and maintenance of both modern and ancient ceramic production using this approach without recourse to a simple kind of ethnographic analogy which requires a direct historical approach to the past or the use of ethnographic homologies.

Is the use of systems terminology just an attempt to obfuscate the obvious with unnecessary jargon? Or, does it say something deeper about the relationships of pottery, environment and society? The use of systems terminology constantly reminds archaeologists that culture and society are systems with varied interconnections. Because the western scientific tradition utilizes an analytical paradigm which breaks phenomena apart into their constituent units, one needs to be reminded that the essential character of ancient social and cultural inference is understanding the links between ceramics and their social, cultural and environmental context. Unfortunately, traditional anthropology does not provide a terminology that emphasizes the systemic interrelationships of culture. One learns detailed categories of technology, subsistence, social structure and religion, but relationships between these categories are not clearly laid out nor understood. In archaeology, one learns the details of ceramic paste, shape and decoration and how to classify such features into types, but the relationships of these entities to the rest of the sociocultural system are based more on traditional archaeological beliefs about the relationships of ceramics and society than on empirical knowledge of such relationships.

A scientific approach is analytical and scientists (especially social scientists) become experts in classifying phenomena into categories and coining new words for entities that do not fit traditional ones. One does not learn about the causal links, nor about the relationships between entities, but rather, one focuses on the entities themselves. One can take a society apart, but can one put it back together again? Can one reconstruct the relationships between parts of culture that one has so painstakingly analyzed, defined and categorized?

Nothing is more illustrative of this dilemma than a childhood memory. During a visit to my grandmother, I discovered some discarded alarm clocks. After taking them home, I disassembled them and enjoyed the thrill of handling shiny brass sprocket wheels and hearing the "twang" of recoiling springs. When I got the clocks apart, however, I could not reassemble them. I do not remember why I thought that I should *want* to put them back together, but perhaps in childish naïvete I thought that I could repair them. I do remember, however, that this same experience was repeated many times with other clocks, and with discarded auto parts from the repair shop across the street. I never could reassemble anything and in frustration, I always ended up throwing the clock and its parts away. Curiously, I do remember that although I took many, many clocks apart, I learned nothing about how they actually worked! Only now, I realize that in my childhood zeal to be analytical, I paid no attention to the relationship of the parts to one another as I took them apart. I never tried to understand how the parts of the clock fit together during disassembly. The point of this story is simple. One can analyze phenomena and never understand how the parts interrelate and how the system actually works.

This study is an allegory for the relationships between ceramics and society. We have focused so much on analyzing ceramics that we have failed to pay attention to the relationship of the ceramics with the rest of culture. In fact, we are so good at the analysis of ceramics that we are now able to describe their constituents in parts per billion. Such trace element analysis is, of course, indispensable, but we fail to recognize that the force of our analytical tradition and that of the language that we use to describe ceramics reflect a way of thinking that makes the discovery of relationships of ceramics, environment and culture difficult.

We need to understand how ceramics are related to the environment and society. The use of systems terminology reminds us that we need to think differently about ceramics and their relationships with the culture we seek to understand. Systems terminology is a constant reminder that archaeologists must develop "systems thinking" about ceramics if they are to use ceramics successfully to interpret the past. Understanding the relationships between phenomena is important, not just the analysis of the phenomenon itself.

Systems terminology also reminds us that the factors (feedback mechanisms) that affect the systems are multicausal. In describing the system, one must first be analytical and identify the units of the system and then describe the relationship between them. In an attempt to be clear, the relationships may seem to be mono-causal. The relationship between climate and ceramic production, for example, may appear to suggest that rainfall prevents ceramic production in all cases and always hinders the development of full-time ceramic specialization. This misinterpretation, of course, is the result of analytical, monocausal thinking that is a part of our western tradition. The use of systems terminology, on the other hand, constantly reminds us that any feedback mechanism is only one of several interacting causative factors that affect ceramic production.

The use of systems terminology has been interpreted by some to mean that cultures are closed, stable systems that have reached equilibrium. On the contrary, cultures are constantly changing. While all cultures must have deviation counter-acting mechanisms that keep the society from falling apart, they probably do not keep the culture in equilibrium. Deviations and cultural evolution will still occur even in the most isolated hunting and gathering societies. Furthermore, such feedback mechanisms are not immutable. They can change as the system gains information. Nevertheless, they provide a basis for cross-cultural comparison because they are rooted in the dynamic formal properties of the system's interrelationships rather than in its static units. These properties thus permit comparison of ceramic production in different cultures in similar ways.

Finally, systems terminology facilitates a way of thinking that permits latitude in the effects of the inputs to the system. Feedback processes, for example, are not a mechanistic, presence/absence, "if this, always that" kind of relationship. A single feedback mechanism is a process which may have a different effect on a system depending on the conditions under which it operates. The kinds of causes and subsequent effects are not fixed; they occur in a continuum, not just as presence/ absence. Systems terminology thus reminds us that the societies of archaeological and anthropological study are fluid and changing, affected by multiple interrelated causative factors.

The complex nature of feedback mechanisms is more comprehensive and generalizable than studying the ceramic phenomenon itself. Feedback mechanisms provide a way to understand the processes of change, for example, in a more comprehensive way than by simply looking at the ceramics themselves. One can describe change by cataloguing its effects at different points in time, or one can explain such change conceptually. Explaining change is facilitated by using systems terminology because it attempts to uncover the underlying processes which cause the change. Such explanations increase the utility of the explanations of the relationships of ceramics, society and the environment by making them more universally applicable as processes which affect the evolution of ceramic specialization.

The unit of analysis

The interrelationships of ceramic production that occur within the ecosystem do not exist in isolation, but occur within the population of potters. The pottery-producing population is the interface between the ceramics and the larger society, on the one hand, and between the ceramics and the environment, on the other. Potters adapt to the environment through ceramic production and also modify this environment by expending energy to obtain the raw materials that are necessary to produce pottery. The pots then serve as channels of matter and energy which flow from the environment to humans in order to meet their nutritional and caloric needs. Ceramics also serve channels of ideological or social structural information between members of the society (Arnold 1985: 127).

Focusing on the population of potters as the locus of the relationships between ceramics, environment and culture is important for three reasons. First, the knowledge of, or information about, production resides within the population of potters and they behaviorally *produce* the ceramics. If any aspect of the society manifests itself in the ceramics, then it is transferred to the pottery in some way by means of the population of potters. Furthermore, pottery is the product of human agents and if any meaning exists in the pottery, it is the result of human action. Unless the relationship of the pottery to that action can be understood, interpretations of the past based on ceramic evidence are limited. Second, in harmony with ecological and evolutionary theory, the processes of ecological interaction and change operate primarily on the population, not on individuals.[13] The unit of adaptation is a population of living organisms and any relationships with the environment occur within that population. The population is thus the interface between the ecosystem, on the one hand, and ceramics, on the other. If one wants to relate ceramics to cultural and environmental systems, on the one hand, and to cultural and evolutionary change, on the other, one must understand the population of potters (rather than just the pots). Third, since cultures are viewed as having the properties of systems, focus on the population of potters is congruent with a systems viewpoint. Using the population as the unit of analysis thus avoids having to reconstruct a system of relationships from what is essentially a static phenomenon, that is ceramics. To use the allegory presented earlier, the dynamics of ancient society cannot be inferred from the statics of disembodied ceramics just as the workings of a functioning clock cannot be reconstructed from its disassembled parts. This problem is nicely embodied in the term "ceramic ecology" which appears to be conceptually contradictory because it links the static material culture (ceramics) with a dynamic, relational perspective (ecology). Nevertheless, it is for precisely this reason that "ceramic ecology" is an essential term for an ecological approach to ceramics because it expresses the paradox that every archaeologist faces in linking static material culture (ceramics in this case) with the dynamics of its contextual systems (society and the environment).[14] If ceramics cannot be viewed in dynamic terms and cannot be used to infer characteristics of the ancient society, there is not much point in using ceramics in archaeological interpretation. They are simply the objects that archaeologists find and have no social significance.

The point is that ceramics need to be understood with reference to a dynamic system if one is to make inferences about an ancient society from its ceramics. The study of the pots themselves will not provide these relationships no matter how many scientific analyses are used nor the number and kind of typologies used to classify them. Only by understanding ceramics as a part of a living system can archaeology begin to understand the relationship of pottery to society in the past. The unit of analysis in an ecological approach to ceramics should thus be the population of ceramic producers rather than the products of that population: pots.

With the importance of the population of potters established as the unit of analysis, it needs to be defined more precisely. The concept of the population used in ecological and evolutionary studies has important analogs with the population of potters. One of these analogs concerns the information in the population. One of the characteristics of a biological population is that it can interbreed and this feature has the effect of mixing and reshuffling genetic information within a common gene pool. Populations of potters also possess an analogous pool of technological information (or knowledge) which is shared through social interaction and learning. Just as genetic information is mixed and reshuffled through interbreeding, technological and decorative information is mixed and shared through social interaction whether it is done deliberately through verbal means or passively through visual means. The population of potters is thus a social group (rather than a biological one) whose numbers have regular social contact with one another. This group should be large enough to have some social interaction, and yet small enough to have this interaction often and regularly. A population of potters also should be geographically localized and be a discrete entity in space; different populations of potters should be geographically separated. Potters may be spread out over a territory in a dispersed settlement pattern, but there should be territorial limits to such a population. This feature makes different populations of potters spatially discrete. To talk about a population of potters in this way is to describe them as a "community" with social cohesion.

In order for this notion of the pottery-producing community to be useful as a unit of analysis, it should have tangible correlates in its ceramic products and these correlates should be archaeologically recognizable. A population of potters ideally should classify and use a particular set of local raw materials in community-defined ways which are distinct from the classifications and behavior of other communities of potters.[15] It should combine raw materials into pastes in ways that are distinct from other communities.[16] Vessel shapes produced in a community should be at least somewhat different from those produced in other communities (see Arnold 1978b, 1978c) and the ceramic decoration in each community should be different from that used in others.[17] Although some raw materials and vessel shape categories may be shared over a larger area with other communities of potters (in the Valley of Guatemala, for example), a community of potters should have similarities in behavior that are distinct from other communities.

While an ecological approach sees ceramic production as an adaptation to the environment, it reveals virtually nothing about the ceramics themselves and how a given ceramic complex should be described. In recent years, the focus on ceramic studies has moved away from systems, adaptation, and cultural processes to concerns about individual decision making, religion and the development of specialization.[18] Although the role of potters' decision making has been recognized as a factor in ceramic production since at least the work of Bunzel (1929) and Watson Smith (1962), the recent concern with potters' decisions in ceramic studies has been stimulated by criticisms of "processual archaeology" that have argued that processual concerns ignored the role of the individual and his/her decisions in ceramic production.[19] This criticism is, of course, true, but inappropriate. No theory or paradigm explains everything. Paradigms are incommensurable; one cannot criticize one paradigm on the basis of another (Lett 1987: 129–133). Differing paradigms are often complementary rather than competitive. For example, the personal history of this research discussed in the preface of this work represents a different paradigm from the remainder of this work. It alludes to the dialogue between the observer and the observed emphasized in the process of interpretation of modern hermeneutics.[20] Although the preface sheds light on the present work and is essential to understand it properly, it is not a substitute for what follows in the ensuing chapters. The preface is complementary, rather than competitive, with a more objective, empirical and rational approach to the data presented in chapters 2–9.

In the same way, one cannot understand the decisions that individuals make until one understands the range of conditions that have favored the outcome of some decisions and not others. Adaptation in human populations represents the end products of individual choices. The social and physical environment exert selective forces for some choices and not for others, but choices are not *determined* by the environment. They are only constrained by it (see O'Brien and Holland 1990, 1992). Human beings still choose, but they must make choices that the environment permits if they want to survive. Some choices will be adaptive while still others are selected against because they cannot be maintained in the environmental and social conditions. Other choices will be neutral as far as environmental selection is concerned and may have no selective advantage nor disadvantage. Still other choices change the environment and create a new set of conditions for adaptation.

The environment of a pottery-making community may affect the number of choices available. In some cases, choices (such as those involving raw materials) may be few, given the technology available. In other cases (such as choices involving design), the choices may be numerous and affected by different selective factors (such as market demand or aesthetic standards) outside of the constraints of the physical environment (e.g. Krause 1985). In summary, then, an ecological approach and an approach which sees ceramic production in terms of the choices that potters make are not competing paradigms, but complementary ones. Potters both make choices and are constrained by the environment.

Although the predominant paradigm described here is cultural ecology, the book also demonstrates the complementary nature of different paradigms for describing ceramic production. Cultural ecology emphasizes the importance of the environment, the adaptation of the potters to that environment and the relationships between the pottery and the society. It shows how the potters have changed the environment in order to adapt. It also provides the unit of analysis (the population of potters), and suggests how that unit is identified in a "real world" pottery-making situation. Since the adaptation of a population to an environment requires choices, this work also utilizes a paradigm which describes the choices potters use. These choices go beyond those choices selected by the environment and include those utilized both in fabrication and decoration. The description of these choices is essential because it is one way of expressing the variability of the ceramics in a way that is complementary to an ecological approach.

The plan of the book
In spite of a great surge of interest in ceramic studies in archaeology, we still know relatively little about the relationships of ceramics to their environmental, social and cultural context. This work utilizes an ecological approach to understand these relationships in a community in the Peruvian Andes in a point of space and time.

The next chapter (chapter 2) lays out the environmental context of the community and its adaptation to that environment. Understanding this environment and its effect on ceramic production also requires seeing it from the perspective of culture history (chapter 3). The unique series of events that occurred in the Ayacucho Valley during the last 1,500 years suggests that the valley occupied a rather unique environmental niche in southern Peru. Ceramic production is also the product of a population of potters which represents an adaptation to a rather unique set of conditions within the environment around a community. Chapter 4 describes this population and its relationships to these unique conditions. While the relationships of ceramic production to its physical environment certainly need to be understood, they tell us little about the ceramics themselves and the following chapter (chapter 5) lays out the technology of ceramic production in the community. One could approach such a description in several ways. One could describe the technology in terms of the broad general patterns. Such an approach, however, ignores the variability of the ceramics produced by the population. Another way to describe this technology is to describe it in terms of the choices that potters have available to them. This approach is an underlying theme in Steward's (1955) original cultural ecology, but it is also important because it expresses the variability inherent in ceramic production. The results of ceramic production (pots) do not exist in isolation, but have important relationships with the community and chapter 6 lays out these relationships to the larger environmental and social system. In order for the potter to eat, his products must be turned into food and the last part of chapter 6 details the distribution and marketing of Quinua ceramics.

The concern with the adaptive nature of ceramic production and its relationship with the environment and society in Quinua raises an important question. If the community of potters is the unit of adaptation and production, is this unit reflected in the pottery itself? Potters everywhere possess almost limitless choices for design, but they choose to decorate their pottery with a restricted repertoire which conforms to certain common patterns. In Quinua, these decorative patterns can be described as a set of design correlates that are characteristic of the community of Quinua and not shared with other potters in the valley (chapter 7). But, is there consistency in such patterns? Why do potters choose one set of design patterns and not others? Chapter 8 provides some explanations as to why such uniformity exists. Such choices reflect basic principles of traditional transmission of design and social interaction. Unfortunately, such explanations fail to account for the variability in the design and the chapter also examines some of the causes of this variability.

The last two chapters of this work apply the results of the ecological approach to archaeology. How does an ecological approach to Quinua ceramic production apply to the archaeology of the Ayacucho Valley? Chapter 9 argues that such an approach has important implications for understanding ancient ceramic production in the valley and in all of highland Peru. The concluding chapter (chapter 10) details the implications of the ecological approach in the preceding chapters to archaeology in general.

There are thus four consequences of the ecological approach used in this work. One shows how ceramic production is an adaptation to local ecological conditions. The second reveals the linkages between the ceramics and the technology, social organization and, to a lesser extent, the religion of the population which produces it. The third consequence shows that the ecological approach uses a unit of analysis (the population of potters) which reveals a set of design correlates of that unit. These correlates are the product of complex processes of individual choices and creativity, on the one hand, and social and aesthetic factors on the other. A final consequence of the ecological approach is its utility in understanding ceramic production in the past.

Quinua and Andean pottery making

Besides its contribution to the interpretation of ancient ceramics in general, this study is also a contribution to the ethnography of contemporary pottery making in the Peruvian Andes – an area that has been the subject of few such studies. Tschopik (1950) studied Aymara pottery making in the village of Chucuito in the Department of Puno. Ravines (1963–1964, 1966) studied pottery manufacture in two villages in the Department of Huancavelica. Spahni (1966) has given a brief description of pottery making in the villages of Checca and Pucara in the Department of Puno and in the village of Quinua in the Department of Ayacucho. LaVallée (1967) briefly described production in Aco in the Department of Junín while more recently, Hagstrum (1988, 1989) made a lengthy study of ceramic production in Quicha Grande and Aco. Karen Chavez (1984–85) has written an extensive description of pottery manufacture, distribution and consumption at Raqch'i in southern Peru. Sarah Lunt (personal communication) has studied contemporary pottery production west of Cuzco while Sillar (1988) has described pottery production in several communities south of Cuzco.[21] Christensen (1955), Collier (1959), Wiesse (1982) and Bankes (1985) made studies of pottery making in several communities on the coast of Peru while Litto's (1976) survey includes a variety of pottery-producing communities on the coast and in the highlands of Peru as well as in several other countries of South America. Many of the foregoing articles plus others about traditional ceramics in Peru have been compiled in a volume edited by Roger Ravines and Fernando Villiger (1989) making it the single most comprehensive source about contemporary pottery production in Peru.

Much has been written about the village of Quinua. Tschopik (1947) wrote a brief description of Quinua, but most of the information about the community comes from the work of William P. Mitchell whose research spans more than twenty years.[22] My own residence in Quinua overlapped partially with Mitchell's and his data and insight about the community have enriched my understanding of Quinua ceramic production greatly.

Unfortunately, relatively little is known about Quinua ceramic production. Spahni (1966: 74–88) and the Ayacucho volume of *Documental del Perú* (Cortazar 1967) briefly describe Quinua pottery making, but the latter is based almost exclusively on the data of the former except for the illustrations. Both works are oriented primarily toward describing pottery produced largely for the artisan market. Illustrations of Quinua pottery can also be found in descriptions of Peruvian folk art along with descriptions of Quinua churches (sometimes called "Ayacucho" churches) and other ritual pottery.[23] More recently, preliminary reports of my own work in Quinua[24] as well as brief descriptions of Quinua ceramics in Ravines and Villiger (1989) have also contributed to understanding pottery production there.

Besides the ecological approach used in this book and its application to archaeological interpretation, a study of pottery production in Quinua is important for two other reasons. First, Quinua ceramics are unique in the Ayacucho Valley. No other pottery made in the valley approaches that of Quinua in the diversity of vessel shapes, flexibility of expression and the complexity of its decoration. These characteristics also make Quinua pottery one of the most complex and diverse contemporary ceramic products of the entire Peruvian highlands. Quinua pottery is also unique in Latin America. Its pottery (churches, bulls, and other shapes) is exported to worldwide markets and is available in import shops in New York, Chicago, San Diego, Milwaukee and Europe.[25] A second reason that the study of Quinua pottery is important is because the community lies very near the ancient city of Huari, the capital of a great pre-Inca state which dominated much of central Peru between A.D. 600–800. Since ancient Huari also produced complex ceramics, the study of Quinua pottery may provide some insight into understanding the ancient ceramics of Huari.

These two reasons to study Quinua pottery, however, beg the ultimate question: Why? Why is Quinua pottery so complex and unique? Why has elaborate pottery production evolved here and not elsewhere in Peru? Why was such elaborate pottery made in ancient Huari and in modern Quinua? Although the answers to these questions are certainly relevant to Peruvian prehistory, they transcend cultural historical explanations that are unique to the Central Andes. Rather, they provide a case study of the power of the ecological approach that is not just relevant to Quinua, but has significant implications for understanding the relationship of ceramics to environment and society worldwide.

Five themes of decreasing levels of abstraction occur in the present work. The first is the ecological approach provided by cultural ecology. Ceramic production is an adaptation to local ecological conditions. The book describes ceramic production in classical cultural ecological format beginning with the environment, the relationships between the environment and the exploitative technology, between the technology and the society, and finally between the society and the ideology. A second theme is subsidiary to the ecological theme and traces the community of potters from chapter to chapter first as the unit of adaptation and then as the unit of analysis. This theme follows potters' adaptation to the environment and their choices used in the fabrication and decoration of their vessels. These choices are not determined by the environment, nor are they uniform across the population, but their presentation provides a comprehensive way of describing the variability of the ceramic products of a population. A third theme recognizes the importance of variability in ceramic production and describes that variability from the adaptation to the environment to the description of the design. The final theme is the simplest, most concrete level of all: the social and environmental context of ceramic production in Quinua. At its most basic level, this book describes the population of potters in Quinua and the ceramics that they produce.

2

The community: its physical environment and adaptation

The village of Quinua[1] lies in the south-central Andean highlands within a large inter-montane valley called the Ayacucho Valley. With an elevation of 3,280 meters,[2] the village is located on the upper portion of the gentle slopes of the eastern side of the valley. Approximately a kilometer northeast of the village, mountains rise sharply to elevations exceeding 4,300 meters (figure 2.1).

The community of Quinua consists of a nucleated village and dispersed rural settlements which together form the District of Quinua. In 1961, the District had 5,348 inhabitants with 394 persons living in the village and the remainder dispersed throughout its rural hinterland.[3] The village is the capital of the district which lies within the Province of Huamanga, one of seven such provinces in the Department of Ayacucho. Although the village is 15 kilometers directly north-northeast of the department capital of Ayacucho, 31 kilometers of winding unimproved road connected the village to the city in 1967. In 1974, the road was relocated, shortened and paved in order to increase the accessibility of the community.

Environment

Geologically, the Ayacucho Valley consists of two main components: a base of effusive volcanic rocks of Quaternary (or possibly Quaternary-Tertiary) origin, and relatively soft Quaternary sediments of fluvial origin. On the northeastern edge of the valley, there is an exposure of intrusive acidic rocks of Mesozoic age.[4]

The terrain around Quinua is the result of the successive deposition of layers of volcanic tuff and clays formed by glacial and alluvial action on rocks at higher elevations. While the gradual erosion of these layers has produced the gentle slopes of the region, streams fed by seasonal rains and lakes in the mountains have eroded deep ravines in the relatively soft beds of clay and tuff, often leaving only fingers of land between deeply eroded gullies (figure 2.2).

Two seasons characterize the yearly weather pattern: a wet season (December through March) and a dry season (May through August) with transitional months of April, September, October and November. The wet season begins in September with the amount and frequency of rainfall gradually increasing until the rains reach their climax in January and February (figure 2.3).[5] Most of the annual rainfall comes between December and March and then tapers off rather abruptly in April. September through December tends to be the time of highest mean temperatures (figure 2.4) although the highest temperature of the year can occur in June and July (Rivera 1971: 34). The average daily cloud cover gradually increases from October onward and reaches its maximum (87.5 percent) in January. In February, the cloud cover decreases only slightly with a daily average of 75 percent of the sky covered (Rivera 1967: 16). Relative humidity is highest from December through April (figure 2.5) while temperature oscillation between maximum and minimum is least during these months. In contrast, the dry season consists of warm sunny days with little or no rain (figures 2.3 and 2.4), although the nights are cold. June through August has the lowest mean temperatures with minimum temperatures dropping below freezing at night during June and July (Rivera 1971: 34; figure 2.4). Temperatures in the rural portions of the district, however, vary according to their elevation (figure 2.6).[6] June and July also have the least cloudiness and hence the most hours of sunshine even though the number of hours of daylight is the least of the entire year. Relative humidity is also lowest during this period (figure 2.5). Like any high altitude area, the Ayacucho region experiences considerable oscillation of

Figure 2.1 The central portion of the Ayacucho Valley (looking northeast) showing the location of the village of Quinua (arrow) taken from a mountain summit (Quehuahuilca) 12 km west of Ayacucho. The lighter shaded area in an oval-shape located to the left of the arrow is the Plain of Ayacucho. The ecological zones on the eastern slope of the Ayacucho Valley are also visible in the photograph as horizontal bands of different shades of gray. The lighter area along the tops of the mountains is the montane prairie (as is the foreground). The darker band along the lower slopes of the mountains is the montane moist forest. The lighter area below it is the lower montane savannah or dry forest, but it is only visible as a shade of gray slightly lighter than the zone above it. Its boundary can be followed across the photograph from a point above the head of the arrow. The lower montane steppe lies in the center of the valley in the center of the photograph, but it cannot be clearly differentiated here from the lower montane savannah above it. The ancient city of Huari lies in the exact center of the photograph in the center of the valley. For a map of the same area and a key to the ecological zones, see figure 2.8.

temperatures between day and night with daily temperature change exceeding the range of the seasonal extremes of maximum (4.6° C) and minimum temperature (7.5° C). Because precipitation comes from the east, the Quinua area receives more of the moisture and inclement weather than Ayacucho and the remainder of the valley to the west (figure 2.7). During February and March of 1967 (a rather atypical year, see the preface), rain fell intermittently almost every day, and, for the most part, Quinua was cloaked in heavy fog and low clouds. There were few days with

Figure 2.2 Aerial photograph of the Quinua area showing its highly eroded character. The dense fields and paths around the village of Quinua are located in the right center of the photograph whereas the plaza of the village of Huamanguilla is located in the extreme top center of the photograph along with the checkered fields and paths around the village. The remains of the ancient city of Huari cover most of the lower left quadrant with its urban core visible as a series of walls and enclosures located slightly left of, and below, the center of the photograph. The District of Huamanguilla lies in the upper half of the photograph and the District of Quinua lies in the lower half. The portion of the District of Quinua described in this chapter (that is the lower montane savannah) occurs in the middle third of the right half of the photograph. Compare this figure with figure 2.8. The top of the photograph is north (photo courtesy of Servicio Geográfico Militar, Lima).

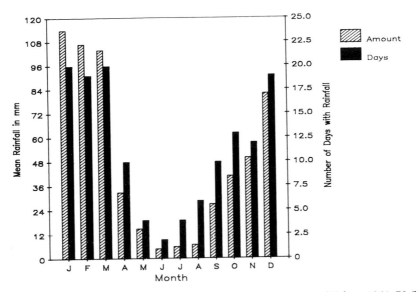

Figure 2.3 Rainfall in Ayacucho showing the mean amount of rainfall from 1961–70 (left scale), and mean number of days with rainfall (right scale) from 1962–70 except for July, August and September of 1969, June of 1970 and 1964 for which there are no data (data from Rivera 1967: 41, 43).

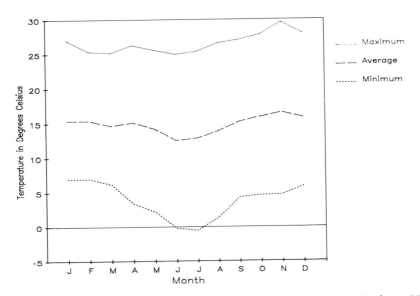

Figure 2.4 The maximum, average and minimum temperatures in Ayacucho from 1962–69. Average (mean) temperatures are for the period from 1962–69 except for January, February and March of 1962 for which there are no data. Maximum and minimum temperatures are for the period of 1962–66 except for January, February and March of 1962 and October, November and December of 1966 for which there are no data (compiled from Rivera 1967 and Rivera 1971: 32).

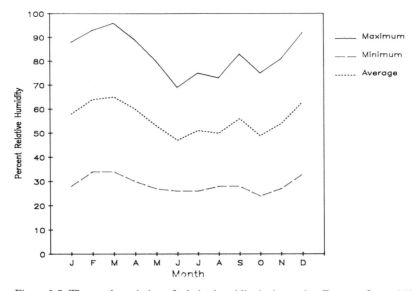

Figure 2.5 The yearly variation of relative humidity in Ayacucho. Data are from 1965–66 except for October, November and December which are from 1965 only. Average relative humidity was calculated from the mean of the maximum and minimum values (based on data in Rivera 1967, 1971).

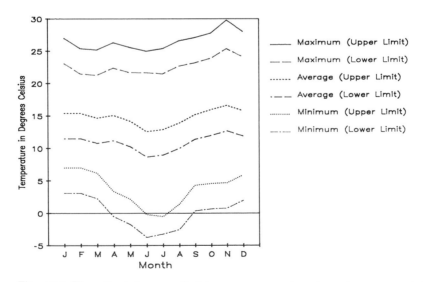

Figure 2.6 The estimated ranges of minimum, average and maximum temperatures in Quinua based on the temperatures in Ayacucho from 1962–66 corrected for elevation. The upper limit temperatures are the Ayacucho values (at 2,761 m) which are probably the highest temperatures for the lower portion of the lower montane savannah in Quinua across the valley (at 2,750 m). The lower limit temperatures are the Ayacucho values corrected for the elevation of the village of Quinua. There is a difference of 0.6° C for each 100 meters of altitude and the village of Quinua is 650 m higher than Ayacucho. So, Quinua temperatures are the Ayacucho values minus 3.9° (chart created from data in Rivera 1967, 1971).

sunshine and the days and nights were generally miserable because of overcast skies and rain. Meanwhile, across the valley to the west, the city of Ayacucho experienced periods of sunshine during this same period – even on days with rainfall. Relative humidity, rainfall and the amount of cloudiness were thus higher on the eastern slope of the valley than in other areas to the west.

Because of the great differences in altitude from the top of mountains to the bottom of the valley, different elevations have different mean temperatures and amounts of cloud cover, sunshine and rainfall. These differences create the five major ecological zones on the eastern side of the valley (table 2.1, figure 2.8 [compare with figure 2.1]). These zones have varying resource potentials for human populations, are exploited differently and have a profound effect on population sizes (figure 2.9).[7]

The alpine rain tundra/subalpine wet paramo dominates the high mountainous area above 4,100 meters. This zone does not support agriculture because of its low mean annual temperature, but rather serves as grazing land for llamas.[8]

Immediately below this zone (between approximately 4,000 and 4,100 meters) lies the montane prairie which covers the upper parts of the steep slopes east of Quinua and extends down into the high valleys above the community (Tosi 1960; figure 2.10). Consisting mostly of bunch grasses, the prairie serves as an important food resource for the animals which graze there, but agriculture is practiced here in

Figure 2.7 View of the eastern side of valley looking southeast from Ayacucho showing rainfall in the mountains on the eastern edge of the valley. Because rainfall comes exclusively from the east, most of it falls on the eastern slopes. Much of the remainder of the valley lies in a rain shadow. Quinua thus gets more rain and more inclement weather than Ayacucho.

Table 2.1. *Major ecological zones in the District of Quinua, Peru*

Zone	Evapotranspiration potential (in %)[a]	Mean annual temperature (in degrees Celsius)	Annual precipitation (in mm)
Alpine rain tundra	less than 0.25	0–3	500–1,000
Subalpine wet paramo	0.25–0.50	3–6	500–1,000
Montane prairie and moist forest	0.50–1.00	6–12	500–1,000
Lower montane savannah or dry forest	1.00–2.00	12–14	500–1,000
Lower montane thorn steppe	2.00–4.00	12–24	250–500

[a] Holdridge's (1947) and Tosi's (1960) estimate of evapotranspiration is controversial (see Frère et al. 1975: 133; Knapp 1988: 28–29). Frère et al. (1975) use a value called *evaporation potential* and discuss several alternative ways of calculating it. In any case, the evapotranspiration for the higher zones utilized here is probably not as low and that for the lower zones not as high as Holdridge (1947) and Tosi (1960) indicate (see Mitchell 1991a: 37). Evapotranspiration increases with a decrease in altitude, but according to the calculations of Frère et al. (1975), the evaporation potential increases only 20 percent from the altitude of the highest zone indicated here (about 4,100 m) to that of the lowest zone (the valley bottom, about 2,500 m).
Source: from Tosi 1960 and Holdridge 1947.

addition to herding. In the upper portion of this zone, bitter potatoes (*Solanum* spp.) are the only crop while in the lower portion, other varieties of potatoes and other Andean tubers like *oca*,[9] *mashua*[10] and *ullucu*[11] are grown (figure 2.11).[12] Agricultural land in this zone, however, must lie fallow for five to seven years for every two years of cultivation. As a result, only a small percentage of this zone is actually cultivated in any one year.[13]

Below the prairie, the montane moist forest consists of dense underbrush of small trees and shrubs 2.5 to 3 meters in height (Tosi 1960). This zone covers the lower portions of the mountains down to where the slopes become more gradual from about 4,000 to 3,400 meters. Agriculture in the prairie is limited to tubers grown in the zone above, a high altitude variety of *quinoa*[14] and a variety of Old World crops like wheat (*Triticum* sp.), barley (*Hordeum* sp.), peas (*Pisum sativum* L.) and broad beans (*Vicia faba*). Much of the land is uncultivated and requires one to five years lying fallow for every three years of cultivation. A considerable variety of wild vegetation grows in this zone and these plants are used for fuel for firing pottery, for making baskets and for culinary and medicinal purposes.[15]

Moving down the slope, the lower montane savannah lies between 3,400 and 2,850 meters and begins at the base of the steep slopes of the mountains. Although the moist forest extends down into the gorges in the upper portions of this zone, the upper boundary of the savannah is best characterized as the upper limit of irrigation and maize agriculture. The boundary between the savannah and the moist forest above is thus not a natural vegetation boundary, but rather one determined by technological criteria. The savannah receives approximately the same amount of annual rainfall as the zones above, but because of more sunshine, higher temperatures and a lower altitude, more moisture is lost from the soil through evaporation and transpiration.[16]

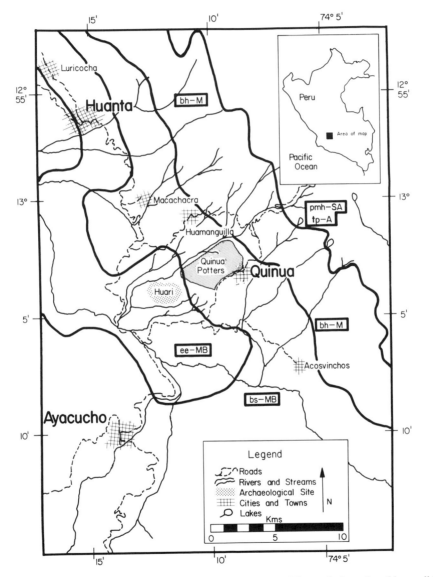

Figure 2.8 The ecological zones in the Quinua area. The symbols enclosed in small boxes identify the zones outlined by heavy lines. These symbols are the abbreviations of Tosi's (1960) Spanish labels: *tp*-A, alpine rain tundra; *pmh*-SA, subalpine wet paramo; *bh*-M, montane prairie or moist forest; *bs*-MB, lower montane savannah or dry forest; *ee*-MB, lower montane thorn steppe. The map was produced by projecting Tosi's zones onto the map of the Ayacucho quadrangle (scale = 1/200,000). Boundaries of the zones in the Quinua region were established by applying Tosi's criteria to the author's data. A photograph across these zones can be seen in figure 2.1.

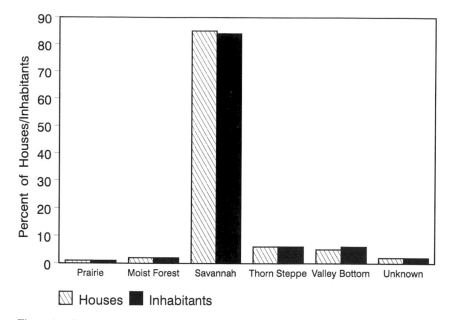

Figure 2.9 Percent of houses (N = 1,370) and population (N = 5,348) in the 1961 census that occurred in each ecological zone in the District of Quinua (adapted from data in Mitchell 1991a: 44).

Figure 2.10 A high mountain valley in the montane prairie above Quinua. This valley contains the stream (lower right) which is the origin of the irrigation system for the Lurinsayuq portion of the community. The origin of the irrigation system for the Hanansayuq portion of the community lies over the mountain ridge on the left (see also Flannery, Marcus and Reynolds 1989: 17). Dark areas on slopes and floor of the valley are cultivated fields.

The savannah is the single most important agricultural zone in the entire region. The largest percentage of the population of the district lives here and it has the highest population density of all of the ecological zones of the district (figure 2.9). The nucleated settlement of the village of Quinua is located here as well as most of the highly dispersed rural households. The savannah is also the highest zone in which maize can be cultivated (see also Tosi 1960: 111), but potatoes, *oca*, *mashua*, wheat, oats (*Avena sativa*), peas, a low altitude variety of *quinoa*, broad beans, squash (probably *Cucurbita maxima*) and beans (probably *Phaseolus vulgaris*) are also grown here. The savannah is also the most important zone for irrigation; no significant irrigation exists in the moist forest zone above nor in the zone below, except in the food plain in the bottom of the valley.

The lowest ecological zone is the lower montane thorn steppe and occurs between 2,500 and 2,850 meters. Less rain falls here and this zone is warmer and sunnier than the zones above. Furthermore, more moisture is lost from the soil through evapotranspiration (Tosi 1960: 72–79). Because of these factors, there is less agriculture here and little, if any, irrigation. Crops are limited to those with low water needs such as wheat, peas, chick peas (*Cicer arietinum*) and barley (Mitchell 1991: 42). If the rains come early and appear to be abundant, however, *quinoa*, maize and

Figure 2.11 A settlement (located in the approximate center of figure 2.10) in the montane prairie above Quinua. Inhabitants of this zone combine herding (largely llamas) with the cultivation of tubers. Tubers are planted on the slopes outside of the settlement and in the nutrient-rich soil of the vacant corrals. Corrals are rotated between tuber cultivation and holding pens for llamas; animals are kept in one corral and then rotated to another so that the former corrals can be used for growing tubers. Former corrals used for tuber cultivation can be seen extending from the left center to the lower right of the photograph.

a type of squash may be grown here, but only with great risk of failure (Mitchell 1991a: 42). Wild products of this zone include the small fruits of the pepper tree[17] and the fruits (called *tuna*) of the prickly pear cactus.[18]

The last major ecological zone of the District of Quinua is the irrigated alluvial flood plain which lies in the bottom of the valley (*c.* 2,500 meters). Crops grown include varieties of those grown in the zones above (such as maize), and various fruits and vegetables (Mitchell 1991a: 42). Cultivation occurs throughout the year.

In summary, as one moves down the slope, the amount of sunshine increases, the mean annual temperature rises and the amount of rainfall decreases. Similarly, the amount of evapotranspiration increases so that effective moisture content of the soil is reduced from zone to zone down-slope (see table 2.1). The lower mean annual temperature and the greater cloudiness of the upper zones serve to inhibit evapotranspiration although these values are not as low as Holdridge (1947) and Tosi (1960) suggest (see Mitchell 1991a: 37–38). Population is concentrated in the lower montane savannah while the remainder of the zones have very low population sizes (figure 2.9).

The spatial organization of the community

One of the ways to describe the adaptation and social organization of a community is to see it in terms of the way in which it organizes space. There are several ways in which the inhabitants of Quinua organize the environmental and social space in their community. The first way consists of the division of the environmental space in the district into a series of horizontal ecological zones. A second pattern consists of the division of one of these zones (the lower montane savannah) into socio-political units. A third pattern distinguishes between residents of the village and the rural inhabitants in the district while a final pattern consists of kin group affiliation organized by both patrilineal and bilateral principles. Each of these will be described in more detail below.

The series of ecological zones on the eastern slope of the Basin (figures 2.8 and 2.1; table 2.1) is the most basic organization of space in Quinua. Each of these zones is exploited differently so that the zonal differences are not just environmental zones, but rather techno-environmental zones. These zones, however, are not distinguished linguistically, but are collapsed into two categories: the *sallqa* or the upper zones consisting of the montane, alpine or sub-alpine zones and the *kichwa* or the lower zones consisting of the lower montane zones and the alluvial river valley[19] (see table 2.1; figures 2.8 and 2.1).

The boundaries of the District of Quinua are arranged to include all of these zones and the inhabitants have access to the products of each in several ways: (1) a family may have fields in more than one zone (see Mitchell 1991a); (2) goods from one zone may be exchanged with products of another zone in the Sunday market; and (3) direct exchange may occur between producers of each zone apart from the formal Sunday market. Inhabitants of the montane prairie, for example, may bring pack trains of llamas loaded with tubers down into the village for sale or exchange (see Flannery, Marcus and Reynolds 1989). Similarly, potters may carry their pots up into the montane prairie or montane moist forest to exchange for tubers. Each zone thus has its unique products which are sold or exchanged with inhabitants of other zones (see Mitchell 1991a: 87–89). The subdivision of the region around Quinua into a series of vertically arranged ecological zones and accompanying exploitative strategies is thus the single most important organizing principle of environmental space in Quinua.

This vertical multi-zonal pattern occurs widely in the Andes and provides a basis of complementary adaptive strategies in which the community strives for (but may never realize) self-sufficiency.[20] In Quinua, this pattern consists of the compressed type of zonation where a steep gradient places different zones relatively close to one another with each accessible within a reasonably short travel time (Brush 1977: 11). In this variant of the pattern, Andeans can exploit the entire range of ecological zones and obtain necessary subsistence items without major migration, trade networks or exchange systems which reach beyond the territorial limits of the community (Brush 1977: 11). This same pattern of vertical zonation is also inter-woven in dreams, mythology, ritual and cosmology in the Pampas River valley to the south of Ayacucho and in highland Bolivia.[21] The widespread occurrence of this zonation principle not only demonstrates its great significance as an adaptive pattern in the Andes, but also reveals its importance in organizing behavior in other areas of Andean society.

The second major pattern of spatial organization in Quinua consists of the division of the community into two sub-sections or *barrios*. This division has a hydrographic basis with profound political and social implications. Each of the Quinua *barrios* corresponds to the boundaries of the two major irrigation systems in the community. These systems begin in the moist forest above the community and extend into the steppe below, but they principally serve the lower montane savannah. Because the flow of water in the irrigation system is based on gravity, the canal network follows the drainage patterns of two adjacent slopes. The water on one slope thus flows into a ravine on one side of the community and the water on the adjacent slope flows into a ravine on the other side of the community. A low ridge between the slopes divides the drainage of the two ravines (figure 2.12). Each of these drainage areas corresponds to each of the two major irrigation systems and each coincides with each of the two *barrios* of the community. One drainage area corresponds to the Lurinsayuq *barrio* and is served by one irrigation system and the other drainage area corresponds to the Hanansayuq *barrio* and is served by the other system (figures 2.13(a) and 2.13(b)). The irrigation pattern thus exploits these drainage differences: the Lurinsayuq system drains into the Huamangura ravine northwest of the community, and the Hanansayuq system drains into Hatun Wayqu, the large ravine to the southeast. The irrigation pattern thus subdivides and organizes social and environmental space in the savannah (Mitchell 1976a).

Until recently, the Lurinsayuq section (or *barrio*) of the community had its own native political organization (called the *varayuq*) which, among other tasks, func-tioned to administer the irrigation system.[22] Currently, the officials of the District of Quinua have assumed this function for both *barrios*.[23]

Although irrigation water in both systems is supplemented by springs, less water is available in the *barrio* of Lurinsayuq, even though the amount of irrigated land there is greater. In both *barrios* of the community, however, the amount of water is limited and sufficient only for a fixed irrigation schedule at the beginning of the main sowing (the *hatun tarpuy*) and for supplementary water after the heavy rains begin. The irrigation system thus cannot supply water to all agricultural land throughout the year (Mitchell 1991a: 61).

Irrigation water is used for each of the two agricultural cycles in Quinua: the dry season cycle and the rainy season cycle. The dry season cycle (the *michka*) produces two successive crops that mature rapidly such as a three-month potato variety followed by barley. The first planting begins in August and depends almost entirely on irrigation for moisture. The second crop is planted in November or December and uses rainfall for moisture. Because irrigation water is inadequate for a dry-season crop throughout the district, the two-crop cycle is utilized only on the upper slopes near the beginning of the canal network (see Mitchell 1976a). The second agricultural cycle (the *hatun tarpuy*) is almost exclusively devoted to maize. It occurs largely during the rainy season, is supplemented by irrigation and begins at different times depending on the altitude (see Mitchell 1991a: 71–73).

Irrigation provides a crucial element of adaptation in the savannah because it expands the amount of land on which maize can be successfully cultivated. Maize is a highly valued crop because it can be stored for long periods of time, has a wide variety of uses (see also Murra 1973) and is an important source of protein which, in contrast to other protein-rich crops, is eaten every day (William P. Mitchell, personal communication). Maize also has symbolic importance and is used to make beer which is crucial in recruiting labor outside of the household (see chapter 6). In the lower montane savannah, climate and rainfall combine to make maize cultivation impossible without irrigation except in a narrow horizontal band. In the upper portion of the savannah, colder temperatures prolong the maturation of maize to a total of nine months. Because rainfall from September through November is insufficient for maize germination and growth, maize must be planted in December when the regular heavy rains begin. The six months between the December rains and the night frosts in early June, however, do not provide sufficient time for the maize to mature before the frost occurs. In order to allow the maize to reach maturity, maize must be planted in September. Because the regular rains do not begin until December, irrigation must be used between September and December in order to provide moisture to extend the growing season into the time of infrequent and insufficient rainfall. For other crops besides maize, however, colder temperatures do not delay maturation enough to extend the growing season beyond the six months period between the beginning of the heavy rains and the onset of frost. Indeed, most of these other crops (or the frost-tolerant varieties of them) are also grown in the montane moist forest above where the growing season is shorter and there is greater danger of frosts. They can thus be grown in the savannah without irrigation.

The lower portion of the savannah presents a different problem for maize cultivation. In this zone, maize requires only six months to reach maturity because the climate is warmer and sunnier. Maize can be planted in December when the regular rains begin and the crop can reach maturity before the June frosts. Because the lower savannah lies close to the drier lower montane thorn steppe, however, moisture availability is less certain here and is insufficient for a successful maize crop. Maize grown in the lower savannah is thus irrigated during the rainy season to provide sufficient moisture.

The irrigation system thus functions in complementary ways in the lower montane savannah. In the upper part of this zone, it permits the growing season to begin earlier during the period of insufficient and erratic rainfall from September through November. This practice allows maize to mature sufficiently before the killing frosts occur in June. In the lower part of this zone, irrigation serves to supplement rainfall during the rains from December through April.

To implement this complementary pattern of water supply, irrigation starts on the upper slopes in September and descends field by field with water reaching the lowest

Figure 2.12 View of the Quinua area (slightly right of center) from above looking southwest towards the city of Ayacucho. The village of Quinua (arrow) lies along a low ridge (not visible here) which extends down the slope and separates two drainage areas. The drainage to the left of the village has its own irrigation system which drains into the ravine on the lower left. This area corresponds to the Hanansayuq *barrio*. The drainage area to the right of the village has its own irrigation system and drains into a ravine out of sight on the right of the photograph. This area corresponds to the Lurinsayuq *barrio*. The uncultivated area in the lower right portion of the photograph at the base of the mountain is the Plain of Ayacucho where the Battle of Ayacucho occurred in 1824. The city of Ayacucho and its airport can be seen in the upper left portion of the photograph.

fields by December (Mitchell 1976a, 1976b). Then, when the heavy rains begin in December, irrigation stops in the upper fields and water is sent down the slope to those in the lower portion of the savannah to supplement rainfall. The system of irrigating different fields in a downward temporal sequence thus represents an adaptation to the moisture and maturation requirements for maize, on the one hand, and the micro-zonal variation in the lower montane savannah, on the other.

In summary, the irrigation system in Quinua helps the local population to exploit

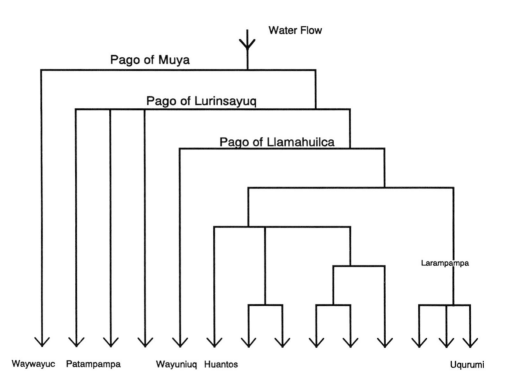

Figure 2.13(a) Schematic diagram of the irrigation system of Quinua showing how the flow of water through the major canals defines the division of the *barrio* of Lurinsayuq into socio-political sub-units. Each of the lines in the diagram represents a major canal in the community with water flowing from the source of the irrigation system at the top of the diagram to the individual hamlets at the bottom. Each *barrio* has its own irrigation system. There is one system for the Lurinsayuq *barrio* (shown here) and another for the Hanansayuq *barrio* (figure 2.13(b)). The source of each system begins in the alpine tundra zone above the community and each drains into one of the large ravines which border the community. In this system, the irrigation system divides the political organization of the community into *pagos* and then into *sitios*. Some of the *sitios* in which potters live occur near the end of the system and are named at the bottom of the diagram. Water in this system eventually drains into the Huamangura Ravine which is the western boundary of the District of Quinua (diagram drawn from map in Mitchell 1976a: 31).

their environment in two ways. First, it raises the altitude of effective maize farming and, second, it increases the productivity of certain areas marginal for maize agriculture by making a two-crop sequence possible where only one crop could otherwise be grown. In the higher portion of the savannah, irrigation increases the area of maize cultivation by extending moisture availability when maturation requirements exceed the period of heavy rains because of the altitude. In the lower portion of this zone, where rainfall is unreliable, irrigation permits maize cultivation by supplementing rainfall during the rainy season when irrigation water is not utilized farther up the slope (Mitchell 1976a, 1976b, 1977).

In addition to the bisection of the rural community into two *barrios* and its sub-division of irrigated land into upper and lower sections, the canal network of the irrigation system also subdivides each *barrio* into administrative sub-parts. Although these sub-parts are topographically defined, the canal network must follow the topography to keep the water running downhill. The canal system thus subdivides each *barrio* into *pagos* which are topographic areas usually bounded by deep gullies. In the *barrio* of Lurinsayuq, for example, the canals subdivide the land into the three sub-sections (called *pagos*) of Muya, Lurinsayuq and Llamahuilca (fig. 2.13(a)).

Source: Yanaqucha Chicha

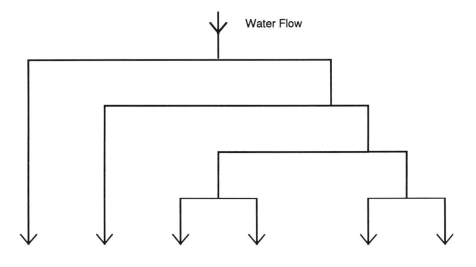

Hatun Wayqu Ravine

Figure 2.13(b) Schematic diagram of the irrigation system of Quinua showing the pattern of the major canals in the Hanansayuq *barrio*. Water in this system eventually drains toward the Hatun Wayqu Ravine which is the major ravine north and east of the village of Quinua. The names of subsections of the community have been left off this diagram because no potters lived in the Hanansayuq *barrio* in 1967 (see chapter 6). For more detailed information, see Mitchell (1976a). The diagram is drawn from a map in Mitchell (1976a: 31).

Muya lies closest to the Huamangura Ravine northwest of the village (see figure 2.2). Lurinsayuq is immediately down-slope from the village to the north and northwest and Llamahuilca is further down-slope from the village to the southwest. Smaller stream cuts and abrupt changes of altitude such as cliffs, gullies, or steep slopes further sub-divide the *pagos* into the relatively flat *sitios* or individual hamlets (figure 2.14).

Another important principle of spatial organization in the community is the distinction between the district capital and the rural portion of the community. This distinction represents a division of space which reflects the basic categories in the Quinua world view.[24] Local people label the inhabitants of the nucleated center of the community as *vecinos* (literally "neighbors") and those of the rural portion as *campesinos* or "peasants." This distinction occurs elsewhere in Latin America as the difference between two types of peasants which represent differences in social class.[25] One type (the *vecinos*) is more acculturated to the national Hispanic culture in terms of language, literacy and dress while the other type (the *campesinos*) is less acculturated in terms of native language, dress and in the lack of ability to read, write and speak Spanish.[26] While these distinctions in Quinua are clear geographically and from the point of view of ideal behavior, the attributes cannot be clearly applied to any one individual because of the change and fluidity in the system. Indeed, Mitchell (1974, 1979) reports that considerable status inconsistency exists within the system.

Finally, a fourth kind of social space used in the community consists of kin group affiliation. Kin groups are both patrilineal[27] and bilateral.[28] All relatives with the

Figure 2.14 The rural hamlet of Añaqata (center) below the village of Quinua (in the *barrio* of Lurinsayuq) in the lower montane savannah. Rural households outside of the village are dispersed in various hamlets (called *sitios*) that are defined by relatively flat areas that are bounded by abrupt changes in elevation.

same patronym (*apellido*) form a kin group called a *casta*. People regard others with the same patronym as kin and form close ties with them, but this group has no corporate functions. More important, however, is the bilateral kin group called the *ayllu*. Each individual in Quinua belongs to an *ayllu* which consists of all of the lineal and collateral kin in one's own generation and in the first and second ascending and descending generations on both one's mother's and one's father's sides. Thus, one's *ayllu* will consist of one's children, children's children, siblings, parents, grandparents, parents' siblings, parents' siblings' children, grandparents' siblings, and siblings' children. Collateral relatives beyond these individuals, descendants of grandparents' siblings and those in the third ascending and descending generations are called *karu ayllu*. Kinship is rarely determined beyond the second generation and thus *karu ayllu* consists of those relatives for whom the precise relationship to the speaker is unknown (Mitchell 1991a: 48).

3

The environment and culture history

Besides a description of the local environment elaborated in the previous chapter, another approach to the ecology of Quinua is to see it from the perspective of the culture history of the region. During the last 1,500 years, Quinua has occupied a unique place in Peru's past and examining its culture history suggests that the environment probably played a significant role in this uniqueness.

There are two environmental factors which are critical for understanding the culture history of Quinua. The first factor concerns the relationship of the Ayacucho Valley to the broader environmental picture of southern Peru. In all of southern Peru, the Ayacucho Valley is one of the largest and broadest valleys of relatively low (less than 3,300 meters) agricultural land (see Onuki 1967: 89, 91). Only the Cuzco and nearby Urubamba/Vilcanota River Valleys may have more high quality agricultural land at a comparable or lower elevation. In the Ayacucho Valley, this arable land consists of the lower montane savannah along the edges of the valley, portions of the montane thorn steppe and a large area of rich alluvial land on the valley floor (figures 2.1 and 2.8). Much of the savannah is relatively flat or located on gentle slopes compared to other areas in the southern Andes and is ideal for the cultivation of maize. If the climate was wetter in the past than it is today,[1] larger amounts of land (for example in the montane thorn steppe) may have been available for agriculture. The Quinua region thus had the agricultural potential for large dense populations with a large amount of land available for maize cultivation.

Second, the Ayacucho Valley is an important travel corridor between the central and southern Andes of Peru. The highland road between Lima, Huancayo and Cuzco goes through the valley today and it is an important node for roads to the tropical forest to the east and the Peruvian coast to the west.

As this chapter will demonstrate, these two factors were critical environmental features which appear to have profoundly affected the culture history in the valley. They were also critical for the production and distribution of ceramics in both the present and the past.

The Middle Horizon
Although human occupation in the valley goes back to the late Pleistocene,[2] the events that relate most clearly to the ecology of ceramic production began in the Middle Horizon Period (A.D. 600–800) when the Quinua area was the center of a great pre-Inca state which dominated the central and southern parts of Peru.

Ceramics reached a high point of development during this time when the valley was the source of a number of complex and highly specialized ceramic styles which utilized a wide repertoire of shapes, slips and paints (figures 3.1 and 3.2). Many of these styles were produced in the ancient city of Huari in association with extensive state-constructed administrative facilities that included temples, storehouses, barrack-like quarters, and community kitchens (Isbell 1988: 189). For about 300 years, Huari was the economic, political and religious center of a vast Andean state

Figure 3.1 A polychrome vessel of the Robles Moqo Style that was probably made in the ancient city of Huari during the Middle Horizon (A.D. 600–800) when a number of complex polychrome styles developed in the Ayacucho Valley. (Vessel photographed in the Museum of the Instituto Nacional de Cultura in Ayacucho.)

that conquered territory, conducted trade, and probably extracted tribute from widespread regions of highland and coastal Peru.

Huari is an enormous urban complex consisting of an urban core of 250 hectares with extensive occupational debris covering an area of 15–18 square kilometers (see figure 2.2). Population estimates of the city vary from a low 10,000–20,000 to a high 35,000–70,000.[3]

This great urban complex lies 5 kilometers down the slope from the village of Quinua in the lower montane thorn steppe (figures 2.1 and 2.2). Quinua potters, however, live much closer to the site. Some reside only one kilometer from the urban core with only a large ravine separating their households from the architectural center of the city. Given the great size of the Huari archaeological zone, it is quite possible that some modern potters now live on what was once the edges of the ancient city.

The development of Huari has its roots in the period between 200 B.C.–A.D. 600 (the Early Intermediate Period) when the first urban settlements emerged in the Ayacucho Valley. These settlements were associated with a pottery style which displayed strong stylistic influences from the Nazca area on the south coast of Peru.[4] Four communities from this period have been identified in the Huari archaeological zone and one of these eventually expanded into a town which ultimately became the city of Huari. This growth may have been at the expense of the other Early Intermediate communities because as nascent Huari grew, other communities nearby were abandoned.[5]

Beginning in the early part of the Middle Horizon (about A.D. 600 in Epoch 1A), Huari became an important ceremonial and residential center with the construction of temples and ceremonial precincts using a technology of megalithic dressed-stones. Although this technology was similar to that used at the Bolivian site of Tiahuanaco located south of Lake Titicaca, the differences between the Huari and Tiahuanaco architecture suggest that Tiahuanaco stone masons were working under the direction of Huari planners.[6]

After this new construction technology appeared at Huari, a new pottery style appeared 8 kilometers away at the site of Conchopata in the southern part of the valley. This novel style consisted of large vessels decorated with mythical themes resembling those carved on the low-relief sculpture at the Bolivian site of Tiahuanaco (figure 3.3).[7]

Tiahuanaco was also the center of a large Andean state (Browman 1981a; Kolata 1982), but rather than being derived from Tiahuanaco, the Ayacucho iconography probably originated from the site of Pucara north of Lake Titicaca.[8] Ayacucho iconography is more similar to that of Pucara than to Tiahuanaco, and Pucara iconography antedates that of Tiahuanaco by several hundred years. One of its themes ("the staff god", see figure 3.3) has its roots in the Chavin style about a millennium earlier. It is unclear why the new iconography was accepted in Ayacucho (and Tiahuanaco), but it is possible that it provided a visual symbol for existing mythical and religious concepts (Isbell 1983) or was the iconography of a revitalization movement.

Figure 3.2 A polychrome ceramic llama of the Robles Moqo Style probably made in the ancient city of Huari during the Middle Horizon (A.D. 600–800). (Vessel photographed in the Museum of the Instituto Nacional de Cultura in Ayacucho.)

Figure 3.3 The carvings on the Gateway of the Sun at the Bolivian site of Tiahuanaco south of Lake Titicaca. Motifs similar to this appeared on pottery at the site of Conchopata in the Ayacucho Valley during the Middle Horizon Period. The central figure with the staff in each hand also occurs in iconography from Pucara during the Early Intermediate Period (200 B.C.–A.D. 600) and in Chavin iconography in the northern Peruvian Andes during the Early Horizon Period (900–200 B.C.).

Once established at Huari, the new iconography occurred on local pottery and on that found in many parts of the central Andes from the Acarí River on the south coast to Huaraz in the north. Monumental architecture expanded at Huari and at nearby Conchopata during this time (see figure 3.4). An urban grid developed at Huari in which walled streets and large block-like, modular units were constructed that were 150–300 meters on a side and surrounded by high walls. This patio-like construction was a product of the remodeling project that focused on a central plan and was probably the outcome of a government which could control substantial amounts of labor. This control over labor and the absence of other sites in the valley with such monumental architecture during this period suggests that Huari was a new center of power and influence in the Ayacucho Valley.[9]

Planned provincial centers were also constructed at this time at Pikillaqta, Viracochapampa, and Jargampata and Jincamocco in widely separated parts of Peru.[10] These planned centers suggest that the Huari state had a centralized administration for the collection and distribution of goods.

By the close of Epoch 1 of the Middle Horizon, settlement patterns in the Ayacucho Valley had shifted. Settlements in the northern, central and southern part

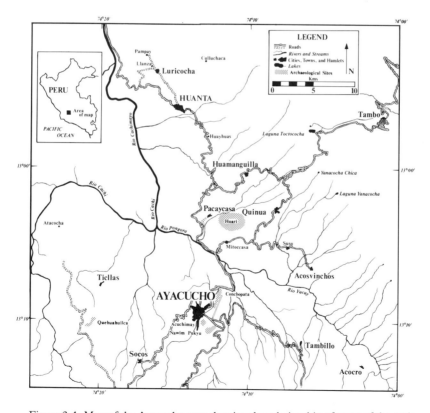

Figure 3.4 Map of the Ayacucho area showing the relationship of some of the major archaeological sites and the modern cities and towns (map drawn from 1:100,000 map of Ayacucho Quadrangle, Instituto Geográfico Militar, Peru, 1970).

of the valley were either abandoned or significantly depopulated and much of the population was living in Huari.[11]

In Epoch 2 of the Middle Horizon, Huari was remodeled again. Immense walls with a thickness of several meters were constructed to enclose architectural complexes. The grid organization and the patio construction of previous architectural phases are absent and in one instance, a large wall was erected across the site as an isolated unit. Rather, trapezoids and elongated triangles seemed to have been the preferred building shapes.[12]

The distribution of Huari pottery reached its greatest extent during this time and planned administrative facilities were constructed at Azángaro in the northern part of the Ayacucho valley.[13] During the early portion of this period (Epoch 2A), however, stylistic disunity began to appear on the coast and this change suggested that new iconographic themes and religious centers were being established outside of Huari. One of these centers emerged at Pachacamac and produced pottery that diluted the Huari stylistic influence on the central coast. A separate center and associated pottery style (the Atarco Style) occurred in the Nazca Valley on the south Coast (Menzel 1974: 70).

After Epoch 2 of the Middle Horizon, the city of Huari was abandoned and large urban settlements in the Ayacucho Valley ended. No large amounts of fancy pottery were made in the valley again during prehistoric times and centralized political power disappeared along with the large dense populations that occurred during the Middle Horizon (Menzel 1964: 72). No large cities arose in the valley again until the emergence of the city of Huamanga (Ayacucho) during the Spanish colonial period.

After the rise and fall of Huari, four significant factors affected the culture history of the region: the Chancas, the Inca conquest, the Spanish conquest and the Battle of Ayacucho. Most of the data about this period comes from historic sources, but the relationship of the historical data to the archaeology of the region is far from clear.

The Chancas

After the Middle Horizon, the Quinua area was dominated by an ethnic group called the Chancas. The Chancas are known from a variety of Spanish chroniclers.[14] Unfortunately, the meaning of the term "Chanca" is not always clear in the historical documents and may have several different meanings (Zuidema 1967: 10). One meaning refers to an historical tribe which lived around Andahuaylas at the time that the Spanish arrived. The Chancas were said to have conquered the Quechuas and established their capital in Andahuaylas.[15] From there, they attacked Cuzco during the reign of Viracocha, the eighth Inca.[16] When the Chancas threatened the Inca capital of Cuzco, the Supreme Inca, Viracocha, fled the city along with his son and the heir to the throne, Inca Urcon.[17] Two generals and several nobles, however, refused to leave Cuzco and mounted a defense against the attacking Chancas.[18] One of these nobles was Yupanqui, another son of Viracocha, who assumed command of the defending troops, rallied the inhabitants of Cuzco to defeat the attacking Chancas[19] and routed them again at their encampment near Cuzco.[20] After this victory, Yupanqui received the title of Supreme Inca, was named "Pachecuti" (which means "cataclysm" or "overturner of the earth") and began his territorial expansion of the Inca state.[21]

Although the Chancas are historically linked with the beginning of the expansion of the Inca empire near Cuzco, there are some data that link their origin to the Ayacucho area. According to Cieza de León, the Chancas believed that their fore-fathers had emerged from a lake called Choclococha located southwest of Ayacucho. They then conquered the surrounding area, and settled in a place called Cuquibamba. After some years had passed, they conquered the Quechuas and moved into the province of Andahuaylas where they remained until the time that Cieza visited them.[22] A corroborative account of the Chanca origin is given by Sarmiento in 1572 who said that the natural inhabitants of the province of Andahuaylas were called Chancas, but the two *cinches* of the Chancas originally came from the edges of Huamanga (Ayacucho) before they settled in the region around Andahuaylas.[23] Guaman Poma states that the group of Anca Uallo Chanca came out of Lake Choclococha and began to rule during the reign of Manco Capac, the first Inca.[24] Another link of the Chancas with the Ayacucho area occurs in the sixteenth-century *Relaciones Geográficas* which reports that there was a tribe of people in the Province of Angaraes (in the Department of Huancavelica north of the city of Ayacucho) who called themselves "Chancas" and were said to be the Chancas of Andahuaylas.[25]

Linking the Chancas to archaeological remains in the Ayacucho area is prob-lematic. Archaeologically speaking, the Chancas were believed to have lived west of the Apurimac River and in the Pampas drainage (Lumbreras 1974: 198). The former location places them in the Ayacucho Valley where their origin may have been the remnants of the Huari state.[26] Two ceramic styles, the Arqalla and Patarajay styles, are associated with hilltop sites to the south of the Ayacucho Valley in the area in which the Chancas were believed to live: around Vilcashuamán in the Pampas River drainage south of Ayacucho and in the Arqalla area 25 kilometers southwest of Ayacucho.[27] Ceramics similar to the Arqalla style also occur on mountaintop sites in the northern drainage of the Rio Pampas south of Ayacucho from Pomabamba to Chuschi (Scott Raymond, personal communication). While archaeological surveys of the Ayacucho Valley are unpublished, there is at least one large mountain top site (Quehuahuilca) on the western edge of the Ayacucho Valley (see figure 3.4) which may be an Arqalla or Patarajay site and thus date to the time of the Chancas.

The Inca conquest

The second significant factor that affected the Quinua area after the Middle Horizon was the demographic changes that resulted from the Inca conquest. After Inca Pachecuti (A.D. 1438–71) defeated the Chancas in Andahuaylas, he turned his attention northwest to the Ayacucho area where several ethnic groups resisted his advances. After conquering this region about A.D. 1460, he pacified it by relocating colonists (called *mitmaqkuna* in Quechua or *mitimaes* in Spanish) there and established political and administrative control centers in Quinua and Huamanguilla (Stern 1982: 20).

Even though these population movements took place well before the Spanish conquest, many of the relocated colonists maintained relationships with their area of origin until the end of the seventeenth century. It is thus possible to discover the sources of these colonists using the Spanish chronicles and local historical documents written after the conquest (Zuidema 1966). Many of these groups came from places as diverse as Ecuador, the Inca capital of Cuzco, and from Cajamarca and Huanuco in northern Peru.[28]

Only two groups of colonists were settled in the Quinua area. One group came from the village of Anta west of the Inca capital of Cuzco and was relocated around the village of Huamanguilla northwest of Quinua (figure 3.4; Zuidema 1966: 71). A second group came from Acos, a small community located 53 kilometers southeast of Cuzco. Both the Acos Indians and the Anta Indians were Incas of Privilege which were tribute-paying ethnic groups in the Cuzco region who lived outside the capital.[29] These groups were subservient to the ruling elite in Cuzco, but supported it by producing food and by occupying low level administrative posts in the Inca state such as maintaining the roads (the Anta Indians) and the bridges (the Acos Indians; figure 3.5).[30] Incas of Privilege were also important sources of populations for resettlement in newly conquered areas (Bauer 1990: 47).

Two historic sources confirm the resettlement of the Acos Indians near Ayacucho (Huamanga). One author (Sarmiento de Gamboa), writing in 1572, describes the circumstances which led to the exile of the Acos Indians:

> There was another pueblo called Acos which is ten or eleven leagues from Cuzco. The *cinches* of this pueblo were two – one called Ocacique and the other called Otoquasi. They were openly very contrary to the views of the Inca and resisted him forcefully. Inca Yupanqui thus fought against them with great military strength. The great difficulty of this conquest became obvious to the Inca because those of Acos defended themselves with a great deal of animosity and hit Pachecuti in the head with a stone. Because of this, the Inca did not want to stop fighting them until he had finally conquered them even though he had already spent a great deal of time in battle. He killed almost all of the people of Acos, and those whom he pardoned and those who survived that cruel massacre, he exiled to the edges of Huamanga where they are now called Acos.[31]

Cieza de León, writing in 1553, corroborates the location of the Acos Indians in the Ayacucho area and mentions that there was a village called Acos along the Inca road north of Huamanga (Ayacucho). The Acos Indians, he said, lived in the craggy mountains to the east.[32]

These statements suggest that communities in the Ayacucho area which are called "Acos" were probably the locations where the Incas resettled colonists from Acos near Cuzco (Zuidema 1966). The "Acos" of which Cieza writes is actually the community of Acobamba north and west of Ayacucho, but the sixteenth-century *Relaciones Geográficas* reports that the Inca colonists in the town were colonists from Huarochiri located 200 kilometers northwest of Acobamba.[33] The Acos Indians, Cieza says, were in the mountains to the east.[34] The precise location of the Acos Indians is not clear from Cieza, but there are two other communities in the area which are also called "Acos" and lie east (and south) of Acobamba: Acosvinchos, a village 15 kilometers east-northeast of Ayacucho, and Acocro (Acos Ocros, see

Figure 3.5 Drawing from Guaman Poma [1615] showing "Acos Inca" who was the Inca administrator of the bridges standing in front of the bridge at Guambo (*Guambochaca*). (The inscription reads "Governor of the bridges of this kingdom" (in Spanish) and "General administrator of bridges, Acos Inca" (in Quechua) [translation and drawing from Guaman Poma 1956: 268]).

Zuidema 1966: 71), a village located 21 kilometers east-southeast of Ayacucho (figure 3.4).

It is also likely that the Acos Indians were settled in the area around Quinua. Two legal documents detailing land disputes from the seventeenth and early eighteenth centuries indicate that the two major divisions of Quinua (now referred to as Hanansayuq and Lurinsayuq) were called "Hananacos" (Hanan Acos) and "Lurinacos" (Lurin Acos).[35] These documents also indicate that the territory of Hananacos extended to the small hamlet of Suso southeast of Quinua and hence to the border of the District of Acosvinchos. The area of Quinua and Acos Vinchos thus appears to correspond to the area east and north of Ayacucho mentioned by Cieza as the location inhabited by the exiled Acos Indians. The area of the resettled Acos Indians thus may have extended from Quinua to Acocro (see figure 3.4).[36]

Because of the important historical relationship of Quinua and Acos, I traveled to Acos in the Department of Cuzco in the hope that a visit to the community would provide some insight into the development of the potters' craft in Quinua (figure 3.6). Much to my disappointment, there were no potters in Acos. Informants indicated that no potters had worked there in recent memory and no potters were reported anywhere in the Province of Acomayo (see also Ghersi 1959: 14). According to informants, the nearest pottery-making communities were two remote hamlets (Charamoray and Yanque, see Sillar 1988) near Santo Tomás in the Province of Chumbivilcas three days' walk to the west.

With no potters in the Acos area, a brief archaeological reconnaissance was carried out to assess whether the ancient pottery of the Acos area showed any similarity (and perhaps relationship) to the modern pottery of Quinua. This reconnaissance revealed no evidence of Late Horizon Inca occupation in and around Acos. Only a single Imperial Inca sherd was found and this occurred on a site within the village itself. The most obvious archaeological sites dated from the Late Intermediate Period (A.D. 1000–1476) immediately preceding the Inca expansion and had surface pottery of a Killke-related style (figure 3.6). This pottery showed little similarity to Quinua pottery except the use of red and black parallel lines – hardly a characteristic that links two pottery styles removed in space and time. Only extensive archaeological testing in Quinua and in Acos could reveal whether there was any relationship of the Late Intermediate pottery in Acos and modern ceramic production in Quinua.

The archaeology of the Inca period around Quinua is much more poorly known than its history because the archaeological surveys of the region have not been published. One published Inca site (called Ñawim Pukyu) near the Lake of Yanaqucha in the montane prairie northeast of the village of Quinua (see figure 3.4) consists of a structure with Inca stonework.[37] Another site with Inca occupation lies near the village of Acocro. A small surface collection from the site made by one of Professor Zuidema's students from the University in Ayacucho included a few sherds of Cuzco Polychrome – the classic pottery style of the Inca empire.

The Spanish Conquest

Spanish contact began in 1532 when Pizarro and his small band of soldiers landed on the north coast of Peru. After marching southward, they captured the supreme Inca Atahualpa at Cajamarca, held him for a ransom of gold, and finally executed him. Then, Pizarro marched on the Inca capital of Cuzco and ultimately subjugated the Incas.

After the conquest of Cuzco, Quinua was the location of the first Spanish settlement in the highland region between Lima and Cuzco. During the early years of Spanish occupation (up to about 1536), the puppet Inca ruler, Manco Inca, escaped to the mountains northwest of Cuzco.[38] His raids harassed Indian groups allied with the Spanish and disrupted commercial routes. These difficulties eventually led Pizarro to expand European control along the highland route between Lima and Cuzco by establishing a permanent settlement intermediate between these two cities (Stern 1982: 28). As a result, during the first few months of 1539, Captain Francisco de Cardenas, in obedience to the mandate of Francisco Pizarro, founded the Villa of San Juan de la Frontera de Huamanga along the road between Lima and Cuzco on or near what is now the village of Quinua.[39] This Spanish frontier town "held out

Figure 3.6 A view of the village of Acos looking east. Acos is located in the Department of Cuzco and is 250 km southeast of Quinua and 53 km southeast of Cuzco. It was the village from which the Incas drew colonists for settlement in the Quinua area. A defensible archaeological site dating to the Late Intermediate Period lies on the mountain on the upper right of the photograph and another lies on the top of the mountain off the photograph to the left (Martina Munsters, personal communication). These defensible locations may have been those from which the Acos Indians tried to resist conquest by Pachecuti and those from which they were exiled to the Ayacucho region after their defeat (see Sarmiento de Gamboa [1572, chapter 35] 1942: 101).

precariously" against Manco Inca and other local groups who supported the Inca cause until Pizarro sent Vasco Guevara and additional soldiers to bolster the settlement's defense and establish Spanish control more firmly (Stern 1982: 28). The cold, humid and rainy climate of Quinua, however, did not agree with the Spanish. Furthermore, the soldiers were concerned that if war broke out with the local population, the deeply eroded gorges around the settlement would provide few avenues of escape (see figure 2.2).[40] Thus, as early as April 25, 1540, the local ruling council in Quinua (that is, the *cabildo*) acted to move the settlement across the valley to the west.[41] The actual change of location, however, may have occurred later since the official title of the new settlement ("San Juan de la Frontera de Huamanga") and its status as a city were not reissued until 1544.[42] Out of this newly relocated community grew the modern city of Ayacucho.

The new settlement across the valley had a number of distinct advantages over the first settlement in Quinua. The elevation was lower, and the settlement was closer to good sources of water.[43] The Spanish found the climate more agreeable and it enabled them to grow fruits and vegetables brought from their homeland.[44] They believed that this advantage would aid in attracting and keeping new arrivals because a stable European population was necessary to counter the threat of local rebellion and neo-Inca raids (Stern 1982: 28). Finally, the Spanish believed that the new location had a peaceable atmosphere.[45]

The Battle of Ayacucho
The only other significant historical event in the Quinua area occurred in the nineteenth century. After Liberator Simón Bolivar declared Peru independent of Spanish rule in 1821, Bolivar's military leader, General Sucre, defeated the forces of the Spanish Viceroy on December 9, 1824 on the Pampa ("plain") of Ayacucho ("corner of the dead") which lies less than a kilometer above the village of Quinua (see figure 2.1). This battle broke the Spanish power in South America (Cortazar, 1967: 135–138) and became such an important milestone in Peruvian and South American history that the name of "Ayacucho" was given to the city of Huamanga across the valley which had been founded almost three centuries earlier in Quinua.

Conclusion
Quinua holds an important place in Peruvian archaeology and history. First, it lies next to the city of Huari which was one of the most important cities in pre-Incaic Peru. Second, it was located in what may have been the heartland of the Chancas against whom the Incas began their imperial expansion. Third, Quinua was the site of the first Spanish settlement in the Andes outside of Lima and Cuzco and fourth, it was the location of the battle which ended the Spanish domination of South America.

Initially, it may seem that such a culture historical background would have little to do with the environment and ceramic production in Quinua. These high points, however, are not random events in Peruvian culture history, but rest on important environmental factors. First, the Ayacucho Valley has one of the largest and broadest areas of relatively low agricultural land in all of southern Peru. The Quinua region thus had the agricultural base for large dense populations with the potential for a significant amount of land for maize cultivation. Second, the position of Huari below Quinua, the foundation of both the Inca and Spanish settlements in Quinua, and the occurrence of the Battle of Ayacucho near Quinua suggests that the village of Quinua was located on an important commercial and transportation route in the past. While the valley is not flat by any means, it is the route of choice from the Mantaro river southward towards the Cuzco Valley and beyond to the Peru/Bolivian Altiplano around Lake Titicaca. Today, the Ayacucho Valley has important foot roads that go to the coast, jungle and elsewhere in the sierra and the only highland road from Huancayo to Cuzco passes through the valley. It is thus probable that ancient travelers found the valley an attractive route as well. Finally, Quinua is located in a strategic military position in the valley and from a position on the plain of Ayacucho above the village, one has a commanding view of most of the valley (see figure 2.12). From there, one can see the city of Ayacucho and its environs as well as much of the southern two thirds of the valley. While the position of modern Ayacucho is advantageous because of its warmer and drier climate, its strategic position is limited. Except from the mountains above the city, it is not in a position to see approaching armies from a distance to warn of impending attacks.

All of these reasons have implications for ceramic production in the valley and the distribution of pottery throughout the Andes. Quinua was the center of a large, relatively low (by Andean standards) agricultural area which provided a maize subsistence base for large, ancient populations. These populations provided an immediate market for ceramic products. Equally important is the fact that Quinua lies along the most important transportation route through the southern Andes. This route was very significant as a channel for the widespread distribution of ceramics in both the present and the past.

4

Ecological interrelationships of the community of potters

The two previous chapters described the environment of the Quinua region. In an ecological approach, the unit of adaptation to this environment is the population and the focus is on the relationships between the population and the environment. In an ecological approach to *ceramics*, the adaptation to the environment occurs through a community of potters. The population of potters is the interface between ceramics and the environment, on the one hand, and the society, on the other. It is thus the unit of description, and it is important to describe this population and its relationships with the environment before one can describe the ceramic production of the community.

The community of potters in Quinua

Although Quinua is known for its unusual pottery, only about one percent of the population was engaged in ceramic production in 1967.[1] All of these potters lived in the Lurinsayuq portion of the community and were roughly equally distributed among each of its three subdivisions, the *pagos* of Muya, Llamahuilca and Lurinsayuq. Like most of the population of the area (see figure 2.9), all of the potters lived within the lower montane savannah (see p. 25), and many within the lower portion of that zone (table 4.1). Almost all resided in the dispersed rural settlements outside of the village and were thus considered to have a low social position relative to others in the community (see p. 32).

The pottery-making population in Quinua is a discrete population distinct from other communities of potters in the valley. Potters live either in or near Ticllas, Huayhuas, Luricocha, and in the *barrio* of Santa Ana in the city of Ayacucho (see pp. 177ff.). None of these potters, however, live near the Quinua potters; the nearest is fifteen kilometers away in the city of Ayacucho (figure 3.4).

Quinua potters say that pottery is also made in the adjacent rural areas (that is *chacras*) of the neighboring District of Huamanguilla. Huamanguilla potters are said to make the same vessel shapes as Quinua potters, but they paint different designs on them. One informant said that Huamanguilla potters made only bowls (*platos*) and water-carrying vessels (*porongos*).

I could never verify the presence of potters in the District of Huamanguilla. It was never clear whether informants were speaking about potters in the rural areas of Huamanguilla or those in the rural sections of the *pago* of Muya in the District of Quinua. This problem is complicated by the fact that the people of Quinua view Muya as distinct from the rest of the district. The potters of the *pagos* of Lurinsayuq

Table 4.1. *Location of potters' residences in Quinua in 1967 according to the quality of agricultural land*[a]

Pago (subsection) of the *barrio* of Lurinsayuq	*Sitio* (hamlet)	Number of households in upper savannah (better land)	Number of households in lower savannah (poorer land)
Llamahuilca	Wayuniuq		3
	Tantarniuq		2
	Sururuyuq		1
	Aquqata		1
Lurinsayuq	Lurinsayuq Pampa	6	
	Añaqata		2
Muya	Waywayuq		1
	Inkaqasa		1
Totals		6	11

[a] This table shows the residence location of potters personally known to the author. More lived in the district than are represented on this table, but most of these lived in the *pago* of Muya, and were not visited. This chart does not include the three potters who lived and worked in the artisan center in the village, but farmed a small plot of land in the rural areas. One has a plot of land in the thorn steppe. A second farms a plot of land in Hanansayuq, and the location of the land farmed by the third is unknown.

These data are confirmed by a survey carried out by the artisan center in 1967 which lists 36 potters in the district. Eleven lived on poor agricultural land in lower Lurinsayuq, ten lived on better land in the upper savannah, and the location of the remainder could not be determined with certainty. Eleven potters, for example, are listed for Muya and the upper half of Muya lies in the upper savannah and roughly half is located in the lower savannah.

and Llamahuilca know very little about the potters of Muya and say that the pottery made there is different from that of the rest of Quinua.

These perceptions about Muya are rooted in the complexities of the relationships between the *pago* of Muya and Quinua, on the one hand, and the adjacent District of Huamanguilla, on the other. Muya is politically part of the District of Quinua, but it has closer relationships with the District of Huamanguilla even though a large ravine (called Huamangura) separates the two districts. There are several reasons for these ties. First, Muya was historically part of Huamanguilla (and thus part of the Province of Huanta) even though it is nearer to Quinua geographically and is part of the Quinua irrigation system.[2] Second, church records in Quinua reveal that marriages between inhabitants of Muya and those from the District of Huamanguilla occurred more frequently than with inhabitants from other areas of Quinua outside of Muya.[3] Third, Muya is ritually more closely tied with Huamanguilla than with Quinua. During the ceremonies for the Day of Pentecost (*Espiritu Santo*) in May, 1967, crosses were taken from four hamlets of Muya (Inkaqasa, Calvario, Patampampa and Kiturada) to Huamanguilla for blessing by the priest while the other hamlets of Quinua did not participate at all. Fourth, some

Muya potters take their ceramics to the weekly Sunday market in Huamanguilla rather than to the one in Quinua. Even though the Huamanguilla market is larger than the Quinua market, it is three times as far from Muya than Quinua is. Since Muya is tied to Quinua politically and closer to Quinua geographically, it would seem more logical for Muya potters to go to Quinua rather than Huamanguilla.

All of these data suggest that the people of Muya interact with the population of the District of Huamanguilla on a more intensive level in social, religious and economic matters than they interact with the people of the other *pagos* of Quinua even though Muya belongs to Quinua politically and is closer geographically. If potters *do* exist in the adjacent regions of the District of Huamanguilla, it is very likely that they produce pottery similar, if not identical, to Muya. They are thus considered to be part of the pottery-making population of the District of Quinua described here.

Most of the potters in the community practice their craft seasonally and then only within their own households. This pattern conforms most closely with the mode of production called "individual workshops"[4] in which potters are predominantly male and make pottery for only part of the year. Potters may also farm in this mode, but pottery making is vital as their main source of income. Production is aimed at the most lucrative markets. Potters in this mode may also utilize technological aids such as a kiln (Peacock 1982: 9).

While almost all potters in the community at the time of my visit worked within their own households, three workshops existed outside of the household. One of these was the government-sponsored artisan center located within the village of Quinua. It began about 1964 or 1965[5] as a plank in the platform of a politician who said he would give work to the potters. The Ministry of Education paid the salary (US $70 per month) of each of the three potters who taught there, as well as that of the director and the caretaker.

In 1967, the artisan center was located in a large colonial-style house which was rented from a former hacienda owner. The house had a large patio with enough rooms for storing raw materials, and for making, drying and storing pottery. There was also an office for the director, and a sleeping room for the caretaker. By 1978, the center had moved into a new building next to the village church nearer to the center of town.

Instruction in the center was free of charge to any who wanted to learn the craft. For the period beginning in March of 1967, at least one potter had to recruit his own students from the rural areas of the community. Teaching methods did not consist of formal classes, but primarily involved students becoming apprentices to the potters. Students observed and imitated the potters and then practiced these skills. Pupils learned all aspects of pottery production and produced a variety of shapes.

The pottery made at the center was not produced for local sale or use, nor was it marketed by local intermediaries. Rather, it was produced primarily for commercial sale and display in Huancayo and Lima and was transported there by the director of the center. In 1967, pottery was being produced for an exhibition at the Museum of Art in Lima.

In 1967, the potters in the artisan center were the only potters in the district who lived in the village. Two of the teachers were potters before they worked at the center, but both had migrated to the village from the rural portions of Lurinsayuq. The third teacher originally came from the rural portion of Hanansayuq and was not a potter, but learned the craft at the center. Because teachers were well paid by local standards, this third teacher obtained his position through political connections even though he knew nothing of the craft. Unlike many political appointees, however, he subsequently learned how to make pottery and was a conscientious teacher.[6]

Besides the artisan center, a pottery workshop also existed at the local grammar school below the village (the *nucleo escolar*). A room was set aside for making pottery at the school and two potters worked there, but they also made pottery in their own households. One potter reportedly worked in the school workshop on Saturday afternoons.

The relationship of the potters to the school was not clear, but they were not school teachers. Informants reported that students paid to watch these potters produce ceramics and then the potters paid the students to make ceramic churches for them. One of these potters, however, said that he taught a class on how to make pottery at the school. Unlike the pottery made in the artisan center, however, this pottery was sold to a merchant who then marketed it to retailers and wholesalers in the national and international artisan market.

One of the potters who worked at the grammar school also had a workshop near his house. Pupils provided cane alcohol and *coca* leaves for the opportunity to observe him make small ceramic churches. Once the pupils learned how to make churches, however, the potter paid pupils to produce them and then sold the vessels to a merchant who came from Ayacucho.

In 1978, informants said that the number of potters in Quinua had increased since 1967. More potters were learning the craft because they could obtain better economic returns from pottery than they could previously. Potters were still restricted to the *barrio* of Lurinsayuq with none in the *barrio* of Hanansayuq. Although potters lived in the same rural *pagos* that they did in 1967, there were more in the *pago* of Lurinsayuq. An informant said that many were moving to the village because of the presence of electricity there and the ease of selling their pottery to merchants and tourists from a position along the road. This commerce was greatly facilitated after the road to Ayacucho was paved in 1974 because tourists frequently came to Quinua by bus and taxi and went from store to store buying ceramics. The local tourist market for ceramics, however, totally disappeared in the 1980s as a result of the guerrilla war.[7]

Relationships of the population to the environment

Besides describing the population of potters as the unit of adaptation, an ecological perspective requires an understanding of the relationships of the population of potters to the environment. A previous volume (Arnold 1985) argued that these relationships can be described as a series of feedback mechanisms which were broadly classed into the categories of resources, weather and climate, degree of sedentariness, scheduling, demand, man-land relationships and technological innovations. Not all of these mechanisms tie ceramic production with the environment and society in Quinua, but most interact with the population of potters in a way that reveals the complex set of relationships between the population, ceramic production, society, and the environment.

Subsistence agriculture

Quinua potters are part-time male specialists who use pottery production to supplement their returns from subsistence agriculture. Although the peasants of Quinua strive for self-sufficiency, they rarely have enough land to support themselves through agriculture alone.[8] One person living in the savannah requires at least 1 *yugada* of land (about 1/8 hectare) to provide food for one year, but the harvest from this small tract does not include expenses of fiestas, *coca* leaves, clothing, medicines, and salt (Mitchell 1991a: 86). Since the average household consisted of 3.9 persons in 1961 and owned or controlled 1 *yugada* of land, even the average household could not feed itself.[9] In 1972, only 15.7 percent of the households in the district were single-person households so that 84 percent of the population of the district could not feed themselves on local agriculture alone (Mitchell 1991a: 48). In 1981, the average household size had risen to 4.4 persons while the average conjugal household had 4.7 occupants. Joint families (N = 12) had an average size of 7.6 occupants and had a very precarious existence if they had no means to supplement subsistence agriculture (Mitchell 1991a: 85–86).

These data paint a bleak picture for life in Quinua. If the average family of 4 owns 1 *yugada* of land, it can barely feed one adult. Households that own 2 *yugadas* of land (the modal frequency of field size proposed by Mitchell's informants) can barely feed two adults and no children. If families own 4 *yugadas* of land (the upper limit of the amount of land available for people who live in the savannah), some children as well as adults can be fed, but this family could not use agriculture to provide cash for seeds, fertilizer, labor, *coca* leaves, alcohol, medicine and school supplies. Furthermore, it would have no food for ceremonial expenditures and would not be able to store food for poor years. Even families with 4 *yugadas* of land would live a precarious existence even though they might be able to live off their subsistence crops in good years.[10]

For those inhabitants who are landless, the picture is bleaker still. These individuals must work in agricultural wage labor for food or have some other means of support. Although a Peruvian government report[11] indicates that only 2 percent of the Quinua peasants are landless, Mitchell's informants consider this amount too low (Mitchell 1991a: 56).

Most of the inhabitants of Quinua thus do not grow enough food on their own land to feed themselves. Many families only produce enough food from their own fields for about half a year and must pursue alternative strategies to supplement subsistence agriculture. These strategies may include activities such as migration, unskilled wage labor, remittances from migrants, specialized occupations (for example carpenters, masons and mule drivers) and craft production such as pottery.[12] In 1965, for example, the marriage records in the District of Quinua indicated that 20.7 percent of the newly wed couples were doing non-farm work, while birth records indicated that 12.5 percent of new parents supported themselves with non-farm activity (figure 4.1; Mitchell 1991a: 104). In the years since 1967, inadequate returns from subsistence agriculture have been further demonstrated by increasing percentages of workers engaged in non-farm work (see figure 4.1; Mitchell 1991a: 105).

Scheduling of production

Pottery making in Quinua largely supplements subsistence agriculture and occurs during the dry season. This scheduling of pottery production is partially related to the yearly pattern of weather and climate and this, in turn, is one important reason why Quinua potters are part-time rather than full-time specialists. Because the molecular structure of clays requires air drying to remove much of the physically-held interlayer water in newly made pots, pottery making requires dry, warm, and sunny days to sufficiently dry the vessels before firing (Arnold 1985: 61). Indeed, several days may be necessary for adequate drying because low temperatures and high relative humidity prolong the drying of pottery. Prolonged drying in the rainy season means more frequent movement of the undried pottery outside and back inside again and this activity further increases the risk of breakage. Without sunny days, the potter cannot dry his pottery sufficiently and, hence, he cannot fire it without substantial cracking and breakage. Vessels that have not been air-dried sufficiently after fabrication may be damaged during firing because residual water in the paste will turn to steam and cause breakage. Potters also believe that vessels must also dry sufficiently before slipping and painting or the vessels will crack during

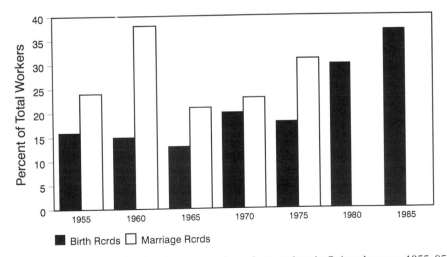

Figure 4.1 Bar graph showing the percent of non-farm workers in Quinua between 1955–85 from birth and marriage records (data from Mitchell 1991a: 105). There are no data available from the marriage records for 1980 and 1985.

decoration. Clays, tempers, paints and fuel must also be sun-dried before use. Fuel requirements for damp kilns also increase during wet weather and the potters say that rain ruins the firing process. Moreover, moisture from humid and rainy conditions weakens vessel walls and increases the risk of damage to the newly formed pots (see Arnold 1985: 61–97).

Potters also consider the rainy season too cold for making pottery (see figure 2.6), but the basis for this belief is not immediately apparent. Like all high altitude environments, diurnal oscillation of temperatures occurs in Quinua (figure 2.6). While temperatures drop to their lowest point during the dry season, these low temperatures occur only at night when pottery is not made anyway. But, pottery left outside at night could crack and break because of the formation of ice crystals in the newly formed pots. During the rainy season, days are often cloudier and rainier than the dry season (see figure 2.3) and daytime temperatures in the wet season may be cooler than those in the dry season even though the average and maximum monthly temperatures do not vary more than 3° to 4° Celsius during the year (figure 2.6).

Some potters may make pottery during the rainy season, but they must store it until it can be dried and fired when the weather changes. Because rainy weather blankets much of the Quinua area during the months of December to April (see figure 2.3), potters risk damage to their pottery from prolonged drying and leaky roofs. Agriculture, however, is still the most secure way for the potters to obtain food during the rainy season when pottery cannot be made successfully. As a result, little pottery is made during the rainy season and it is both necessary and convenient for the potter to pursue agriculture at this time in order to provide food for his family if he has agricultural land. Those few potters who do manage to make some pottery during the rainy season must wait for a sunny day to fire. Generally, days with a substantial amount of sunshine begin to occur in April. When a suitable day arrives, a potter can fire as many as three to four kiln-loads of pottery in one day. The rainy season thus provides deviation counteracting feedback for the craft between December and March, limiting production for all potters except those who want to risk the problems of delayed drying and increased breakage.

Even the work in the artisan center ceases during the rainy season (figure 2.3). It is not clear whether this pause is designed to coincide with summer vacation for the grammar school to allow students and teachers to meet the unique labor requirements of agriculture during this time, or because of the limiting effects of the rains on pottery production. In any event, the teachers at the center make enough money from the rest of the year to support themselves during the vacation months and the vacation *does* coincide with an environmentally difficult time to make pottery.

Potters generally do not try to mitigate the limiting effect of inclement weather through the use of technological innovations (see Arnold 1985: 211–213). In 1967, potters did not use drying racks or sheds and did not dry their pottery over a fire. There was only one potter who tried to lessen the adverse effect of rainy weather by building a roof over his kiln so that the rain would not damage his pottery during firing.

The regulatory feedback of rainy weather from December through March is further complicated by the household-based production in Quinua. Since potters make their pottery inside their own household, the space required for making and storing pottery competes with the space needed for living, sleeping, eating and general storage. With the necessity of being indoors during rainfall, drying more than a few green vessels indoors increases risk of breakage. A potter could only store a limited number of fired vessels in his household before they would get broken by playing children, domestic animals (for example dogs), and clumsy adults. The construction of special structures for drying (such as special racks and sheds) would alleviate the problem of space for drying and storing pottery, but this technical innovation requires capital which potters did not possess in 1967. If they did have capital, they did not use it to intensify their craft.

The main adaptive problem for Quinua potters thus consists of changing the conditions under which the pots are made, dried and fired in order to mitigate the adverse effects of the rainy season. In situations in which the space used for pottery production is used mainly for living, a potter is limited in the amount of pottery he can produce and dry before firing. If the potter builds additional rooms in his household, they can be used to fabricate, dry and store green pots and store fired vessels before they are sold. The construction of additional space thus could alleviate the competition of living space and that needed for ceramic production. Potters would thus not be as limited in making pottery during the rainy season as without such space, but they still must wait for the dry season to fire their pottery. In order to totally alleviate the regulatory effects of rainy weather on ceramic production, however, the potter must have sufficient space available to make, dry and fire all the pottery indoors under relatively controlled conditions as in a modern pottery studio or ceramic laboratory. Indeed, the evolution of pottery production to the modern ceramics industry involves (among other things) the control of the environment in which ceramics are produced from the drying of raw materials to the firing of the finished product.

Seasonal weather patterns also affect the availability of resources for firing pottery. Although potters prefer to use a woody shrub called *chamizo* (see chapter 5) for firing, they may also use straw or dung. Straw, however, is only available at harvest time which occurs during the beginning of the dry season, and would not be available in the quantities necessary for firing throughout the pottery-making season. Further, crops that produce straw (for example oats, barley and wheat) are cash crops, not subsistence crops, and are grown in limited quantities. Dung is not generally available in the rainy season because animals graze in the montane prairie and moist forest zones away from the pottery-making households in the lower montane savannah. Any dung that is available during the rainy season, however, cannot dry out sufficiently for use as a fuel. Sufficient dung for firing is thus restricted to the dry season (May through October or November, see figure 2.3) when animals are brought down from the montane zones in order to graze in the fields in the lower montane savannah.

The use of straw and dung for firing, however, competes with other more important uses.[13] Straw is used for making adobe bricks and for fodder for cattle and burros. Dung is used for fertilizer because farmers can avoid crop rotation by staking animals in their fields to provide fertilizer for the next season's crops.[14] Dung can also be burned for cooking as it is elsewhere in Peru. So, besides its seasonal availability, straw and dung have more important uses than pottery firing. *Chamizo* is thus the most reliable and consistently available fuel resource which is utilized by all potters visited in Quinua. It, too, requires drying before firing and this requirement places a further restraint on pottery production limiting it to the dry season.

Potters could choose to "toast" their pottery over a cooking fire to avoid problems of prolonged drying.[15] If potters are dependent on the craft to make a living, the amount of pottery that could be dried and fired in this manner is negligible. Given the size of a cooking fire, very limited amounts of pottery could be fired in this way without increasing the size of the fire. If the size of the fire inside the house was increased, it would put the safety of the house and its occupants in jeopardy. Since cooking involves simmering soups and boiled tubers and grains for long periods of time, toasting of pots would compete with cooking time. Furthermore, the same constraints that limit the drying of clay and fuel would effectively limit the availability of these resources during rainy weather. Little pottery could thus be dried over the fire during the wet season because of the lack of large amounts of dry fuel. Pots would still have to be stored for firing and storage of more than a few pots would compete for living space and risk of breakage would increase. Totally dry pots are less fragile than freshly made ones, but they still can be damaged easily by moisture and household occupants.

The potters who live in the lower portions of Lurinsayuq (like those who live in Huantos near the ancient site of Huari) have more favorable weather conditions for making pots. They live closer to the lower montane thorn steppe and have more sunny days in which to fire their pottery than the potters who live upslope nearer the village. As a result, potters from lower Lurinsayuq may be able to fire their pottery during the rainy season when little pottery is available and obtain higher prices for it. It is not unusual, then, to find more potters living downslope than living farther up.

Quality of agricultural land

The residence location of Quinua potters also suggests a relationship between pottery production and the quality of the agricultural land. Potters generally live in the areas of poorer agricultural land. This poor land is the result of two factors: erosion and lack of moisture for agriculture. In 1967, most of the potters lived in lower Lurinsayuq – an area of steep slopes within the lower montane savannah affected by extensive stream cutting (see figure 2.2; table 4.1) and sheet erosion due to its sloping character (figure 4.2). By way of contrast, land further up the slope (in upper Lurinsayuq) is much flatter with much less stream cutting and erosion.

The second factor that affects agricultural potential in this region is the relative scarcity of water for agriculture. Part of this deficiency rests with the nature of the weather, which provides more rainfall on the upper edges of the valley than it does farther down the slope in the lower montane thorn steppe (see table 2.1; figures 2.7

and 2.8). Since more potters live in the lower portion of the savannah and thus close to the thorn steppe with its reduced rainfall and higher amounts of evapo-transpiration, their fields receive less rainfall than the agricultural land farther up the slope. Lower Lurinsayuq also loses more water from the soil through evapo-transpiration (see table 2.1) because it receives more sunshine and has a higher mean annual temperature than the upper portions of the savannah near the village. Potters, then, generally live on agriculturally marginal land which is sloping, eroded, and has insufficient moisture from low rainfall and excessive evapotranspiration.

The potter-agriculturalists of Quinua adapt to this environmental problem of reduced moisture in the lower savannah by utilizing irrigation to supplement rainfall (see chapter 2). In comparison to the upper slopes of the barrios of Hanansayuq and Lurinsayuq, however, the lower slopes of Lurinsayuq lie in a less favorable position for obtaining adequate irrigation water for agriculture. First of all, since the amount of irrigation water is limited, inhabitants of the lower savannah cannot utilize the early planting during the dry season (the *michka*, see chapter 2) because it requires irrigation.[16] Planting the *michka* is advantageous to Quinuenos because they can receive twice the price for potatoes harvested from the dry season planting than they

Figure 4.2 Part of the eroded portion of the *barrio* of Lurinsayuq below the village of Quinua looking north from the hamlet of Huantos (see figures 2.2 and 4.9). Many potters live in this area and most of this land is sloping and cut with ravines and gullies. This eroded land, however, exposes abundant ceramic resources, and in the area shown here, there are three clay sources, and one temper source is out of sight in the ravine below the center of the photograph. Flatter, less eroded land occurs above this area immediately below the steep slopes of the mountains in the background. (The darker area on the lower two-thirds of the mountain slopes is the montane moist forest [see figure 2.8]. Above it lies the montane prairie and, beyond it, the sub-alpine and alpine zones.)

can from potatoes planted during the wet season cycle, the *hatun tarpuy*.[17] Second, because the irrigation canals are made of earth and the canal system is long, much of the water which flows through the system is lost through seepage before it reaches the end of the system. This problem could be alleviated by increasing the volume and flow of water, but these changes would damage the canals and would make the delivery of water to lower portions of the community even more difficult if not impossible (Mitchell 1973: 15). Third, less water is available in the Lurinsayuq system than in the Hanansayuq system (Mitchell 1973: 13) and there is more land to irrigate in Lurinsayuq than in Hanansayuq. All of these factors suggest that the lower parts of Lurinsayuq lie in the least favorable position of the community with respect to the availability of moisture.[18] The lower savannah thus has lower agricultural productivity relative to the areas farther up the slope that include the upper parts of the *barrios* of Hanansayuq and Lurinsayuq. This problem is not unique to the areas in which potters live, but is shared by all of the households in the lower portion of the savannah. Inhabitants of the lower savannah thus must supplement their subsistence activities. Besides making pottery, they are also involved in trading and in making guitars and hats.[19]

Since the inhabitants of lower Lurinsayuq do not plant the early two-crop cycle (the *michka*) in August and begin the irrigated rainy season cycle (*hatun tarpuy*) in December, they have few agricultural responsibilities between August and November. Potters in this section of the community thus can make pottery for three

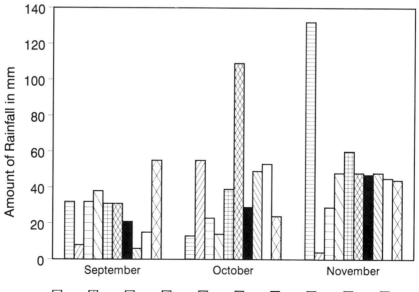

Figure 4.3 Year to year fluctuations of rainfall in Ayacucho during the months of September through November in the ten year period from 1961 to 1970 (data from Rivera 1971: 43). The amounts of rainfall shown here correspond more closely to the rainfall in the lower portions of the lower montane savannah in the District of Quinua than to areas further up the slope, but they do show the general pattern of fluctuation during these months (see chapter 2).

months longer than potters who live farther up the slope. While conditions for making pottery are excellent here during the dry season (June through August), they are also favorable from September through November. Temperatures are the highest of the year (see figure 2.6) and rainfall and relative humidity are still limited. Indeed, year-to-year fluctuations in rainfall between September and November in this section of the community favor pottery making over agriculture without irrigation (figures 4.3 and 4.4).

Besides weather and climate, scheduling conflicts with agriculture is a second reason for the seasonal pattern of pottery making. These conflicts mainly occur during the months of January and February when the maize and potato fields must be cultivated and weeded. These activities take place almost simultaneously for all fields. Even those fields planted two to three months later must be cultivated and weeded at the same time as others because the crops at lower and warmer altitudes mature more rapidly than those at higher elevations (Mitchell 1991b).

Rains restrict the days available for weeding still further. Farmers do not work in their fields during rainfall nor immediately after it, but they must wait until the ground dries out sufficiently. Because January and February are also the time of heaviest and most frequent rainfall, days with rain can reduce work in the fields to only a few days. The average number of days without rain during this period was nine to ten from 1962–1970, so that the time actually available for agricultural work during the height of the rainy season is greatly restricted (figure 4.5). Males weed their own fields or work in the fields of others to meet reciprocal work obligations

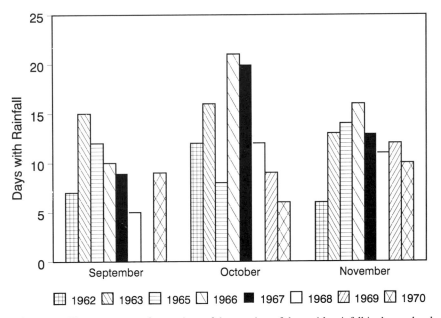

Figure 4.4 The year to year fluctuations of the number of days with rainfall in Ayacucho during the months of September through November in the period from 1962 to 1970 (data from Rivera 1971: 41; there are no data available for September of 1964). These values reveal the unpredictability of rainfall for agriculture during this time in the lower portion of the lower montane savannah.

(Mitchell 1991b: 199). Since each *yugada* of maize requires 6 person days of labor for cultivation, those few days without rain during January and February create a great demand for labor (figure 4.5). If the potters have fields of potatoes, the labor demand is 8.25 person days per *yugada* of land during this time (Mitchell 1991a: 211). Since most agriculturalists grow both maize and potatoes, potters who are also farmers would probably not be able to make pottery at all during the rainy season considering both the inclement weather and the labor requirements of weeding and cultivation. If there are only *two* days without rain during January and February as there were in 1967 (see preface), then potters would not be able to make *any* pottery and would need to invest all of their labor in their fields.

The harvest and storage of maize and potatoes require even more labor than weeding, but households have less difficulty completing harvest tasks with only the members of their household than they do with weeding. The reduced rainfall during the harvest months of May through July allows a greater number of days for agricultural tasks than the height of the rainy season from January through March and many of the harvest tasks are accomplished by women (figure 4.5; Mitchell 1991a). The wheat harvest, however, may require large amounts of male labor. If, for example, animals are used to thresh the wheat, men will be needed to control the animals, turn the stalks of wheat and fork the straw from the threshing floor (Mitchell 1991a).

The scheduling of agricultural labor for planting, weeding and harvesting is critical and therefore once labor has been invested in agriculture, agricultural responsibilities must take priority over making pottery. If crops are planted too soon, they may not receive sufficient water. If planting is delayed too long after the start of the rains (or irrigation), then the crops will not have enough time to mature before the onset of frost. If the cultivation of tubers is delayed for lack of manpower, they will rot because of insufficient drainage, or during a dry year, will not receive enough moisture. Unharvested crops left too long in the field may be stolen, or destroyed by frost or hail, and thus harvest responsibilities rather than making pottery must have priority for labor (see Brown 1987: 227).

Potters who attempt to make pottery during the rainy season thus must be landless, or those with very little land (figure 4.5). Given the regulatory effect of rainy weather on pottery production and the scheduling conflicts with cultivating fields of maize and potatoes, potters who are also farmers are weeding or cultivating their own fields or working in the fields of others during those few days without rain during the rainy season. Those potters who made pottery during the rainy season would thus be those without agricultural land or labor obligations to work on the land of others or would have to make pottery during rainy days and risk breakage and delayed drying. Potters with large families, however, may be able to effectively meet labor obligations, and still have the labor to make pottery.

Pottery making is thus primarily a source of income during the dry season between harvesting and planting. Although harvest begins as early as April for some crops, most potters begin making their pots in mid-June after the harvest is completed. Although Quinua potters practice their craft between June and

September when there are few scheduling conflicts with agriculture, there are still some agricultural responsibilities during this time which may interfere with pottery production (figures 4.5 and 4.6). First, the cleaning of the irrigation canals occurs in late July and early August[20] and all who want irrigation water for the following year must participate in the cleaning. This activity would conflict with the optimal time for ceramic production for potters who use irrigation for agriculture. A second scheduling conflict occurs at the time of the onset of the irrigation water in the upper portions of the savannah. Irrigation water comes to Muya during August 1–15, to Lurinsayuq Pampa during August 16–30 and elsewhere in the upper portion of Lurinsayuq in September.[21] In preparation for the arrival of the irrigation water, the fields must be plowed and planted. Although weather and climate are favorable for making pottery from June through November, scheduling conflicts with agriculture may also preclude pottery production during this time in the upper portion of the savannah. Potters who live in the lower section of Lurinsayuq, however, can make pottery during this entire period because irrigation water does not arrive in lower Lurinsayuq until the rainy season begins in December and fields do not need to be plowed and planted until November. Potters in lower Lurinsayuq thus have fewer scheduling conflicts with agriculture from August through October than farmers/

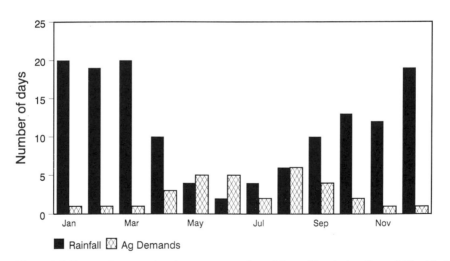

Figure 4.5 Bar graph comparing the average number of days with rain (see figure 2.3) with the number of days of labor required for maize cultivation in the upper savannah. Data are for 1,250 square meters (one *yugada*) of maize for the rainy season cycle (*hatun tarpuy*) and come from Mitchell (1991a: 204–215). If the number of days required for potato cultivation rather than maize cultivation were used, the number of days required for agriculture would double because the time required for plowing fields and for cultivating, harvesting and storing potatoes is 1.5–2 times the amount of labor necessary for maize. If the data for the dry season cycle (*michka*) were included, the number of days required for agricultural responsibilities in January and February would increase greatly because of the labor required for the potato harvest. Since agricultural responsibilities generally do not occur when it is raining, the amount of time that a farmer/potter with one *yugada* of land has available to make pottery can be roughly estimated by adding the days with agricultural responsibilities for each month with the days with rain for that month and subtracting the sum from the total days in the month. These calculations suggest that a combination of weather and subsistence responsibilities can provide almost total regulatory feedback for pottery production during the rainy season for farmers in the upper savannah.

potters in the upper savannah (compare figure 4.5 with figure 4.6). Weather may also be favorable for ceramic production from April through May, but again scheduling conflicts with harvest preclude ceramic production. To resolve this dilemma women may work in the fields while the men make ceramics (Mitchell 1991a: 63), but ceramic production mainly occurs between harvest and planting. Landless potters would not have these difficulties, but would work in agriculture as wage laborers to make up for loss of income during the rainy season when weather and climate limit ceramic production.

Resource locations

A significant relationship also exists between the location of potters and their resources. The location of potters in the barrio of Lurinsayuq corresponds closely to the availability of ceramic resources in the area. Much of Lurinsayuq lies in the area of the greatest stream cutting. In some of the lowest portions of the barrio, streams have cut deep gullies and canyons into the geological deposits of the valley exposing thick beds of clays and volcanic ash which potters mine for body clay and tempering material (figures 2.2, 2.14, 4.2, 4.7 and 4.8). Indeed, all of the temper sources in the region occur in the lower portions of the *barrio* of Lurinsayuq (or nearby) and occur in thick beds of volcanic ash exposed through stream cutting and erosion (figures 4.8 and 4.9). Besides the stream cutting, the steep slope of much of the land between the gullies makes it very susceptible to sheet erosion (figures 2.14 and 4.2). As a result, seasonal rains have removed much of the topsoil in many of these locations, exposing the clay beds underneath and making them easily accessible from the surface. Potters take advantage of these exposed deposits obtaining clay in a variety of locations, but seldom digging deeper than 25 centimeters to extract it. All of the clay sources recorded in Quinua in 1967[22] occured on sloping land in Lurinsayuq

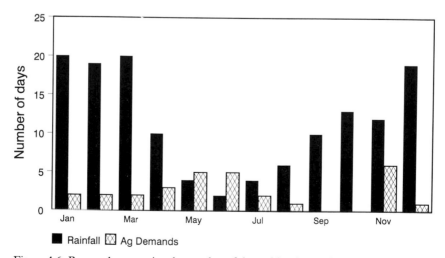

Figure 4.6 Bar graph comparing the number of days with rain (see figure 2.3) with those required for maize cultivation in the lower savannah. Data are for 1,250 square meters (one *yugada*) of land for the rainy season cycle (*hatun tarpuy*) and come from Mitchell (1991a: 204–215).

Figure 4.7 A thick bed of volcanic tuff exposed by erosion in the hamlet of Utkuchuku (see figure 4.9) below the village of Quinua. Volcanic ash is abundant in the community and is used as a pottery temper.

that has been exposed to sheet erosion. The geological and erosion patterns in Quinua thus provide widespread and abundant ceramic resources.

Local land tenure patterns and the highly eroded character of the terrain create great problems for potters who want to obtain clay from a nearby source. Since clay mining leaves holes in fields and ruins agricultural land, local agriculturalists who are not potters do not allow potters to mine clay on their land.[23] One reason for this refusal is that much of the agricultural land is already marginal because of its sloping and eroded character. Mining ceramic resources further contributes to the demise of agricultural land setting processes into motion which will eventually destroy it.

Since landowners are reluctant to permit potters to obtain raw materials on their land, potters must often procure their raw materials surreptitiously because they fear confrontation with recalcitrant farmers. Two potters, for example, may conspire together in order to obtain clay from another person's land. One potter will get the landowner drunk on cane alcohol in order to divert his attention while the other potter extracts the clay, fills the hole with rocks and earth and puts fertilizer on it. Potters say that such an activity is not considered stealing and does not destroy the land, but actually improves it.[24] In the *pago* of Llamahuilca, taking clay is not considered stealing because it is not used by the landowner. One potter reportedly purchased land with abundant clay in the hamlet of Wayuniuq (in Llamahuilca) so that he would not have to worry about the problems of land rights in obtaining clay.

Figure 4.8 A thick bed of volcanic ash in the hamlet of Utkuchuku showing the two openings created by mining the ash for pottery temper (see figure 4.9). This particular source is the only evidence of sustained, intensive mining at any of the raw material sources visited in the District of Quinua.

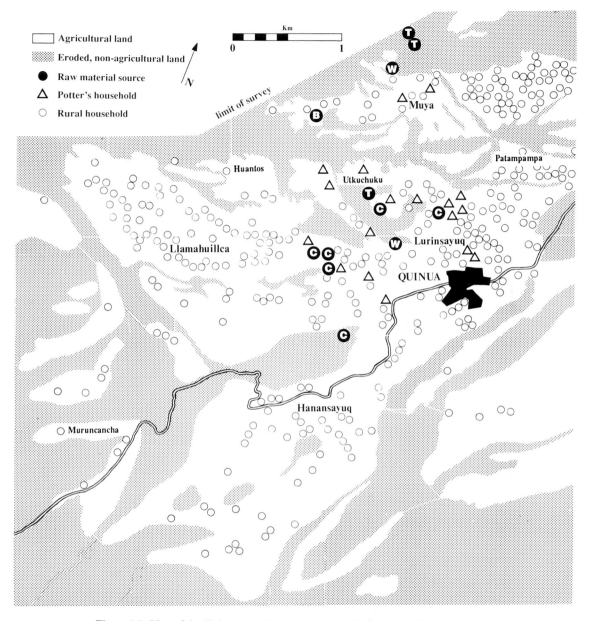

Figure 4.9 Map of the Quinua area showing agricultural and non-agricultural land, the locations of potters' households and the source locations of raw materials. The symbols in the black circles refer to the source locations for ceramic raw materials: "T" is for temper, "C" is for clay, "W" is for white paint and "B" is black paint. Note the highly dissected land caused by erosion in the upper portion of the map. Compare with the aerial photograph in figure 2.2.

On a visit to the hamlet of Larampampa, one potter showed me a clay source in a maize field where he had procured some clay, but he would not allow me to collect a sample while some women were watching us from a nearby house. Similarly, when I visited the temper mine in the hamlet of Utkuchuku, my informant told me that although a relative of his "owned" the temper mine, I should hurry with my sample collecting and examination of the mine so that the owner would not come and disturb us.

Another case of surreptitious procurement of raw materials is illustrated by my visit to the source of white paint. We left the village very early in the morning and walked down the slope. My informant told me that he would have gone later in the day if he was obtaining the paint for the artisan center (where he worked). But, since the paint was for his own use, he said that he needed to obtain the paint when he was not working for the center. Later, however, he admitted that he could not dig the paint during the day because the owner would harass him. While he was mining the paint, he was repeatedly concerned about barking dogs and other indications that people were approaching. He then confided to me that the owner of the source now lived on the other side of the village. With the owner living so far away from the source and by digging the paint so early in the morning, my informant was virtually assured that he could proceed undisturbed. As if to underscore his surreptitious activity, we returned to the village a different way than we had come.

Local religious beliefs are also intertwined with the exploitation of ceramic resources. Some resource locations may be sacred because they are inhabited by the mountain god (*urqu taytacha*). The mountain god is the single most important deity and inhabits the high mountains. He also manifests himself as an eagle so that any location visited by an eagle is also sacred. If a ceramic resource exists in a sacred location, the mountain god must be placated with an offering (*pagapu*) of *coca* leaves or cane alcohol before any raw material is removed.

One such sacred location is Ankaptiana (*chaqta parada*) "the place that the eagle site," a promontory below the village in the *pago* of Lurinsayuq. Two ceramic resources occur in this location. One consists of a laminated deposit of semi-consolidated volcanic tuff that potters formerly used as a base upon which to form their pottery. The other resource is a white slip/paint which is mined on the slope across a small stream from the promontory.

The role of religious beliefs in the acquisition of ceramic raw materials is best illustrated by means of a personal experience. During my residence in Quinua, my principal informant took me to all of the major sources of ceramic raw materials in the area. On one occasion, we visited Ankaptiana to obtain white paint (described above). Several days after our visit to this source, my informant told my colleague (William P. Mitchell) that when he procured the white paint, he should have made an offering to the mountain god. As a result of this oversight, he told Mitchell that the mountain god had sent him a dream. He dreamed that he, his wife, his young son and his employer (the Director of the Artisan Center) were in the jungle on the eastern slopes of the Andes and had gone into a cave without giving an offering of *coca* leaves and cane alcohol to the mountain god. Inside the cave, they met a white man and a white woman which the potter believed were representations of the mountain god. The white man touched his hand and said that he would not eat him, but would eat his friend, the Director of the Artisan Center. The potter turned to run and escape from the cave, but as he did, the roof collapsed. He and his wife managed to escape although his wife injured her face in the disaster. His son and the Director of the Artisan Center, however, had been eaten by the deity.[25]

The raw material for white paint procured during this trip was unusable and the potter had to return to the source to obtain more paint. One can only surmise whether the potter saw a relationship between the inferior quality of the paint and his unintended snub of the mountain god. But, when the potter returned to Ankaptiana to obtain white paint a second time, he said that he provided an offering.

Resource locations in the high altitude areas (the montane, alpine and sub-alpine zones) above the village are also sacred because these zones are believed to be the residence of the mountain god. On one occasion, a local potter and I were preparing to travel by truck up into the montane prairie (the *sallqa* or *puna*) with an engineer from the Peruvian government. The potter wanted to obtain some white paint from a source near the lake of Yanaqucha Chica (see figure 3.4) and I wanted to observe the source and collect some samples. Knowing that all of the terrain in the high altitude zones above the village was the domain of the mountain god and therefore sacred, I was curious whether the potter would leave an offering (*pagapu*) for the deity. I noticed a bottle of cane alcohol in his pocket and asked him if the alcohol would be his offering. "No," he replied, it was for a more mundane purpose: the alcohol, he said, was for "warming himself" in the cold *puna*. He then pulled *coca* leaves out of his pocket and said that the *coca* was for the offering. Unfortunately, the trip never materialized, and so it was not possible to observe the offering at the white paint source above the village. It was clear, however, that potters were serious about the necessity of making an offering to placate the mountain god when ceramic raw materials were procured from sacred locations.

Religious beliefs and land tenure patterns thus provide deviation counteracting mechanisms for over-exploiting ceramic resources to the point of ruining agricultural land. Since clay resources are dispersed over a wide area and procured from deposits on the surface of the ground, fear of divine retribution and recalcitrant landlords help randomize the population's procurement of ceramic resources. Clay and temper sources thus tend to be spread out without intensive exploitation in any one location.

The distances to the ceramic resources of clay, temper and fuel provide a deviation amplifying feedback for ceramic production in Quinua. Clays and tempers occur well within a universal catchment area for these resources established from a cross-cultural comparison of such distances for pottery-making communities world-wide.[26] In Quinua, clays may be obtained from one's own fields, and many sources occur within a preferred threshold distance of 1 kilometer from potters' households.[27] All the clay sources in the community are not known, but based on the known sources, potters never travel more than 2 kilometers to obtain clay. Temper sources are more restricted in distribution than clay sources, and exist within 1 kilometer of few potters (figure 4.9). Potters may thus travel as much as 3 kilometers to obtain temper, but this distance is within the maximum threshold distance of 7 kilometers identified for pottery-making communities worldwide.[28]

The distance that potters must travel to the source of the clay for cooking and brewing pottery generally exceeds the distance to the sources of clay for the non-cooking pottery. Clay for making cooking pottery comes from one source – a location called Uqurumi. If Uqurumi is the *only* source of this clay, then most of the potters would have to travel more than 1 kilometer to obtain it (figure 4.9) and this distance exceeds the preferred threshold distance to clay for the non-cooking pottery. Little, if any, cooking pottery is made in Quinua and one possible reason for this lack of production may be the increased energy inputs that require potters to travel a greater distance to the source of this clay than to sources used for the non-cooking pottery.

Potters find an abundant supply of fuel for firing in the montane moist forest above the village. Several kinds of brush grow there, but potters prefer only one type (*chamizo*) because of its drying and burning characteristics (see p. 100). Threshold distances to fuel resources derived from cross-cultural studies are not available because of limited data (Arnold 1985: 36–37). Very few Quinua potters, if any, are located within 1 kilometer of this resource, but all would travel no more than 4 kilometers to procure it. Quinua potters thus must travel greater distances to obtain their fuel resources than other ceramic raw materials.

The eroded areas of Lurinsayuq are somewhat less important as a source for the slips and paints. Almost all of these materials exist within the preferred distance of 10 kilometers (Arnold 1985: 56) identified from a worldwide sample. Sources exist in the eroded areas of Lurinsayuq for black, white, and, to a lesser extent, red paint. All of these sources are less than 3 kilometers from every potter. There are, however, other sources of paints in Hanansayuq (probably less than 5 kilometers distant), and in the montane prairie above the village (less than 10 kilometers distant). Both of these more distant sources, however, are within the first threshold distance of 10 kilometers. The source of red paint at Culluchaca near Huanta, on the other hand, is 19 kilometers away, but it is still within the second threshold of 30 kilometers for worldwide distances to paint resources.

Distances to paint resources are uniformly greater than distances to clays and tempers, but since pottery making requires much smaller amounts of paint than of clay and temper,[29] potters need not live near all of the paint sources. Materials for paint can be easily transported and are not used as rapidly as identical amounts of clay and temper.

The location of Quinua potters also provides accessibility to other kinds of ceramic resources. A meter or so below a weathered promontory (Ankaptiana) down the slope from the village, potters mine flat pieces of a laminated, semi-consolidated volcanic tuff which they formerly utilized as a base for forming the pottery. This resource lies within a distance of 1 kilometer for many potters and no potter would have to travel more than 3 kilometers to obtain it.

Distances to ceramic resources in Quinua are not affected by either modern transportation or pack animals. Only sources accessible by road can be transported by motor vehicles (such as a truck) and in 1967, none of these resources were accessible by road. In 1978, however, one potter reported that his temper was brought to his house in the village by truck. Burros also may be used to transport clay (Spahni 1966: 74) and temper, but they are more important for transporting fuel for firing because the brush (*chamizo*) used is bulky and great amounts are required for firing even one kiln-load. Potters may also transport all ceramic raw materials to their household on their backs. While potters thus may use pack animals and motor vehicles to bring their raw materials to their households, these methods of transport do not affect the distance traveled to the source locations.

The ecological niche of Quinua potters

Quinua potters live in an ideal ecological niche for pursuing a combination of pottery making and agriculture. The climate is generally favorable for agriculture, but without capital-intensive drying facilities, the production of fired pottery is limited to the few months of the dry season and is prevented from developing into a full-time craft. Consequently, potters must turn to agriculture for subsistence. The agricultural land available to them, however, is marginal because it is eroded and lacks access to sufficient moisture for maize agriculture. At the same time, it provides potters with basic ceramic resources (clay, temper, and paints) and because it yields a single wet-season crop, it gives them more time for making pots than they would have elsewhere. Pottery making thus helps compensate for the low productivity of the agricultural land upon which many potters live and provides a means for them to supplement their subsistence activities. Potters who are also farmers and live on limited or poor agricultural land must thus turn to pottery making (or some other craft) during the dry season to supplement subsistence activities. The combination of pottery making and agriculture in the Quinua region therefore represents a complementary adaptation to a marginal agricultural area.

If potters lived outside of their present ecological zone, they would experience difficulties in carrying out both agriculture and pottery production. Living in the zone above (the montane moist forest) would place them nearer their fuel source, but the lower mean annual temperature (see table 2.1) would limit crop repertoire and lengthen the growing season. In addition, fewer areas of suitable agricultural land occur in this zone than in the zones below because of the steep terrain and long fallow times. Potters' residences would lie beyond the preferred distance (1 kilometer) to their clay and temper resources. Distances to these basic resources would not only exceed present distances, but would approach the maximum threshold distances of 6–9 kilometers known for these materials cross-culturally. Fabrication and firing of pottery would be even more restricted to the dry season than it is now because of increased cloudiness and fog. Finally, the lower temperatures would make pottery making unpleasant, delay the drying of unfired pottery and make breakage more likely. Lower temperatures at night during the dry season would cause unfired pottery to crack and break due to freezing and force potters to store unfired pottery indoors where it would compete with space for living and the storage of subsistence crops.

Potters living in the upper part of the lower montane savannah also have disadvantages in practicing their craft. Although the conditions for agriculture and irrigation improve in this zone, potters living there have less time to make pottery because of increased agricultural responsibilities between August and December required by the irrigation cycle. Indeed, agriculturalists with irrigated land in this zone would have little time for pottery making, and could live on agriculture alone if the amount of land was adequate for subsistence. Potters who already live in this sub-zone probably possess no agricultural land and thus have no agricultural responsibilities to conflict with pottery making during optimal climate for pottery making.

If potters lived in the lower montane thorn steppe (below the savannah where they now live), the agricultural potential would be much reduced. The subsistence base would be more precarious because of soil erosion and the reduced amount of moisture available from rainfall and irrigation. During the dry season when there is no irrigation, there is little or no water in this zone except in the river at the bottom of the valley. Potters in this zone, however, lie within the preferred threshold distance of 1 kilometer from their clay and temper resources, but would live more than 7 kilometers from their fuel resources in the montane forest. Nevertheless, weather and climate would act as deviation amplifying feedback for pottery production to a greater degree here than in the zones further up the slope and potters should be able to make pottery nearly all year.

In the alluvial flood plain of the valley floor, abundant water, flat land and rich soil combine to make it a prime agricultural area. Although the distances to the modern sources of clays and tempers extend beyond the preferred distance of 1 kilometer, ceramic raw materials *do* occur here. Alluvial clays are found in the flood plain (near Chacco) and are currently exploited for brick and tile production. Temper could be easily procured in the many beds of volcanic ash which flank the flood plain. Potters who are also agriculturalists, however, would experience chronic scheduling conflicts with farming responsibilities because irrigation and warm temperatures permit farming almost year round.

Conclusion

The systemic relationships linking the population of potters in Quinua to its environmental and cultural context are complex. Climatic patterns provide regulatory feedback for the craft so that ceramics cannot be dried and fired during the rainy season. Small houses also limit production during this time because the household space required for making and drying vessels competes with living space. Production cannot increase in the rainy season without the capital to build special structures for making, drying and firing pottery and to separate drying space from living space. Furthermore, potters live on poor agricultural land, which has limited moisture from both rainfall and irrigation, and is sloping, cut with gorges and eroded. The erosion that creates poor agricultural land, however, also exposes raw materials for ceramic production providing abundant local resources for an alternative to subsistence agriculture. Environmental factors in Quinua thus combine to make agriculture and pottery making complementary in both the seasonality of production and the location of many of the potters' households. The rainy season with its almost daily rains is crucial for local agriculture, but it limits ceramic production. When the harvest ends and there are no rains, however, dry weather favours production. Similarly, although agriculture is possible in the marginal agricultural area in which potters live, the eroded land provides resources of clay, temper, paints and slips. Because of the dispersed settlement pattern, the access to these resources by any one potter is affected by energy costs, religious beliefs and reluctant landowners who do not want to have their land destroyed. All of these factors help randomize the exploitation of clay across the landscape, limit the destruction of agricultural land and maintain the complementary relationship of agriculture and pottery making.

The systemic relationships between the population of potters in Quinua and their ceramic production have also contributed to the changes in Quinua ceramic production during the last twenty-five years. Population growth, the reduced value of peasant farm production in the national economy (Mitchell 1991a) and the presence of abundant resources have all affected the expansion of the craft from about 40 potters in 1967 to approximately 500 in 1988 at a time when peasants became even more marginalized through declining agricultural production (Mitchell 1991a: 9, 104). Increased participation in the cash economy has also helped potters to mitigate the deviation counteracting effect of weather and climate by providing capital for them to build workshops away from their living area for making, drying and storing pottery during inclement weather. Increased production has provided increased economic returns and, as a result, given Quinua potters a higher social status in the community.

5

Ceramic production in Quinua

The previous chapter described the community of potters as the unit of adaptation and elaborated its relationship to the environment and society in Quinua. While understanding this relationship is essential for an ecological approach to ceramic production, the method of cultural ecology also requires an "analysis of the behavior patterns involved in exploitation of a particular area by means of a particular technology" (see Steward 1955: 40). Since the production of ceramics entails a heavy exploitation of the environment through the procurement of raw materials, an ecological approach to ceramics should also consist of an analysis of the behavioral patterns involved in the production of the ceramics themselves.

While an ecological perspective is essential to understand ceramic production within its socio-cultural and environmental context, it is less than useful in describing the ceramics themselves. The systemic and relational character of cultural ecology must thus give way to a more analytical paradigm. This different theoretical slant to ceramic description, however, does not compete with an ecological one, but rather complements it by focusing on the specifics of ceramic production beyond the broad patterns of the ceramic-ecological relationships. One such paradigm views human cultural behavior, and ceramics in particular, as a series of choices.[1] This chapter thus describes the production of Quinua ceramics as a series of choices that potters make in producing their vessels. Even though these choices are cognitive and are not available to the archaeologist, they are partly based on material criteria and their end products have material manifestations. While the focus of this chapter is on the material correlates of these choices, the choices themselves have been inferred.

A second analytical paradigm that has grown tremendously in recent years is the use of the techniques of the physical sciences to analyze ceramics.[2] Some of these techniques have focused on the chemical and mineralogical composition of the pottery[3] while others have focused on the properties that make ceramic vessels amenable for cooking, storage or some other such use.[4] In and of themselves, the techniques of the physical sciences contribute little to understanding human behavior. What is needed is to understand the relationship of the analytical results of the scientific approach to the actual choices of the potter. Besides the focus on the potters' choices, this chapter will thus describe and evaluate the choices of the potter in terms of scientific criteria derived from the physical sciences.

Selecting raw materials

The first decision that a Quinua potter faces when he desires to make pots is the class of pottery he wants to produce. Does he want to make cooking/brewing pottery or does he want to make non-cooking pottery? These two choices are not equally desirable, however, because the potter does not choose to make cooking/brewing pottery very often. Although potters may produce it for their own use, only two examples of cooking pots from Quinua were observed being sold in the markets of the valley. While other communities of potters in the valley (Ticllas, Huayhuas, Ayacucho, and the Luricocha area) produce cooking ware in shapes similar to those made in Quinua, no potter was observed producing cooking ware in Quinua in 1967. Most often, Quinua potters choose to produce the decorated non-cooking pottery which is distinct from pottery made elsewhere in the valley.

Once the potter makes the basic decision about the kinds of pottery he wishes to produce, he needs to obtain the appropriate raw materials. Pottery for cooking (and for brewing maize beer called *chicha*) requires a special clay which potters say has small "gold-like" particles in it. This clay occurs only at Uqurumi, a hamlet below the village in the *barrio* of Lurinsayuq in the *pago* of Llamahuilca. Pottery for carrying water, holding food, for ritual, for the tourist, or any other purpose besides cooking or making maize beer requires a different clay (*llinku*) which does not contain these "gold-like" particles. This type of clay is abundant and occurs in many locations.[5] Some potters dig it in their own fields whereas others go elsewhere to obtain it. Most potters interviewed, however, say that they prefer to use the clay which is mined along the banks of an eroded stream bed in the hamlet of Tantarniuq near the village cemetery.

Clays used for the non-cooking pottery contained both clay minerals and non-clay minerals and were varied in mineral composition (figures 5.1 and 5.2). It was not possible to easily characterize this clay in terms of the relative amounts of minerals that occurred in it.

Only one sample of the clay for cooking pottery was collected. Mineralogical analysis of this sample revealed that it, like the clays for the non-cooking pottery, also contained both clay minerals and non-clay minerals. The analysis (by X-ray diffraction) of this clay along with four sherds of cooking pottery revealed that a somewhat different combination of minerals occurred in this clay than in the clays for the non-cooking pottery (compare figure 5.3 with figures 5.1 and 5.2).

Potters say that the clay with "gold-like particles" is needed for vessels used for cooking and making beer so that they will not crack or break. These "gold-like" particles are flecks of the gold-colored mica mineral phlogopite which were identified macroscopically in all sherds of the cooking pottery. Although the black mica mineral biotite occurred in the single sample of the clay used to make this pottery (figure 5.3), both phlogopite and biotite reflect light in such a way that potters can readily distinguish clays with abundant mica from those without it. Although phlogopite also was observed microscopically in two samples of the clay for non-cooking pottery, it occurred in such small quantities that the potter normally would not be able to detect its presence.

The belief that gold-like particles are important for cooking and brewing pottery has an objective scientific basis because micaceous pottery is technologically superior to non-micaceous pottery for cooking. A micaceous paste is more resistant to thermal fracture, has improved heat transfer and is stronger than other pastes because the plates of mica reduce crack propagation and deflect the energy of crack initiation (Wallace and Viana 1982: 8–9). In a laboratory experiment of mica-tempered clay using an impact tester, test tiles made of mica mixed with refractory clay in a proportion of 1:5 tested 19 percent stronger than the plain refractory clay.[4] Even though these same test tiles showed cracking, they did not break; the first fracture did not move throughout the entire tile enough to cause breakage. Separation did not occur until the tiles were turned over and impact tested again. This superior strength of micaceous clay appears to be related to the nature of the mica itself. Mica particles impede fracture because they bind with the clay and resist the tensile forces occurring along the planes of the mica particles (Wallace and Viana 1982: 8). A cooking pot made with micaceous clay thus would probably crack long before it would break, permitting the contents of the vessel to be saved before total failure of the vessel walls. Micaceous pastes thus appear to lower the chances of failure from thermal fracturing. These experiments suggest that the vessels made with the micaceous clay in Quinua are stronger and more durable for cooking and beer preparation than vessels made with non-micaceous clay.

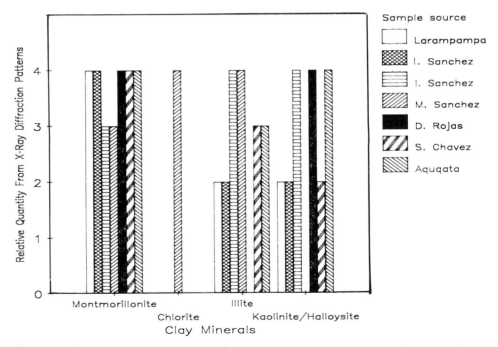

Figure 5.1 Bar graph of relative quantities of clay minerals in the samples of clays for non-cooking pottery. Relative quantities (Y axis) are based on the analyses of the X-ray diffraction patterns and are arranged according to the following key: 1= trace amount present, 2 = minor component of the sample; 3 = secondary component of the sample and 4 = major component of the sample (from data in Arnold 1972a: 95).

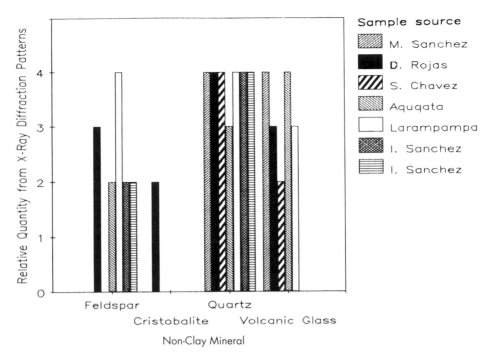

Figure 5.2 Bar graph of relative quantities of non-clay minerals in samples of clays for non-cooking pottery. Relative quantities (Y axis) are based on the analyses of the X-ray diffraction patterns (see figure 5.1 for key) (from data in Arnold 1972a: 96). In addition, the mica mineral phlogopite was identified in two samples using a binocular microscope.

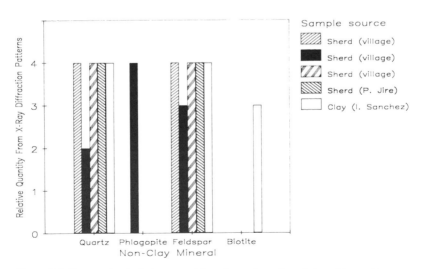

Figure 5.3 Bar graph of relative quantities of non-clay minerals found in cooking pottery from analyses of one sample of clay and four sherds. Relative quantities (Y axis) are based on the analyses of the X-ray diffraction patterns (see figure 5.1 for key) (from data in Arnold 1972a: 96). Besides being identified by X-ray diffraction, phlogopite was also identified in all of the sherds of the cooking pottery using a binocular microscope. The clay sample shown here also contained montmorillonite and illite as major clay mineral components. The clay minerals in the sherds, however, could not be identified because clays lose their crystalline structure on firing and this structure is the feature identified by X-ray diffraction.

Besides the presence of large quantities of mica, another important physical difference between the clay used for the cooking pottery and that for non-cooking pottery consists of the amount of naturally occurring non-plastics in these types of clay. The percentage of non-plastics in the one sample of clay used for cooking pottery was 51.57 percent whereas the mean percentage (N = 6) of non-plastics in clays for the non-cooking pottery was 5.3 percent (Arnold 1972a: 96). The clay for the cooking pottery was thus more than 50 percent non-plastics while the clay for the non-cooking pottery contained less than 10 percent non-plastics. Potters did not verbalize this distinction between the amount of non-plastics present, but the fact that they did not add non-plastics to the clay used for cooking pottery indicates that potters recognized that plenty of non-plastics occur naturally in this clay.

The only other qualitative differences between the two clay types do not appear to be recognized by the potter. Volcanic glass, cristobalite, kaolinite (or halloysite) and chlorite occurred in the clays used to make non-cooking pottery (figures 5.1 and 5.2), but did not occur in the cooking pottery clay (figure 5.3). Moreover, the potters did not recognize the properties of the minerals (montmorillonite, illite, quartz, and feldspar) found in both types of clay (figures 5.1, 5.2 and 5.3).

If the potter chooses to make pottery that is not used for cooking or making beer, then he must also procure sand (*aqu*) to mix with his clay (see Spahni 1966: 74). Sand is abundant in the area and occurs at several locations. It is mined at

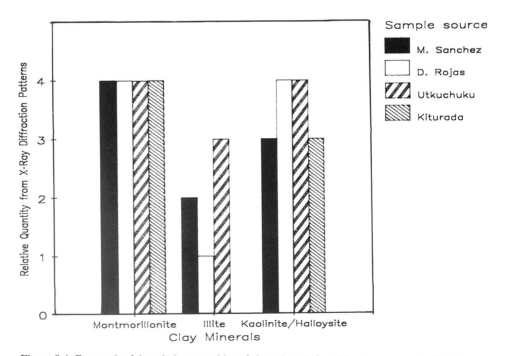

Figure 5.4 Bar graph of the relative quantities of clay minerals found in temper samples. Relative quantities (Y axis) are based on the analyses of the X-ray diffraction patterns (see figure 5.1 for key) (from data in Arnold 1972a: 98).

Utkuchuku (in the *pago* of Lurinsayuq) below the village and at Kiturada on the north side of the Huamangura Ravine along the trail to Huamanguilla. Potters also report sand sources near Muruncancha along the road below the village and at Chaqiri near Muya. Evidence of mining occurs at both Kiturada and Utkuchuku where small cave-like openings occur in the cliff faces. Most potters interviewed, however, preferred to procure their temper from the hamlet of Utkuchuku.

The mineralogical composition of the temper samples was also highly variable. Like the clays in the area, tempers contained both clay minerals and non-clay minerals (figures 5.4 and 5.5). The clay mineral montmorillonite occurred in each of the temper samples. Several clay minerals in the tempers (figure 5.4) were identical to those present in the clays used for non-cooking pottery (figure 5.1). Chlorite, however, occurred only in the clay samples.

The non-clay minerals in the temper were also identical to those in the clay used for non-cooking pottery except that the mineral apatite occurred in one sample of sand, but not in the clay, and cristobalite occurred in one sample of clay, but not in the sand (compare figure 5.5 with figure 5.2). Volcanic glass occurred in each of the sand samples and was the major non-plastic component in these samples. The mica minerals of biotite and phlogopite were identified microscopically in all samples of sand, but they occurred in very small quantities.

Potters did not know anything about the mineralogical similarities or differences between clay and sand used for non-cooking pottery. They did not identify the mineralogical similarities between temper and clay (montmorillonite, illite, kaolinite [or halloysite], quartz, feldspar, and volcanic glass) nor did they comprehend the

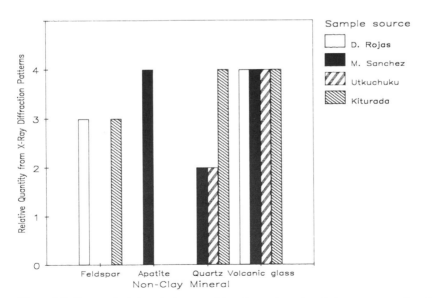

Figure 5.5 Bar graph of the relative quantities of non-clay minerals in temper samples. Relative quantities (Y axis) are based on the analyses of the X-ray diffraction patterns (see figure 5.1 for key) (from data in Arnold 1972a: 98).

qualitative differences between the two classes of materials. Finally, they did not recognize the presence of apatite that occurred in one sample of sand, but not in the clay, nor did they realize the presence of cristobalite that occurred in one sample of clay, but not in the sand.

Since there is such a mineralogical similarity between clays and tempers, how do potters distinguish between the two types of materials? Quinua potters distinguish between the sand and clay on the basis of source location and texture: clays and temper are found in different kinds of locations and clays are plastic while the temper is sandy or granular. Indeed, Quinua potters use the Quechua word (*aqu*) for temper which means "sand." This distinction suggests that the physical difference between temper and clay rests upon particle size and the relative proportion of non-plastics present in these materials (figure 5.6). The great differences in the relative amounts of non-plastics present in each of these materials are probably the objective bases of the potter's distinction between temper and clay.

The lack of the potters' recognition of specific minerals in their raw materials and their apparent concern for the relative amount of non-plastics is further reflected in the innovative behavior of individual potters. One potter used a brown sand obtained from the clay source in Tantarniuq as a temper supplement to the white sand obtained from Utkuchuku. He believed that the brown sand prevented the pottery from cracking when it was wet and sticky and caused the pottery to dry quickly without damage. He further explained that potters may use this sand as the only kind of temper in preparing the paste, but that he usually added only a small amount to paste that was already tempered with white sand.

In order to compare this temper variety with the clays and other tempers used in the community, samples of brown sand temper were analyzed to determine their mineralogical composition. Two samples were collected: one from the potter who used it and another from its source in Tantarniuq. The two samples were almost identical mineralogically except that the sample collected from the potter contained the clay mineral illite as a secondary component and the sample obtained from the source did not contain it. Both samples contained kaolinite or halloysite as the major clay mineral component and montmorillonite as a minor component. The major non-plastic component in both samples was quartz with volcanic glass as a secondary component.

Brown sand showed both similarities and differences with the raw materials used for the non-cooking pottery. Like all of the clays and tempers, it consisted of clay minerals and non-clay minerals. More non-plastics were present than in the clays used for the non-cooking ware, but there were fewer than those in the white sand temper and in the clay used for the cooking and brewing ware (figure 5.6).

Even though the samples of brown sand temper came from the same source (Tantarniuq) as the clays used for non-cooking pottery, they were not qualitatively nor quantitatively identical to the clays. Although some minerals (like quartz and volcanic glass) occurred in both the clays *and* the brown sand temper, the relative amounts of these minerals differed. Quartz was the major non-plastic component of both the clays and the brown sand temper. While no mica minerals were detected in either sample of the brown sand, the mica mineral phlogopite was identified visually in two of the clay samples. The clay minerals in the brown sand also varied quantitatively and qualitatively relative to the clay samples. Kaolinite (or halloysite) was the only major clay mineral component in both samples of brown sand, while montmorillonite occurred as a minor component.

Great differences also occurred between the samples of brown sand temper and white sand temper. Volcanic glass tended to be the major non-plastic component in white sand temper, but it was only a secondary component in samples of the brown sand temper. While quartz was the most abundant non-clay mineral in the samples of brown sand temper, it occurred in only a few samples of white sand temper and then only in greatly varying quantities. Small amounts of the mica minerals phlogopite and biotite occurred in all the white sand temper, but no mica minerals were identified in the samples of brown sand temper. Feldspar, apatite, and the clay mineral chlorite occurred only in the white sand temper. While some minerals were thus common to both tempers, they varied both qualitatively and quantitatively between each type.

The complexity of the similarities and differences between brown sand temper and clay, on the one hand, and brown sand temper and white sand temper on the other suggests that mineralogical similarities and differences between brown sand,

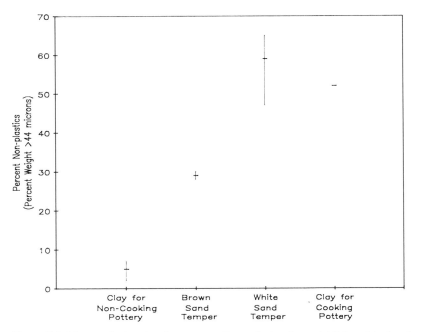

Figure 5.6 Line graph showing the percent of non-plastics (by weight) found in the clays and tempers in Quinua. (Non-plastics were materials operationally considered to be particles greater than 44 microns which was the screen size used to physically separate the non-plastics from the plastic materials.) Horizontal lines indicate mean values, while the vertical lines show the range of the values in each sample. While potters do not distinguish between the mineralogical components of their raw materials, this graph suggests that they behaviorally distinguish raw materials by the approximate amounts of non-plastics present (from data in Arnold 1972a).

clay and white sand temper are of little importance to the potter. Potters distinguish brown sand from the other raw materials on the basis of source location and the relative amount of non-plastics (figure 5.6).

Quinua raw materials thus exhibit a substantial amount of mineralogical variability (figures 5.1–5.5). This variability is related to the highly dispersed sources of clay and temper which are spread out over a horizontal distance of approximately 6 square kilometers and over a vertical distance of 300 meters. This mineralogical variability suggests that considerable variability also exists in physical properties of these raw materials. These varying physical properties make the potters' predictions of raw material suitability inconsistent except to say that micaceous clay is better to use for making cooking pottery than non-micaceous clay. Potters thus have no common, nor consistent criteria for identifying a suitable clay. One potter said that good clay was solid, hard and very dark with some black spots in it while other potters said that good clay contains few, if any, rocks. Such a clay, it is said, comes from the hamlet of Tantarniuq. A clay free of rocks is very important because during firing, rocks may expand at different rates than the clay matrix and cause vessels to crack and break (see Rye 1976). If a clay is found to contain too many rocks during mining, it is simply discarded at the source and another clay is obtained elsewhere. Even so, during paste preparation, the paste is kneaded thoroughly in order to remove any remaining rocks.

The lack of a common criterion defining suitable clay necessitates considerable experimentation by potters when they obtain raw materials from new sources. Some potters experiment with unknown clays by making test vessels to see if they crack or break before they use the clay on a large scale. One potter at the artisan center told about a white clay he found near the hamlet of Utkuchuku below the village. The clay was very workable, but one test vessel made with it cracked during drying and another cracked and broke during firing. Another potter at the artisan center had obtained a green clay (called *ichma ukri*) above the village where the road from Quinua to Tambo meets the road from Huamanguilla. He tested it as a slip on a candle holder and it fired to a tan/cream color, but it had a slightly different texture than other paints. X-ray diffraction analysis of this paint revealed that it was composed of quartz and the clay mineral illite and was thus different from the other Quinua slips which contained montmorillonite (see discussion of decorating pottery, p. 98) and had different physical properties.

Fabricating pottery

After the potter procures temper and clay, he needs to prepare them properly. Since temper is mined in large chunks and then transported to the house in this form, the potter must break up the chunks and prepare them by grinding. Then, both the clay and temper need to dry in the sun. Two or three days may be necessary for thorough drying. If it rains while the clay is drying, it must be taken inside and dried again outside. The potter then soaks the clay in water, and mixes it with the dry temper in proportions of approximately five parts temper to four parts clay (or slightly more temper than clay). After the paste has been prepared, the potter rolls it into large cylinders and stores it until it is needed. The potter is then ready to begin shaping the pottery.

Quinua pottery is formed on a lime and cement slab (called a *teapu* in Quechua). Each object is made on a separate slab in order to facilitate removal of the newly constructed object from the forming apparatus without damage. A potter may have a dozen or more of these slabs available in his household. Some potters, however, prefer to use flat chunks of *qiqatu* (a semi-consolidated volcanic tuff) as the base for forming pottery (see Spahni 1966: 75) because the vessels do not stick to it and can be removed easily.

The lime-cement forming slab rests on a very low, circular ceramic plate. The potter turns the slab and the ceramic plate as a unit on a broken piece of mosaic tile or a flat stone (figure 5.7). The entire apparatus rests on the ground (or floor of the house) and the potter works in a seated position on a mat or animal skin. Men never sit directly on the ground because it is believed that they will become sick due to the earth vapors which will enter their body through their testicles.[7]

Quinua potters form their pottery using modeling and modified coiling. Modeling shapes the clay with only the fingers and hands. Modified coiling draws the clay up from a thick coil and thins it to make the walls of a vessel. More coils or portions of coils are added as needed to achieve the desired shape and size.

The vessel forming techniques used in Quinua appear to be well adapted to the local clays. The plasticity and strength of the clay and resulting paste is evident from

Figure 5.7 The three-part forming apparatus used to make pottery in the District of Quinua: the lime-cement or *qiqatu* slab lies on top with the clay dish between the slab and a piece of mosaic tile. The slab and dish turn as a unit on the piece of tile. The scale around the chalkboard is in 1 inch units.

the fact that the vessel walls are relatively thin, can be drawn upward and formed from a single coil and show no evidence of sagging.

In producing cooking and brewing ware, the potter can choose to fabricate only four vessel shapes: *manka*, *urpu*, *maqma*, or *tumin* (figure 5.8). Each of these four vessels has important uses. The *manka* is primarily a cooking vessel. It can also be used as a container for: (1) selling and dispensing hot food (stew and corn-on-the-cob) at roadside eating places; (2) storing various objects in the house; and (3) storing white paint for decorating pottery. The second shape made with this micaceous paste is the *maqma*, and it is primarily used as a vessel for making maize beer (*chicha*). It also serves as a general storage vessel for agricultural produce like maize, grain or other seed crops and provides protection against mice predation inside the house.[8] Potters frequently use it for: (1) storing raw clay and chunks of temper; (2) soaking raw clay; and (3) storing and resoaking broken pieces of unfired vessels and scraps of paste trimmed from newly-made pottery. For these purposes,

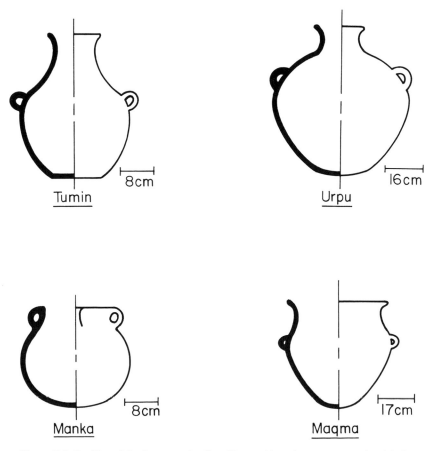

Figure 5.8 Profiles of the four vessels of cooking and brewing pottery made with the untempered clay in Quinua.

the *maqma* may be partially buried (usually to within 8 centimeters of its mouth) either inside or outside the potter's house. Like the *maqma*, the *urpu* is used for making maize beer. The *tumin* is used primarily for transporting and storing beer and water. When the *tumin* contains beer, the mouth of the vessel is stuffed with bark, leaves of the pepper tree (*molle*) or wadded up pieces of plastic to prevent spilling during transport and to keep foreign matter out of the liquid. When the bark or leaves of the pepper tree are used, they serve as a strainer through which the liquid is poured when served.

Quinua potters say that the three types of beer jars (*maqma, urpu,* and *tumin*) are distinguished by the size of their mouth. The *maqma* has the largest orifice, the *urpu* is next in size and the *tumin* is the smallest (figure 5.8). Since no cooking pottery was being made during the course of the field work, no data were available concerning the fabrication of these vessels and therefore the data used here come from photographs of these vessels already in use. Comparisons of the ratio of mouth diameters to greatest diameter showed a clear difference between the *urpu* and the *maqma* (figure 5.9), but even with a sample size of one, differences between the *urpu* and *tumin* did not appear to be mouth diameter, but rather size and perhaps the shape of the vessel base (see figure 5.8).

Every other vessel made in the potters' shape repertoire is produced with a paste that is behaviorally tempered with volcanic ash. This paste category includes other utilitarian shapes which are not used for cooking or maize beer, and includes

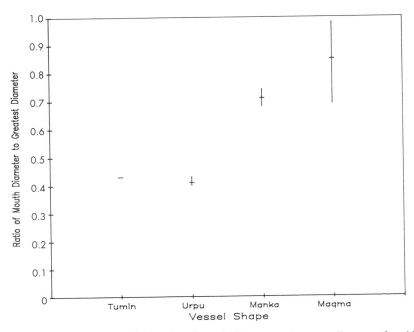

Figure 5.9 Comparison of the ratios of mouth diameter and greatest diameter of cooking pottery based on photographs of the vessels: *tumin* (liquid-carrying jar, N = 1), *urpu* (beer-brewing jar, N = 2), *maqma* (*chicha* storage jar, N = 4), *manka* (cooking pot, N = 2). Horizontal lines indicate mean values, while the vertical lines show the range of ratios for each dimension.

all shapes used for ritual and ornament as well as those made for the artisan market.

In making non-cooking vessels, the potter must first decide which class of shapes he wishes to make. He can either make utilitarian shapes or decorative or ritual items. Utilitarian shapes include the bowl (*plato*), the liquid-carrying vessels (*aysaku*)[9] and a variety of less important shapes. Each shape has a variety of uses. The bowl is utilized primarily as a serving vessel (roadside food vendors use it to hold hot maize-on-the-cob) and for storing miscellaneous items in the house (figure 5.10). All of the liquid-carrying shapes (the *yukupuynu*, *puynu*, *tachu*, and *tumin*) are produced primarily for local consumption and are employed for storing, carrying, and dispensing water or other consumable liquids. People utilize the *tachu* (figure 5.11) for carrying water from the irrigation ditches to the house; roadside food vendors use it as a receptacle to hold water for washing dishes and hands. It can also be used to carry and dispense the maize beer into individual cups. One finds the *yukupuynu* in the markets where vendors use it for carrying and storing water (figure 5.12). It is particularly valued for carrying water long distances because the narrow neck prevents spillage. The *puynu* is used to hold water at roadside food vendors and as a pitcher to serve beer (*chicha*) (figure 5.13). The *tumin* is used for transporting and storing water and *chicha* and can also be made with the paste used for cooking pottery. When *chicha* or water is dispensed from the *tumin*, it is usually poured into *tachus* or *puynus* which are then used to fill individual cups.

Potters say that all of the *aysaku* vessels have the same shape except for the size of

Fig. 5.10 The *plato* shape. The diameter of the measuring tape is 2.5 cm. For dimensions of vessels of this shape, see figures 5.14–5.16.

the mouth. This belief is supported by the measurements of these shapes. Comparisons of the ranges and means of their greatest diameters (figure 5.15) and heights (figure 5.14) reveal that the *aysaku* shapes have similar size ranges. By way of contrast, when the mouth and neck diameters of the shapes are compared, the means are different although the ranges show some overlap (figures 5.16 and 5.17).

Since these shapes have different size variations, measurements of absolute mouth sizes do not take these size variations into account. Furthermore, the potters' perceptions of mouth size as the distinguishing characteristic of the shape are probably not just based on the absolute size of the mouth, but rather on its relative size in comparison to the vessel diameter. Indeed, comparisons of the ratios of mouth and neck diameters to the greatest diameters suggest that ratios rather than absolute sizes distinguish one *aysaku* shape from another (figures 5.18 and 5.19). This observation is congruent with the cross-cultural data that show that ethnographic vessels with the same utilitarian function can be characterized by ratios of mouth diameter to greatest diameter (Henrickson and McDonald 1983).

Figure 5.11 The *tachu* shape. The scale is in centimeters. For dimensions of vessels of this shape, see figures 5.14–5.17.

The potter's belief that the *aysaku* shapes are the same except for the size of the mouth suggests that all of these vessels went through identical stages of production except for shaping the neck and the mouth. Further, the similarity of the greatest diameter of the bowl (*plato*) to the greatest diameter of these vessels suggested that the bowl form was an early stage of the production of these shapes (figure 5.14). One can thus construct a hypothetical fabrication grammar (figure 5.20) to show the choices that the potter had available as he fabricated these shapes.

Besides the bowl and liquid-carrying shapes already discussed, there are other utilitarian vessels made in Quinua that were observed less frequently.

> The *tinaqa* (figure 5.21) is an open-mouthed jar with a flat bottom; its mouth is only slightly smaller than its greatest diameter. The neck of the vessel tapers gradually from the point of greatest circumference to its mouth. Either two or four strap handles are attached to the vessel wall slightly above the point of greatest circumference. Most often *tinaqas* were used as receptacles for a sweet drink and for hot food at roadside food vendors, but at one family fiesta, a *tinaqa* served as receptacle for holding maize

Figure 5.12 The *yukupuynu* shape. For dimensions of vessels of this shape, see figures 5.14–5.17.

beer. At the house of one potter, it was partially buried in the ground and
used for storing the raw material for white paint.

The *chaysaku* has straight sides and a flat bottom. On some vessels, two strap
handles are attached to the vessel below the rim, but on others there is
only one. Potters use this vessel for holding water when they are making
pottery.

The *vasinika* (Spahni 1966: Lamina V, no. 10) is a chamber pot. It has a
shape similar to a cooking pot (see figure 5.8) except that the chamber pot
is generally smaller and has its handles placed well below the rim of the
vessel whereas the handles for the cooking pot are always attached from
the rim of the vessel to the upper body.

Other vessels of utilitarian value that have lesser importance are the teapot (*tetera*),
the wash basin (*lavatorio*), the cup, a food dish for dogs (*latu*), and a fancy pitcher
called a *papaya* which can be filled from the bottom and then turned upright without
the water spilling out. There are a variety of other shapes which have uncertain
utilitarian usage and will not be described here.

Figure 5.13 The *puynu* shape. For dimensions of vessels of this shape, see figures 5.14–5.17.

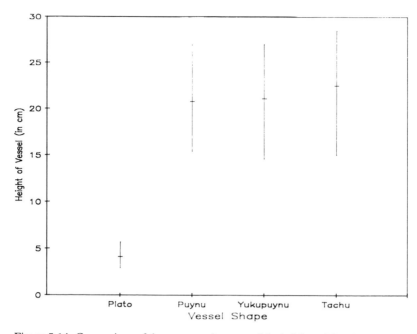

Figure 5.14 Comparison of the means and ranges of the heights of the *plato* and *aysaku* shapes (*plato*, N = 5; *puynu*, N = 11; *yukupuynu*, N = 7; *tachu*, N = 7). Horizontal lines indicate mean values, while the vertical lines show the range of the values for each dimension.

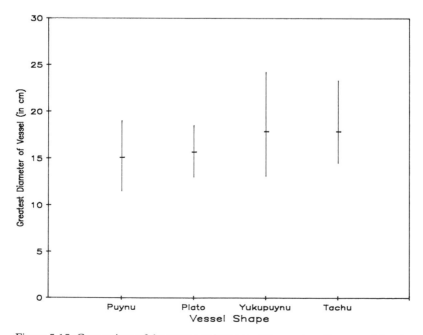

Figure 5.15 Comparison of the means and ranges of the greatest diameter of the *plato* and *aysaku* shapes (*puynu*, N = 11; *plato*, N = 5; *yukupuynu*, N = 7; *tachu*, N = 7). Horizontal lines indicate mean values, while the vertical lines show the range of the values for each dimension.

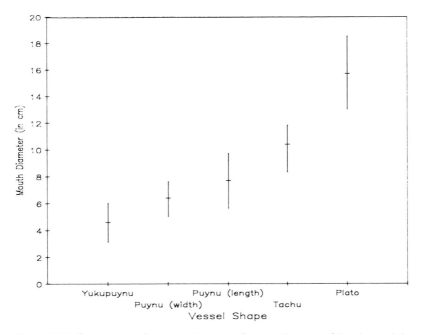

Figure 5.16 Comparison of ranges and means of mouth diameter of the *plato* and the *aysaku* shapes (*yukupuynu*, N = 7; *puynu*, N = 10 for spout width and N = 7 for spout length; *tachu*, N = 7; *plato*, N = 5). Horizontal lines indicate mean values, while the vertical lines show the range of the values for each dimension.

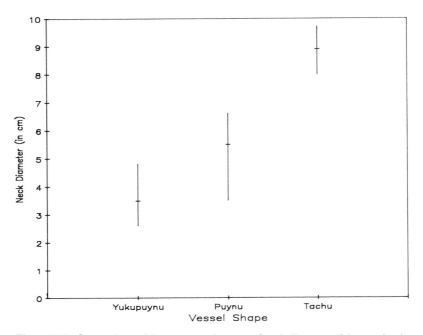

Figure 5.17 Comparison of the means and ranges of neck diameter of the *aysaku* shapes (*yukupuynu*, N = 7; *puynu*, N = 11; *tachu*, N = 7). Horizontal lines indicate mean values, while the vertical lines show the range of the values for each dimension.

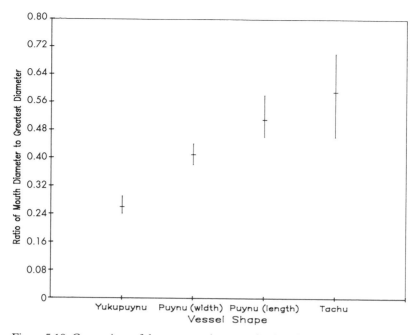

Figure 5.18 Comparison of the means and ranges of ratios of mouth diameter to greatest diameter for the *aysaku* shapes (*yukupuynu*, N = 7; *puynu*, N = 10 for spout width and N = 7 for spout length; *tachu*, N = 7). Horizontal lines indicate mean values, while the vertical lines show the range of the values for each ratio.

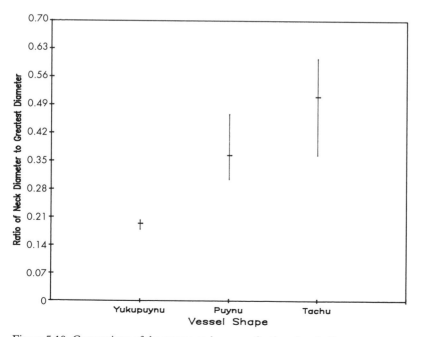

Figure 5.19 Comparison of the means and ranges of ratios of neck diameter to greatest diameter of the *aysaku* shapes (*yukupuynu*, N = 7; *puynu*, N = 11; *tachu*, N = 7). Horizontal lines indicate mean values, while the vertical lines show the range of the values for each ratio.

Another category of Quinua pottery consists of ritual or ornamental vessels which generally have no utilitarian purpose. The most important of these items are described below.

> Churches: The ceramic church (figure 5.22) comes in a variety of forms, but most usually has two towers. Some tend to be similar in appearance to the twin-towered cathedral in the city of Ayacucho. In 1967, churches were Quinua's most famous ceramic product (Spahni 1966: 84). In the commercial artisan market outside of the Ayacucho Valley, these churches are known as "Ayacucho" churches.
>
> *Chunchu*: This figure (figure 5.23) is a ceramic representation of the jungle Indians (such as the Campa) who live in the tropical forest to the east of the Andes.
>
> *Ukumari*: This figure is the ceramic form of the mythical being of the same name which lives in the tropical forest east of the Andes (figure 5.24). The *ukumari* has exceptional strength and is half-man (or woman) and half-bear.
>
> Bulls: The bull is considered to be an animal representation of the *amaru* (a

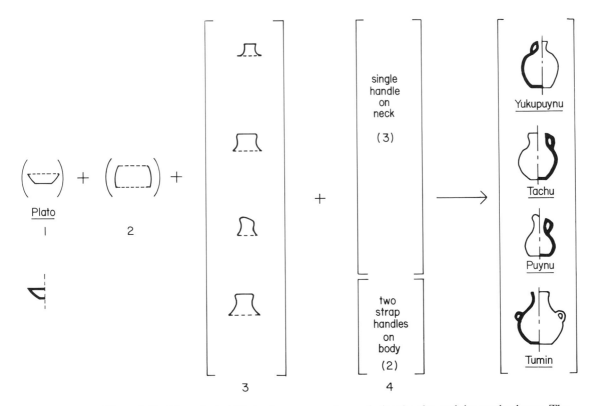

Figure 5.20 A hypothetical fabrication grammar for producing the *plato* and the *aysaku* shapes. The parentheses indicate that the items within them are selected for any vessel shape, while the brackets indicate that choices must be selected in a horizontal line with those options in other brackets.

powerful spirit) which can also take the form of a duck, serpent, pig or chicken (William Mitchell, personal communication).

Musicians: These figures (called *musicos*) are ceramic representations of musicians playing the drum, the trumpet, or the guitar.

Double pot: This vessel consists of two small cup-like portions which are joined together at the base so that the liquid contents of one cup can pass into the other (figure 5.25). On one side of the vessel, there is a small handle with a cylindrical cross-section which is attached to each cup.

Llama: This vessel is made in the shape of a *llama* and has a circular opening on the back of the animal (Spahni 1966: Lamina VI, no. 4).

Even though all of the non-cooking pottery in Quinua described so far is used for indigenous utilitarian, decorative or ritual purposes, most of the pottery produced in Quinua in 1967 (except the *aysaku* shapes) was not used locally, but was sold to merchants for the domestic and foreign artisan market. In 1978, this practice continued except that one potter reported that only vessels that were "ugly" and crudely executed escaped being exported from the community and were sold locally.

The flexibility of the modeling and modified coiling technique used in Quinua allows potters to innovate easily and make copies of virtually any object (see Spahni 1966: 78). So, it is not difficult for potters to keep up with changing demand for new and innovative shapes. In addition to the traditional utilitarian, ritual and

Figure 5.21 A *tinaqa* decorated with the black-and-white-on-buff painting scheme. The match box is inserted for scale and is 3.4 cm wide.

Figure 5.22 A church which is decorated in the black-and-red-on-white painting scheme. The match box is inserted for scale and is 3.4 cm wide.

ceremonial shapes described above, potters produce a variety of other shapes which do not have any local use, but are produced entirely for the tourist market. These shapes include elaborate crosses, candelabras, candle holders, jet planes, helicopters, boats, swans, crucifixes, nativity scenes, local scenes, and models of the saint and its pedestal carried in the procession on Easter morning in Ayacucho. In 1978, one potter reported that potters produced a greater variety of tourist ware than they did in 1967. In the 1980s, the variety of shapes has increased even more as more people produced ceramics, and constantly changed their designs in order to maintain their market share (Mitchell 1991a).

Figure 5.23 A *chunchu* decorated in the white-on-red painting scheme. The scale is in centimeters.

Decorating

Ceramic decoration in Quinua consists of both plastic and painted decoration. While most decoration involves slipping and painting, potters also use modeling, stamping and molding while the clay is still damp and plastic. Some figurines (like churches, bulls, llamas, and musicians) are made entirely by modeling. Potters also model small objects like *chunchus* which are fastened to larger ceramic objects. Modeling is also used to modify the shape of the vessel walls (on churches, for example) which have been fabricated by modified coiling. Stamping using the ends

Figure 5.24 An *ukumari* (legendary half-human/half-bear) painted with the white-on-red painting scheme. The scale is in centimeters.

of bamboo tubes is used to form the faces on some individual figures like *chunchus* (figure 5.26).

Up until this point in the production process, pottery making is almost exclusively a male activity. Although there were two female potters in Quinua in 1967, males almost always procure and mix raw materials, and fabricate and fire the vessels. Both males and females, however, slip, polish, and paint the pottery.

When the potter has completed shaping a vessel, he places it aside to dry. After it has become leather hard, he (or his wife) trims the excess clay from its base and then makes the exterior surface smooth with his wet hand. The clay trimmed from the vessel is resoaked for future use.

Before the potter slips and paints his vessel, however, he must obtain and prepare the appropriate raw materials. Depending on the style he wishes to paint, the potter must obtain one or more of the following colors – white, red, black or buff (Spahni 1966: 76). White paint (*ruyaq ichma*) occurs in three locations: in Ankaptiana, in the canyon of Huamangura below the hamlet of Incaqasa (in the *pago* of Muya) and near "little black lake" (Yanaqucha Chica) in the montane prairie above the village. Most potters interviewed, however, preferred to procure their white paint in Ankaptiana which lies directly below the village in the *pago* of Lurinsayuq. There are several shallow holes in the fields of this hamlet from which potters procured their paint, but potters say that it can be obtained anywhere in Ankaptiana.

The raw material for the white paint looks like tan clay. To procure it, potters first remove the surface overburden and then only select material from 15 centimeters below ground level. After removing the roots from the excavated material and separating the tan clay from the green and red clays, the potter tastes it to determine

Figure 5.25 A double pot which is painted with the black-and-red-on-white painting scheme. The scale is in centimeters.

if the paint has its distinctive taste. If so, he packs it into balls which are placed in his carrying bag.

Potters can obtain red paint (*ichma puka*)[10] in four locations: in the *pago* of Muya, near "little black lake" (Yanaqucha Chica) in the montane prairie above the village, near the battlefield of Ayacucho above the village, and at Culluchaca (see Spahni 1966: 76) in the mountains northeast of the town of Huanta, 17 kilometers northwest of Quinua (see figure 3.4). Of these locations, potters prefer the paint from Culluchaca because they say it is superior to the paint obtained locally. Potters say that red paint from the Quinua sources flakes off the vessels when they are dry or blackens easily with firing. Potters make a three day trip to Culluchaca to procure their paint and obtain it through purchase or trade (usually for local pottery).

Red paint from the different sources may have slightly different colors when fired and thus may have different compositions. A red slip on some *tinaqas* was darker than that used on bowls (*platos*) and it is said that potters from the hamlet of Wayuniuq use the paint from Culluchaca while those from the *pago* of Muya use the paint obtained in Muya itself.

Less information was available on black and buff paint. Black paint occurs only in the hamlet of Waywayuq in the *pago* of Muya. Buff paint is yellow in its raw state and turns tan or buff with firing. Informants were not in agreement about the

Figure 5.26 A potter using a mold to produce a face for a small modeled *chunchu* that will be placed on a *candelabra* (see figure 5.34).

sources for buff paint, but sources were said to occur in the Huamangura Ravine (in the hamlet of Waywayuq) and in the montane prairie above the village (near the lake of Yanaqucha Chica).

The potters' choice of raw materials used for slips and paints reveals an understanding of physical properties of these materials. Mineralogical analyses of the paints by means of X-ray diffraction (Arnold 1972a: 99) indicated that all of these paints contained montmorillonite as the major clay mineral component. Montmorillonite is known for its excellent film-forming properties which gives the paint a superior spreading quality.[11]

The presence of certain minerals in the paints produces their color (Arnold 1972a: 99). All of the non-clay minerals present in the white paint are colorless or white (volcanic glass, quartz, cristobalite and feldspar). The clay minerals in the paint (montmorillonite and smaller amounts of kaolinite or halloysite) are also white. Goethite is primarily responsible for the color of the black paint and is the chief non-clay constituent of this paint. The other minerals present (volcanic glass, montmorillonite and beta iron oxide) do not alter the black color. Hematite is the primary non-clay mineral in the red paint and is responsible for its red color. Goethite is a secondary component of this paint and darkens the red color, but feldspar and the clay minerals (montmorillonite and smaller amounts of kaolinite or halloysite) may lighten it making the red not quite as dark as it would be with the goethite and the hematite alone.

Potters must prepare raw paints properly in order to use them on pottery. Since the material for black paint is a rock, it must be ground into a fine powder. The raw material for white paint is not white when mined and the potter tests it at the source by rubbing it on the handle of a pick to see if it dries to a white color.

After the potter returns to his house with the paint, it must be dried in the sun. Then, it is mixed with water before being used to decorate the pottery. Potters say that if the paint has not dried enough, it will fall off the vessel after it has been applied. If white paint retains its tan or buff color after drying, or if the paint flakes off the vessel, the potter discards it, returns to the source again and obtains the paint from a slightly different location.

In trying to control the quality of white paint, the potter is relying on the physical properties of two different minerals. First, it is probably the absence of sufficient quantities of montmorillonite that is responsible for the failure of white paint to adhere to a vessel and flake off the vessel when it dries. As stated earlier, montmorillonite is known for its film-forming properties and case-hardening structure which would make this mineral superior for slips. Secondly, while the adherence of the raw paint is the desired characteristic, the potter is relying on the presence of certain iron minerals (like limonite) to indicate it. The presence of even a small amount of limonite causes the paint to remain a buff color after drying or change from white to buff or yellow after firing. This characteristic is not related to the presence of montmorillonite in the paint. Potters cannot always obtain a truly white-firing paint because "white" paints often turn cream or pale yellow during firing.

After the newly formed vessels are leather-hard and the potter has prepared the paints, the pottery is ready to be decorated. Decoration follows a definite plan (figure 5.27); only non-cooking pottery receives decoration. If it is necessary to place a slip on the vessel, it is applied with a damp piece of cloth and then burnished with a smooth stone. If the vessel to be burnished does not have a slip, the outside of the vessel is dampened with water during burnishing. Some vessels, however, are not burnished at all.

Whatever the intent of the potter, burnishing has the effect of increasing the strength of the pottery. In experiments comparing burnished with unburnished pottery (Wallace 1989), cylindrical test tiles of a terracotta clay burnished on all sides were an average of 21.8 percent stronger than those which were not burnished. Similarly, test tiles of a buff-firing clay were 21.5 percent stronger than unburnished tiles. Since ceramic vessels are not often burnished on all sides, the experiment was repeated with burnishing on only one side and then impact tested. Test tiles that were burnished on the impact side (or compression side) of the tiles were

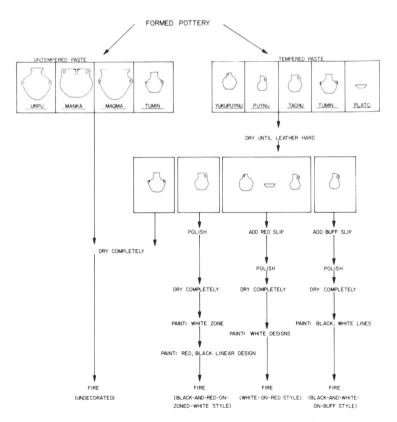

Figure 5.27 Diagram of utilitarian and service vessels showing the sequence of painting, burnishing, and slipping used to produce the undecorated pottery and three painted schemes in the community. (These steps are inferred from the most frequent patterns of decoration [or lack of it] and are not rigid rules, but rather appear to be behavioral guidelines which are occasionally violated and modified (see chapters 7 and 8 for variations].)

13.7 percent stronger than unburnished tiles while those tiles that were burnished on the tension side of the impact were 21.7 percent stronger than the unburnished tiles (Wallace 1989: 39). The results of these experiments suggest that burnishing increases the strength of vessel walls and makes them more resistant to breakage. Furthermore, burnishing the inside of the vessel will make the outside wall more resistant to breakage from an external blow (Wallace 1989: 37).

Potters do not decorate their vessels further until they have dried completely because they believe that the pottery will crack if it is painted before drying. Most decoration besides slipping is delayed until the day the pots are fired when both men and women paint the designs using a feather for smaller lines and a brush for larger lines (figure 5.28).

The varied use of burnishing, slipping, and painting in definite combinations produces three distinct painting schemes in Quinua. The most common painting scheme used in Quinua is the white-on-red scheme. Its main characteristics consist of bands and motifs[12] of relatively thin white lines on a burnished red slip. Potters use this scheme almost exclusively on *platos*, *puynus* and *yukupuynus* (figures 5.10, 5.12, 5.13), but they often use it to decorate *tinaqas*, bulls, cups, teapots (*teteras*), *chaysakus*, and most figurines other than churches (see figures 5.23 and 5.24). In addition, many of the new and innovative shapes made in Quinua are decorated in this scheme.

The second most common type of painted decoration used on Quinua pottery consists of the black-and-red-on-white scheme. In this scheme, red and black lines are drawn on an unburnished (matte) white background. The lines may be straight or zigzag and are sometimes arranged in parallel to form a design. Designs consist of bands or a central motif dominating a major design zone; they are almost always oriented vertically. Potters use this style exclusively to decorate the ceramic churches (figure 5.22), *tachus* and double pots (see figure 5.25) and occasionally use it on *tinaqas* and other figurines besides churches. The unburnished matte white background defines the design zone and for some shapes like churches (see figure 5.22) and figurines like llamas and sheep, the white background covers the entire vessel. For other shapes (*tachus*, *tinaqas* and double pots, see figure 5.25), the white background is restricted to a particular zone on the vessel. The remainder of the vessel is generally unslipped (or perhaps slipped with buff paint) and may be either burnished or unburnished.

The third and least common kind of painted decoration in Quinua is the black-and-white-on-buff scheme. This type consists of black and white designs painted on a burnished buff slip (or burnished body clay). Few data exist on this scheme, but some *puynus* (figure 5.29), cups, and *tinaqas* (figure 5.21) are decorated with this painting scheme. The main motifs consist of plants outlined in black and white lines.

Firing

In preparing to fire his pottery, the potter must first obtain the proper fuel. Of all the potential fuels available, potters prefer to use the shrub *chamizo* (*suqusuqu* in Quechua) because it is available in large quantities, relatively easy to obtain and costs virtually nothing. *Chamizo* grows in the montane moist forest above the village along with a variety of other shrubs (collectively called *chaqu*). The latter have disadvantages which makes them relatively inferior to *chamizo* for firing. The thorns of the *chiqchi* make it unpleasant to handle. The *chinwicha* possesses an insufficient amount of leaves which fall off when the plant is dried. The *chilca*[13] also has insufficient leaves. The *taya*[14] has a great many leaves which dry well, but they do

Figure 5.28 Painting a design on Quinua pottery using a small feather. This red-on-white color scheme is a non-traditional variation of Quinua painting. The vessel being painted is non-traditional and is an example of a vessel being produced for the artisan market.

not produce much flame. A potter *could* thus use some of the *chiqchi*, the *chilca*, and the *taya* for firing, but potters recognize *chamizo* as superior for firing and prefer it in comparison to these shrubs because it dries well without losing its leaves and it burns with a hot, quick flame.

Potters travel to the montane moist forest in the early morning to obtain their *chamizo* because it is easier to cut before the sun gets too hot. Potters cut it close to the ground and load it on their backs or on burros for transport to their houses.

Besides *chamizo*, potters can also use straw for firing or the dung of cattle or burros, but these fuels are either relatively unimportant or infrequently used. Informants only used straw in starting the fire and occasionally during the remainder of the process. One potter considered burro dung as a superior fuel for firing, but said it should be used in conjunction with *chamizo* and then only a little should be placed on the floor of the kiln. Burro dung, however, can be used for firing small items and small amounts of pottery. In these cases, he said, the dung is placed between the vessels, stacked up in the kiln or allegedly plastered on to the pottery.

After the potter obtains his fuel, he must dry it in the sun. While he prefers to have two days for drying the *chamizo*, he needs at least one sunny day for drying both pottery and fuel. At this time, he places his pottery on straw mats, sheets of plastic or large animal skins (from cattle) while he finishes decorating the pottery (figure 5.30).

At this time, the potter may repair vessels which have been damaged by the rains. Potters repair vessels by moistening the edges of the break, applying clay to the area, and shaping it to the vessel contours by using a flat scraper. Then, the objects are set aside to dry. Although potters say that any pottery can be repaired before firing, in practice, they only repair objects like *candelabras* which do not hold liquids.

Quinua potters fire their vessels in a permanent adobe kiln. Kilns are basically cylindrical in shape, but sometimes their form corresponds more to a truncated cone. The top of the kiln remains open and often the plane of the opening is not parallel to the ground level (figure 5.31).

The Quinua kiln is more complex and technologically sophisticated than open firing where nothing separates the fuel from the pottery during the firing process. The fuel is placed in a firebox below the pottery and is separated from it by a piece of adobe, pottery or metal. The potter stokes the fire through a hole into the firebox and this feature gives the potter several advantages over open firing. First, it reduces losses due to firing clouds which occur when burning fuel touches the pottery. Second, the firebox provides more control than a potter would have with open firing, permitting the potter to add more fuel as it is needed. Adding fuel is not beyond his control as it is when potters place all the fuel together with the pottery in open firing.[15]

There are several lines of evidence that suggest that the Quinua kiln is an introduction dating to historic times. First, Quinua potters do not use a Quechua word for their kiln and this suggests that their kiln is not an item of indigenous material culture. Second, the Quinua kiln is an updraft kiln which provides more control over

Figure 5.29 A *puynu* (pitcher) painted in the black-and-white-on-buff painting scheme. The scale is in centimeters.

the firing process than open firing or firing within a low wall. Although common in the Old World (e.g. Rye and Evans 1976), updraft kilns are unusual in traditional pottery-making communities in the New World and do not occur in most of the other traditional pottery-making communities in Peru.[16] Updraft kilns similar to those of Quinua, however, are found in the pottery-making communities of Aco (LaVallée 1967) and Quicha Grande (Hagstrum 1989: 172–173) in the central Peruvian highlands. A more modern kiln occurs in the coastal region of northern Peru (Wiesse 1982: 232). The general lack of association of updraft kilns with traditional pottery production in Peru, however, suggests that these devices were not indigenous to Andean ceramic technology, but were introduced from Spain (see Hagstrum 1989: 172–173).

When the potter has completed all of the preparations for firing, he stacks the vessels upside down (or on their sides) on the support in the bottom of the kiln just above the firebox. Then, he fills the kiln with vessels up to a point just below the top

Figure 5.30 Pottery spread out on skins and straw mats to dry prior to slipping, painting and firing. There is a wide variety of pottery in the photograph including utilitarian vessels (such as the *yukupuynu* in the lower center), traditional figurines (for example the two bulls in the center of the photograph) and new pottery produced exclusively for the artisan market. All of this pottery (except that of poorer quality), however, was purchased by a trader for export to Ayacucho and Lima. *Chamizo*, the brushwood used for firing, can be seen drying on the ground in the lower left hand corner.

Figure 5.31 The Quinua kiln during firing. The person on the left (with a cigarette in his right hand) is a visiting North-American. Pottery to be fired lies at the lower left of the photograph while the fuel for firing (*chamizo*) lies at the lower right.

of the kiln (figure 5.32). Finally, he places sherds over the pottery to keep the flames and heat from escaping from the spaces between the vessels.

To initiate firing, the potter places some *chamizo* and straw in the firebox and ignites the fire. At first, he proceeds slowly and waits for long periods before adding more *chamizo*. Sometimes the fire goes out and he has to light it again, but he continues to add fuel at a slow pace. When the flames reach the top of the kiln and heat the sherds on top of the pottery, the potter touches the sherds on top of the kiln with his hand to see if they are warm. If so, it signals the end of the water smoking stage and the beginning of the oxidation stage (Shepard 1956: 81–83). After this transition point, the potter continues to place *chamizo* into the kiln, but does so at a more rapid rate than previously. During this stage, the potter maximizes the rapid burning characteristics of *chamizo* by letting the fire burn off the leaves of the shrub and then recovering the unburned stalks before adding more fuel.

If the unfired pottery gets in contact with moisture, or if the fire in the kiln is extinguished, the pottery will either be irreparably damaged or it will have to be refired. If it begins to rain during firing, the potter must take special care to keep both the kiln and the fuel dry. He prevents the rain from entering the kiln by covering the top with an animal skin or very large piece of broken pottery. The fuel is kept dry by covering it with sheets of plastic, animal skins or straw mats. To be sure that the *chamizo* is kept sufficiently dry during rain, the covering on the kiln is removed and bundles of chamizo are placed over the opening before they are placed in the firebox.

Adding fuel at a rapid rate continues until the potter sees the red-hot glow of the pottery through the spaces between the sherds on the top of the kiln. The firing process is then complete and the potter ceases to add fuel. At this point, he scrapes the ashes out of the firebox and places them on the sherds on top of the kiln taking care to cover all of the holes. After about half an hour, these ashes have burned off and the potter can see the color of the fired pottery between the sherds. Then, he removes the covering of sherds and unloads the kiln.

The potter's perception of the end of the firing process as the red glow of the pottery has a technologically sound foundation. Shepard (1956: 86) points out that potters may use several criteria to judge the completion of firing: burning a pre-determined amount of fuel, the passage of a predetermined period of time or the appearance of the fire or the pottery. One way of evaluating the appearance of the pottery is by its color. Shepard suggests that there are two basic reference points for judging the completion of the process by color: temperature and degree of oxidation. Temperature can be judged roughly by color because the light emitted by a black body is proportional to the fourth power of its absolute temperature. Pottery is close enough to a theoretical black body for rough temperature estimates to be made by color (Shepard 1956: 86). Using color to evaluate the progress of the firing process also reflects the degree of oxidation of the pottery. Shepard says that using the color of the pottery to indicate the progression of the firing process is really a monitor of the degree of oxidation of the vessels. This criterion is also used by potters in Ticul, Yucatan (Mexico) where the red glow of the pottery inside the kiln indicates that the firing process is complete. It is clear from both the Ticul data and the Quinua data, however, that there are a variety of behaviors used to bring the firing process to completion and the potter must follow these before he evaluates the color of the pottery.

The time needed for firing varies. One potter said he needed one hour to fire when the kiln was hot and three hours when it was cold. Another said only two hours were necessary for firing (see also Spahni 1966: 76). From the potter's viewpoint of the process, however, the amount of firing time is really a secondary consideration. Firing time is dependent upon two factors which potters recognize as: (1) the warming of the sherds on top of the kiln which signals the transition from slow, gradual warming of the kiln to a more rapid firing process; and (2) the presence of red-hot pottery at the top of the kiln which signals the end of the process.

If some of the newly fired vessels are black, the potter sets them aside to be refired. Potters say that this problem is caused by too much fire in the kiln. This explanation, however, is erroneous. Blackening of pottery during firing is due to one or more causes. It may be due to a carbonaceous clay that has been incompletely fired. Some Quinua potters use a black clay which is highly carbonaceous.[17] If the firing atmosphere during the latter stage of firing does not contain a sufficient amount of oxygen, the carbonaceous material in the paste will not burn out sufficiently and the pottery will remain entirely or partially black. A second cause of blackening may be from incomplete firing. In the early stage of the firing process, the pottery is blackened by the smoke from the burning fuel. In the latter stage of the process, this

Figure 5.32 Loading the kiln prior to firing. Vessels are carefully stacked in the kiln with their mouths downward to take greatest advantage of the heat from the fire.

carbon is burned off, but a sufficient amount of oxygen is necessary to remove all of the carbon present on the surface of the pottery that was deposited in the early stage of the process. If the firing atmosphere during the latter stage of firing does not contain a sufficient amount of oxygen, the pottery will remain black. If fuel touches the pottery during firing or if the pottery is stacked too closely together, small pockets of inadequate oxygen may exist in the kiln and black smudges will occur on the vessels. Since the fuel is separated from the pottery in the Quinua kiln with the use of a firebox, fire clouding from fuel contact is not as much of a problem as the lack of care in stacking. Finally, an inadequate oxygen supply in parts of the kiln may blacken red-slipped vessels. Potters say that this result stems from using an inferior red slip (that is a paint which does not come from Culluchaca). Such fire clouds, however, are most likely related to the firing atmosphere. The lack of oxygen during the latter stage of the firing process creates a reducing atmosphere and may cause the red hematite in the slip to change to the black-colored mineral magnetite which has a metallic luster (Shepard 1956: 38–39). If the lack of oxygen is relatively localized during the latter portion of the firing process, a blackened pocket of pottery could be the result.

In brief, the potter's beliefs about the quality of his paints have an objective basis and are generally practical. He recognizes that higher quality paints adhere to the surface of the vessels. This characteristic corresponds to the presence of montmorillonite in the paints. Furthermore, his recognition of the raw material color is based upon the actual color of different minerals. While the potter has practical knowledge of the selection and use of his raw materials, his knowledge of the firing process does not have a scientific basis. Firing accidents, for example, which have their origin in the firing process itself are often erroneously attributed to the quality of raw materials.

Making pottery at the artisan center

Making pottery at the artisan center (p. 50) is essentially the same as the process used in the rural areas. The most obvious differences consist of technical innovations which require capital that is either not available to rural potters or if it is available, is not used to intensify the craft. With capital available to pay them on a regular basis, potters in the artisan center are freed from the adverse effects of innovations that may provide no monetary return. They thus have time available to experiment with new and innovative raw materials, techniques and vessel shapes.

One innovation at the artisan center consists of an elaborate clay filtering apparatus which uses a fine screen in combination with ceramic containers (*maqmas*) on each of three different levels (figure 5.33). Raw clay is first soaked for twenty-four hours in the highest vessel and drained through a small hole near its base into a screen over the next vessel. The clay slurry is then allowed to pass through the hole in the bottom of this vessel over a screen into a third vessel. In actual practice, however, the soaked clay is removed with a bucket from the top receptacle and placed manually in the middle vessel. Periodically, the flow of clay slurry from the middle vessel was interrupted in order to clear the screen and then resumed until the screen clogged again. The rocks, roots and other particles caught by the screen were discarded while the smaller particles caught by the screen were shaken through it. The filtered clay was then placed in the top vessel, soaked for another twenty-four hours and then filtered again. When the bottom vessel was full of filtered clay, it was emptied into a wheelbarrow dusted with temper (*aqu*) to prevent sticking and then taken to be mixed with the temper.

Because large amounts of temper are used and the transportation of the temper is paid by the center, it is brought to the center via truck. When available, temper

Figure 5.33 The series of vessels used for soaking and filtering clay at the artisan center. Clay is placed in the top vessel for soaking and then passed into the second and third vessels.

comes from a location near Muruncancha because it is the most accessible source for a truck. If a truck is not available, temper must be brought by burro from the Utkuchuku source because this source is not accessible by truck.

The potters at the artisan center also grind their temper and sift it through a fine screen. If it does not readily pass through the screen, it must be dried in the sun again until it can be sifted with ease. The screenings are either ground and sifted again or discarded.

The necessity of drying the temper after grinding, but before sifting indicates the presence of clay minerals in the raw temper. Damp clay particles tend to clump together, inhibit sifting and mask the presence of larger rocks in the temper which causes breakage during firing.

Filtering raw clay and sifting temper has two important effects on pottery. First, it creates a fine-grained paste. The texture of the paste produced at the artisan center is so fine that it can be rubbed between the fingers without feeling any grit or granular particles. Secondly, filtering and sifting raw materials effectively eliminates rocks in the paste which cause the pottery to crack and break during drying and firing. Many rock types expand[18] and contract at different rates from the surrounding clay matrix during firing, creating weaknesses in the vessel wall and causing vessels to crack and break. This problem was evident in Quinua because small rocks were noted along the broken surfaces of sherd wasters found around local kilns.

The sifted temper is strewn on the floor in one of the rooms of the center, and a wheelbarrow of damp clay is dumped onto the temper. The paste is then kneaded with the feet until the wet clay is mixed with the temper. The prepared paste is then stored before fabrication.

Clay and temper at the artisan center are mixed with no attention to measured quantities of clay and temper. This lack of attention to precise amounts of temper and clay is probably due to the fact that the clay in Quinua contains a variable amount of non-plastic materials. Although the potters claim that they use more sand than clay to prepare the paste, there was no evidence of measuring either sand or clay except the amount used to fill the receptacle during soaking and filtering the clay.

The salary of potters at the artisan center permits the potters there to assume the risks of innovations in another way. Innovations by rural Quinua potters who depend upon their craft for their livelihood require considerable risk. They may, for example, invest their time and effort in producing an item that may not bring monetary return. Taking this risk, however, may reap rewards. In 1967, one potter produced a *candelabra* (figure 5.34) which had no local use, but it combined some traditional shapes (the ceramic church and the *chunchu*) into an innovative combination. The potter fabricated these as an experiment in spite of the fact that the buyer of his pottery said that he would not buy them. The potter thus took a great risk in going ahead and making them anyway. When the vessels were painted and fired, however, the middleman changed his mind and did buy them. This potter, as well as others, then produced more of these shapes and successfully sold them all.

The risks taken by this potter, however, were not as great as those of a rural potter.

Figure 5.34 An innovative *candelabra* first made by a potter in 1967. This shape consists of a bulbous base upon which a miniature church as well as modeled *chunchus* (see figure 5.26) were placed. It continued to be made in the 1980s and was seen in 1989 in the museum shop at the Milwaukee Public Museum. The match box is inserted for scale and is 3.4 cm wide.

The potter who produced the innovative candelabra worked in the artisan center and was paid by the Peruvian government, but he made the candelabra at home during vacation periods to supplement his income. Even though his risk was rewarded, he could afford to take the risk because he was not economically dependent upon selling the innovation.

The potters at the grammar school (the *nucleo*) also used a number of innovations unique among Quinua potters. First, they used an elaborate scheme of mixing and testing clays for plasticity and the effect of firing. One potter said that he taught students how to select the proper clay for making pottery churches. He recognized that the clay/sand ratios had to be varied depending on the amount of non-plastics naturally present in the clay. Five kilograms of ordinary plastic clay, for example, requires six kilograms of sand while a sandy clay (like that from Larampampa) is mixed with temper in a ratio of 3 to 2. To test clays, he said, one must mix the clay to be tested with white clay and sand and with sandy clay. Then, the test clay must be rolled, molded into a long flat briquette and then doubled over. If it broke, then the clay was suitable for making churches. If not, it was not good for churches. This potter also tested the firing properties of the clay and if the test piece cracked and broke during firing, the clay was considered to be inferior for making pottery. If the test piece did not break, the clay was acceptable.

A second innovation used by the grammar school potters was the use of molds. In 1967, these potters began to use molds made from local clays that were formed around figures of ceramic dogs, swans and horses that had been purchased commercially.

The innovation of using molds is probably one of the most important innovations in Quinua. In 1967, only two potters used molds, but by 1978, other potters had begun to use them and they appeared to be one of the factors responsible for the great growth of the craft since 1967. Not all of the shapes in Quinua lend themselves to fabrication by molds, however. While some figures of animals (like those mentioned above) may be easily produced using a mold, other pottery, like churches and the utilitarian vessels, is more difficult, if not impossible to make in a mold.

The relationship of molds and the growth of the craft in Quinua between 1967 and 1978 is not coincidental. Knowledge of two-piece molds can be learned more quickly than most traditional pottery-making technologies because they do not require the skill in motor habit patterns that are necessary with most traditional techniques (see Arnold 1985: 202–224).

Implications for archaeology

Since the information encoded in ancient ceramics consists of technological information about the ceramics themselves, understanding the potters' choices of raw material selection, vessel fabrication and firing can enhance and refine the interpretations of ancient ceramics. There are two kinds of applications of the technological data from Quinua to archaeological ceramics: (1) the ancient ceramics of the Ayacucho Basin (particularly Huari and the surrounding area); and (2) the study of ancient ceramics in general. The application of these data to the ancient ceramics of the Basin will be discussed at the end of this book (chapter 9) along with the implications of the ecological approach in general to ancient ceramic production. This discussion will now turn to applying these data to the study of ceramics in general.

Paste uniformity is not just based on the potters' degree of specialization, but is also dependent on the geological variability of an area. In a diverse geological setting like Quinua where clay and temper sources are diverse and spread out over a horizontal distance of approximately 6 square kilometers and over a vertical distance of more than 500 meters, potters probably will not select raw materials that are mineralogically uniform nor consistent from a qualitative or quantitative viewpoint. Ancient pottery from this area would not be expected to have chemical nor mineralogical uniformity, but rather would be expected to have great variability.

In a different geological setting with a singular source of clay and temper, the sources may be discrete and the raw materials each may contain different minerals. The potters' selection criteria may not only result in discrete groups of minerals in each raw material category, but the potters' practical knowledge may correspond to the actual physical properties of those minerals. Potters in Ticul, Yucatan, for example, use highly discrete raw material sources which are 10 kilometers apart. The raw materials in these sources have limited mineralogical variability and consist largely of different minerals. Ticul potters can separate their raw materials into mineralogical groups by the unique physical properties of the materials (Arnold 1971a). As a result, both the source from which the raw materials come and the potters' selection criteria enable them to predict clay quality by using simple methods.

The Quinua data on paste preparation behavior also suggest that the use of scientific categories to describe ceramic pastes may not necessarily reflect the potter's categories of raw materials. Archaeologists like to utilize scientific categories like non-plastics, plastics and the presence or absence of minerals like calcite, quartz, volcanic glass or mica. The potter, of course, does not think in these terms, but rather is concerned with obvious physical properties of his raw materials like plasticity, the presence of "gold-like" particles, whether the clay feels too sticky or tastes salty (Arnold 1971a). His distinction between different materials is not based on the scientific categories of the ceramic technologist, the chemist or mineralogist, but rather on obvious physical properties learned from experience which he uses to separate one kind of material like clay from another kind of material like temper. Such properties also serve to separate suitable clay for making pottery from inferior clay. The point here is not just the obvious one that potters see their raw materials differently from mineralogists, ceramic technologists, and archaeologists, but that the selection of pottery materials is influenced profoundly by a cognitive structure that largely disregards mineralogical categories except where the amount or quality is significant enough to affect the physical properties which the potter can detect. It thus does not matter to the potter whether both clay and temper contain clay materials, or whether these materials have a few minerals or many minerals. Rather, the Quinua potter separates clay for cooking pottery from non-cooking pottery by practical criteria. He recognizes only the presence of large quantities of mica and the relative amount of non-plastics in these materials. Since the relative amount of non-plastics in the clay and temper is obscured when the two materials are mixed together, the presence or absence of large amounts of mica is probably the only culturally significant mineral of Quinua pastes recognizable by archaeologists.

Not all potters have a sophisticated knowledge of their raw materials.[19] Potters obviously have a technologically adequate knowledge so that they can select suitable clays, tempers and paints to make pottery. But, while their knowledge is practical and useful, it does not always have a scientific foundation. While potters' categories of raw materials may correspond to scientific categories at times (as in Ticul, see Arnold 1971a), their knowledge is not based on a scientific paradigm and thus is not generalizable outside of their own community and its geological setting. It is predictive enough to select appropriate raw materials in their local area, but their knowledge does not explain why one raw material is better than another beyond the practical criterion that a particular raw material produces pots that will not crack or break.

Potters' behavior of selecting raw materials may be consistent with their own knowledge of the materials, but the archaeologist should not expect that this behavior will have consistent nor precise qualitative or quantitative mineralogical correlates in the paste. Paste analysis will thus reveal more information on the geological and geographic location of the pottery-making communities than cultural or behavioral information relevant for cultural or social reconstruction.

The Quinua data can also help in evaluating assumptions and terminology used in analyzing and describing ancient pottery. Standard archaeological practice defines "temper" as "non-plastics added by the potter" or sometimes as "all non-plastics in the paste" (see Shepard 1956: 25). This terminology is not accurate, does not adequately reflect the potters' tempering behavior, and may obscure the behavioral significance of certain inclusions in the paste (such as mica). Plastic minerals and non-plastic minerals occur in both clays and tempers. The difference between the clays and tempers is not so much the absolute difference between plastic minerals in clays and non-plastic minerals in tempers, but rather the relative amount of plastics or non-plastics present in each of these materials. The data presented here and those from Ticul, Yucatan (Arnold 1971a) indicate that the notions of "temper" in pottery may be confusing or ambiguous. The notion of temper as "non-plastics" should be dropped by archaeologists in their description of ancient pottery and more descriptive terms used. Descriptions should refer to the non-plastics like mica naturally present in clays as "mica inclusions" or "micaceous paste" and avoid the behavioral ambiguities of the term "mica temper" (see Arnold 1975c).

Probably the most important implication of this chapter for archaeology is an approach pioneered by F. R. Matson: an ecological approach to ceramic production in antiquity must involve a study of local clays and, if possible, the modern ceramic production of an area. Such a study can provide important interpretive tools for the analysis of the ancient ceramics of an area. The downside of this approach to ceramics, however, is that except for understanding the processes of selection of raw materials and the processes of manufacture, the application of these data outside of the area under consideration is limited.

Conclusion

The description of Quinua ceramic technology from the point of view of potters' choices provides an insight for understanding the details of the pottery production and how that production may relate to the ancient ceramics in the Ayacucho Valley. Although this approach is the more traditional approach of ceramic ecology (Matson 1965a), a broader ecological approach to ceramics has profound implications for the study of ceramics which, as we have already seen, involves the relationship of the ceramics to environment, culture and society.[20] In addition, however, an ecological approach to ceramic production must also involve an exploration of the relationship of the *products* of ceramic production to the environment and culture and that is the subject of the next chapter.

6

Ceramic products and society

Besides the adaptation of the community of potters to the physical environment (chapter 4) and its methods of producing ceramics (chapter 5), an ecological approach to ceramic production involves the adaptive role of the ceramic products of the population. In order to sustain themselves using ceramic production, potters must create a ceramic product which relates in some way to the society and which members of that society will desire. An ecological approach to ceramic production thus involves describing the relationship of the ceramics themselves (rather than just the population of potters) to human social and cultural activities, on the one hand, and the environment, on the other.

Unlike subsistence agriculturalists, potters cannot eat the fruits of their labor and must convert their ceramic products into food. In order to eat, potters must thus create an item that consumers will want. So, they must adapt their ceramic products to the values and cultural patterns of the society, and then find a way in which these products can be placed into the hands of consumers who will exchange food for them.

Channels of matter, energy and information flow

One of the ways in which ceramics enables populations to adapt to their environment is by using ceramic vessels as channels of matter and energy. Human biological processes require matter such as water and essential nutrients such as proteins, vitamins and minerals. Energy in the form of calories is also required to do work (Moran 1982: 5, 12). From an ecological perspective, then, one kind of adaptation involves creating ceramic vessels through which matter and energy flow from the environment to human beings. Besides the transfer of matter and energy, however, pottery may also serve as channels of information flow between members of the society, a process which involves the communication of ideological and social knowledge using ceramics as nonverbal symbols (see Moran 1982: 332).

The shape repertoire of Quinua ceramic vessels is related to their role as channels for the flow of matter and energy (see also chapter 5). First, some vessels serve as channels for the movement of water from the environment to individuals and these vessels are part of the community's adaptation to a specific set of topographic and cultural circumstances. The repertoire of four water-carrying vessels (the *aysaku* shapes), for example, is related to the settlement pattern and the distance to water sources. Rural households are spread out over a large area and access to adequate water for domestic consumption is a significant adaptive problem. During the rainy season (which lasts about three to four months), rural settlements collect rainwater in cisterns (Mitchell 1976a: 32) and/or by placing discarded pottery under the eaves. Households may also divert irrigation water into cisterns and use this water for household use. During much of the year, however, rural inhabitants must walk to a stream or an irrigation ditch to obtain water, but these sources can provide water for only three to six months a year (see Mitchell 1976a). The most reliable sources of water, however, lie at the bottom of steep-walled gorges (the Huamangura and Hatun Wayqu ravines) that are distant from most households. Descending into these gorges and ascending again involves walking along narrow paths where a misstep could cause a vessel to fall and break. The topography thus creates a great risk of breaking ceramic vessels and vessels apparently do break often enough to provide a continued demand for water-carrying vessels. Quinua potters respond to this demand by producing four shapes (the *aysaku* shapes) which can be used for transporting water. The different sizes and shapes of these vessels create a multipurpose repertoire which broadens the channel of nutrient flow (in this case, water) from the environment to human consumers.

In recent years, people have also obtained water from the municipal water supply in the village of Quinua, but the same kinds of risks are present. Few of the inhabitants in the district live in the village and those who live in the rural settlements must still walk to the village to obtain their water and risk breaking their vessels in transit.

Ceramic vessels can also be a more circuitous channel for nutrient flow. Quinua peasants require water while they are working in their fields. Since fields may be located some distance from both households and water sources, water for human consumption must first be transported from the sources to households and then to the fields. Multiple shapes for carrying liquids facilitate this transfer and again broaden the channel of water flow from the environment to human consumers.

A second way in which Quinua vessels are related to the flow of matter and energy consists of enhancing nutrient flow by removing toxins that produce an adverse physiological response for humans.[1] Ceramic vessels serve to detoxify and make palatable a number of Andean crops that contain natural toxins which adversely affect human populations (table 6.1; see also Arnold 1985: 128–135). Cooking is the most obvious process that detoxifies these toxins, but soaking can also be used in some cases. Cooking vessels (*manka*) thus serve as channels that enhance nutrient flow by modifying (in this case, detoxifying) plant products for human physiological processes by sustained heating and cooking.

A third way that pottery is related to the flow of matter and energy involves using ceramic shapes as a channel for maize beer (*chicha*). Beer is a crucial component for recruiting labor. Labor is a scarce resource in Quinua and rich and poor alike need to obtain preferential rights to it. Plowing and weeding, for example, need to be accomplished within a relatively short time. When workers are needed for such agricultural tasks, the sponsor who requests help will almost always provide maize beer as well as cash, cigarettes, and *coca* leaves as an incentive to recruit labor (Mitchell 1991b). In the reciprocal work group (*ayni*), the festive work group (the *minka*), and the corvée labor group (the *faena*), beer is an essential part of the

Table 6.1. *Toxins in plants grown in Quinua destroyed by the use of ceramics*

Toxic constituent Plant	Effect of toxicity	Treatment necessary to significantly reduce or eliminate toxicity	Source
Protease inhibitor			
Maize (*Zea mays*)	Inhibits activities of enzymes that break down proteins	Heat	Liener and Kakade 1969
Barley (*Hordeum vulgare*)		Heat	Liener and Kakade 1969
Oats (*Avena sativum*)		Heat	Liener and Kakade 1969
Potato (*Solanum tuberosum*)		Cooking	Browman 1981a: 112
Broad bean (*Vicia faba*)		Heat	Liener and Kakade 1980: 34–37
Hemagglutinins			
Broad bean	Agglutinates red blood cells	Heating, but heating of soaked beans most effective	Jaffé 1969, 1980
Garden pea (*Pisum sativum*)		As for broad bean	Jaffé 1969, 1980
Red, kidney, or black bean (*Phaseolus multifloris*)		As for broad bean	Jaffé 1969, 1980
Cyanogenic glucoside			
Maize	Cyanide has a strong affinity for cytochrome oxidase which inhibits cellular respiration. Death results from cytotoxic anemia with the brain being most susceptible organ (Montgomery 1969: 14)	Hydrolysis occurs when plant is chopped, soaked in water, and thoroughly cooked (Hydrocyanic acid volatizes on boiling with lid removed). Cooking water should be discarded	Montgomery 1969: 14; 1980
Garden pea		As for maize	Montgomery 1969: 14; 1980
Beans (especially lima beans)		As for maize	Montgomery 1969: 14; 1980
Common bean (*Phaseolus vulgaris*)		Soaking and cooking	Browman 1981a: 106

Hydrocyanic acid Quinoa (*Chenopodium quinoa*)	Same as for cyanogenic glucoside	Chopping, soaking, and cooking	Browman 1981a: 106–13
Anti-vitamin E Kidney bean	Interferes with effectiveness of vitamin E causing liver necrosis and muscular dystrophy in animals	Heating for 60 minutes	Liener 1980b: 443
Metal binding constituents Peas	Binds with zinc, manganese, copper, and perhaps iron thus increasing the physiological requirements of these metals	Heating	Liener 1969
Nitrate accumulator Quinoa	Irritates mucus membranes of gastro-intestinal tract. If absorbed into the blood can cause destruction of red blood cells	Grinding and repeated washing	Browman 1981a: 106–13
Micro toxins Common bean	Interferes with calcium metabolism	Cooking	Browman 1981a: 106

informal contract for obtaining labor and will be supplied to workers by the sponsor. *Fiesta* sponsorship also requires the provision of maize beer and creates a reciprocal obligation for the attendees to work for the sponsor at a future time.

Maize beer is also part of the contract for labor in other kinds of reciprocal obligations. Economic transactions between inhabitants of different ecological zones generally occur between people who know one another and are maintained by a series of reciprocal relationships that are established and perpetuated by gifts of maize beer (among other things).

The transport and drinking of maize beer is thus an important part of economic transactions and those that involve the recruitment of labor. This value is expressed in the use of a variety of ceramic vessels for the production (*maqma*, *urpu*), storage (the *aysaku* shapes, *tinaqa*), transport (the *aysaku* shapes) and drinking (cups, double pots, animal effigy pots) of maize beer.

A fourth way that pottery is related to the flow of matter and energy is through the shape of the channel. Many Quinua vessels are associated with food preferences that involve maize consumption. In contrast to a wide variety of other cultigens available (such as tubers), maize is highly valued because it can be stored for longer periods of time than tubers (Murra 1973). It is probably the most important source of dietary protein in Quinua[2] and is prepared in several ways. Fresh unshelled maize (*choclo*) or kernels of shelled maize (*mote*) can be boiled. Maize kernels can be toasted (*camcha*) and certain types can be popped. Finally, maize can be prepared as a drink called *chicha*. There are two kinds of maize *chicha*, a fermented kind made of germinated corn and a non-fermented kind made of dark red or purple maize.[3] Maize *chicha* is important for religious rituals and these rituals reinforce the high value placed on maize (Murra 1973).

These maize products require preparation techniques which are associated with particular ceramic vessels. Cooking pots (*manka*) are used for the preparation of boiled maize like *choclo* and *mote*. Several variations of ceramic toasters (*tuqtu*) are used for toasting and popping maize, while brewing maize beer requires two large ceramic vessels (*maqma* and *urpu*). Maize beer is stored and transported in tall, narrow-mouthed jars (*tumin*) to avoid spilling (figure 5.8). Both wide and narrow-mouthed pitchers (*puynu*, *tachu*, and *yukupuynu*) can be used for transporting and serving *chicha* (figures 5.11–5.13). Finally, there are a number of ceremonial vessels produced specifically for the ritual distribution and drinking of maize beer (such as double pots, parrot pots, bulls and other animal effigy pots). More shapes are thus used for preparing, serving and carrying maize products than for any other single crop and more vessels are used for preparing, carrying and serving maize beer than any other commodity.

An additional way in which the flow of matter and energy is affected by the shape of the ceramic channel is the relationship between mouth diameter and liquid transport. In order to maximize the flow of liquid in the ceramic channel during transport, vessels have to be constructed to minimize spillage. Liquid-carrying vessels in Quinua (that is, the *aysaku* shapes) thus have mouth diameters much smaller than their greatest diameter.

Ceramics are not simply channels of matter (water, vitamins, minerals) and energy (calories), but they are channels accompanied by human agents. While ceramics provide a channel for nutrient flow, part of the movement of these nutrients from the ecosystem *to* humans involves their transport *by* humans from the environmental source of the nutrients to the consuming location. The channel of nutrient flow thus not only involves the vessel as a container for the modification and transport of its contents, but also involves the congruency of this channel with human patterns of transport. These patterns involve particular motor habits and carrying positions as well as the placement of pottery during use.

Motor habit patterns are unconscious, but customary muscular patterns which result from the habitual use of certain muscles that become strengthened relative to other muscles. Any body posture or activity pattern that requires muscles other than the habitually strengthened ones is difficult to execute and if performed, is difficult to maintain. Such patterns may also be sex-linked due to a variety of factors (see Jenni and Jenni 1976) such as differences in role behavior between men and women (men may never carry water pots) and sexual dimorphisms like differences in hip width and shelf (for example women carry water jars on the hip more easily than men).

Particular motor habits are not universal, but vary with culture. Of the almost unlimited variation of muscular movement, relatively few motions are restricted by anatomical considerations. Few muscles are customarily used, however, and these are systematically applied to a variety of situations.[4] These patterns are learned by members of a culture, tend to be rigid and are altered only with difficulty (Spier 1967: 97–98). They are thus culturally linked, are characteristic of a given culture, and can vary from culture to culture.

The use of pottery by humans requires vessel shapes that are congruent with the patterns of muscular use in a population. If these patterns are not present or developed in the society, the ceramic shape cannot be used properly, efficiently or with ease. Persons who have not developed motor habit patterns required by a particular ceramic shape will find it difficult or impossible to use that shape.

The potential of pottery as a channel for the flow of matter and energy is thus greatly affected by its congruency with particular motor habit patterns of a culture. Because ceramics have the potential to be molded into a wide variety of forms, the shape of a given vessel has the potential to reflect the motor habit patterns of the society (see Arnold 1985: 147–151). Motor habits, carrying positions and placement patterns are not universal, but vary according to the culture involved and profoundly affect the shape of a ceramic vessel.

In Quinua, three of the four shapes for transporting liquids (the *aysaku* shapes) are carried using one hand grasping the handle of the vessel. This pattern is consistent with carrying liquids (usually water or *chicha*) short distances. The fourth shape, the *tumin*, has a more specialized pattern because it is larger than either of the other *aysaku* shapes and has a long narrow neck. Both of these features make it ideally suited to transport liquid over long distances with limited spillage. In fact, the *tumin* will carry much more liquid (probably three or more times as much) than any of the other *aysaku* shapes.

In order to transport this increased amount of liquid, the *tumin* requires a set of muscular patterns that are different from those necessary for the other *aysaku* shapes. These patterns involve carrying the vessel on the back and are dependent upon the existence of the vertical strap handles on this vessel. Carrying involves passing a rope through one of the strap handles, around the vessel and then through the other handle. The remainder of the rope is wrapped around the chest and upper arms of the carrier and tightened as the vessel is lifted toward the back. This position requires the use of the muscles of the upper arms (the biceps and triceps), shoulders (the deltoids), chest (the pectorals, rhomboids and erector spinae) and the back to support the weight of this vessel. These same muscles are used to carry other kinds of heavy loads elsewhere in highland Peru and Ecuador (figure 6.1).

These carrying patterns contrast with those used for carrying water jars in other areas of Latin America. In northern Yucatan (Mexico), water jars are carried on the hip (figure 6.2) and their construction with a flat bottom and horizontal strap handle reflects this pattern. In Guatemala, water jars are carried on the hip, back or head.[5] Vessels carried on the back in northwestern Guatemala use a tumpline and most of the weight occurs on a strap placed on the head (figure 6.3). This pattern utilizes the frontalis muscle with stress also placed on the trapezius, levator scapulae, sterno-cleidomastoid and anterior flexor neck muscles and is used to carry a variety of other objects in Mexico and Guatemala. To relieve some of the pressure on the head and neck muscles, the rope of the tumpline may be partially supported by lifting the rope with the hands. In sum, the muscles used for carrying the *tumin* are totally different from those used for carrying a water pot in northern Yucatan and other areas of Mesoamerica. The muscles used for carrying in a society thus affect the shape of the ceramic channel for the flow of water from the physical environment to humans.

The shape of the cooking pot (figure 5.8) is also related to its role as a channel of matter and energy. Cooking pots have slightly constricted necks which prevent their contents from boiling over. Cooking pots must avoid the problems of thermal shock if they are to prove useful for cooking. Besides the advantage of micaceous clays (chapter 5), cooking vessels are best adapted to withstand thermal shock if they are formed in a spherical shape with a rounded bottom and no sharp changes in direction. This shape minimizes the different thermal gradients from one part of the vessel to the other when the vessel is heated (Rye 1976: 114, 207).

The placement of the handles on this vessel is related to its use on the fire as a channel accompanied by human agents. The handles on the cooking pot consist of short vertical strap handles which are attached from the rim to the extreme upper portion of the upper body of the vessel. This position helps prevent burning one's hands when it is lifted on and off the fire. There are few other handle configurations on cooking vessels which could minimize accidental burning, and one of them occurs on cooking pots made in the Aco area near Huancayo[6] to the north of Ayacucho.

The handle configuration on cooking pottery contrasts with that of other pottery.

Figure 6.1 A boy carrying a load of sticks, using muscles of the upper arms, shoulders and chest, along a road near Quinua. Such carrying patterns are also used to carry large pots (such as the *tumin*) and occur throughout highland Peru and Ecuador in contrast to those used in Mesoamerica (see figures 6.2 and 6.3).

Vertical strap handles occur on several other vessels such as the *tumin,* the *tinaqa* and the chamber pot *(vasinika).* On these latter vessels, the handles are placed lower than the rim and usually occur nearer the point of greatest circumference of the vessels. This placement facilitates carrying of the contents rather than just lifting vessels on and off the fire as is required by cooking pots.

In addition to serving as a channel of nutrient flow, ceramics also serve as channels for mythological and ritual information which flows between members of a community. First, ceramics are channels for the flow of ideological content. In some cases, they are expressions of folk catholicism like the ceramic church (see figure 5.22), the crucifix or a simple empty cross. In other cases, they are channels for the flow of indigenous non-Christian mythology. One such mythological expression is the ceramic *ukumari* (figure 5.24) an exceptionally strong creature which is a half-man (or woman) and half-bear who captures women (or men, if the creature is a woman) and keeps them in a cave for the purpose of having sexual

Figure 6.2 One of the carrying patterns used to carry water jars in Yucatan before piped water eliminated the demand for these vessels. The vessel may also be carried with the base resting on the hip and the arm around the neck of the pot.

relations with them. The *amaru* is another indigenous, mythological being which lives in the ground and causes landslides when it moves. The *amaru* is a very powerful spirit which is manifested in living form as a bull, duck or serpent and expressed in ceramic form as a bull or a duck.

Still another example of ceramics serving as a channel for the flow of ideological information is the ceramic representation of jungle Indians called the *chunchu*. *Chunchus* are a ritual symbol of the jungle Indian (such as the Campa) who live east of the Andes (figure 5.23). For certain religious observances in Quinua[7] and in neighboring communities like Huamanguilla,[8] inhabitants dress like Indians from

Figure 6.3 A woman carrying a water vessel near the hamlet of Coya, in the *municipio* of San Miguel Acatán in northwestern Guatemala. The muscles used in this pattern consist primarily of those of the neck and head. This pattern of muscle use, which is widespread in Mesoamerica, contrasts with that used for carrying in the Andes (compare with figure 6.1).

the tropical forest (east of the Andes) wearing authentic long brown *ponchos*, feather headdresses and accessories such as monkey skins, bows, arrows and shell necklaces (see Mitchell 1991a: 138). During the celebrations of the Day of the Holy Cross (*Santa Cruz*) at Luricocha (see figure 6.4), for example, groups of *chunchus* accompany residents who carry crosses to the local church for blessing by the priest. The *chunchus* play panpipes as they walk, but do not enter the church because they are ritually "savage" (*sic*) and thus non-catholic. Rather, they remain outside the church until their companions emerge with the cross.

While the precise symbolism of the jungle in Quinua (or in the rest of the Ayacucho Valley for that matter) is not clear, the *chunchu* may be a symbolic manifestation of the ecological relationship of the community with the tropical forest east of the Andes.[9] Quinuenos obtain *coca*, peanuts, chili peppers and fruits from the tropical forest and travel there to obtain palms for Palm Sunday festivities (Mitchell 1991a: 152). Some Quinuenos have land in the tropical forest (Mitchell 1991a: 223) because of the inadequate agricultural land locally. The District of Quinua, however, is not adjacent to the jungle, so the utilization of *chunchus* may reflect (and perhaps symbolize) the use of the archipelago model of ecological complementarity in which Andean communities try to achieve community self-sufficiency by utilizing ecological zones that are physically removed from their community (Murra 1972). In Luricocha (figure 6.4), for example, the heavy use of *chunchus* may also be a manifestation of the relationship of that community with the tropical forest. In contrast to Quinua, Luricocha lies in the lower montane thorn steppe (see figure 2.8), a zone which is lower and drier than the lower montane savannah around Quinua. The land is rather poor for agriculture and many agricultural products probably come from elsewhere in order to feed the community. It is thus possible that the massive use of *chunchus* in Luricocha during the Feast of the Crosses may not only indicate a relationship with the tropical forest, but its great economic dependence upon it to supply food (probably maize) to the community. It thus appears that the ceramic *ukumari* and *chunchus* in Quinua are tangible mythological manifestations of the close ties between Quinua and the tropical forest even though their precise meaning may be more general, varied and complex than simply a manifestation of the archipelago model of ecological complementarity.

A second way that ceramics serve as a channel for information flow consists of their use for ritual purposes. One such use is the placement of ceramic objects on the tops of houses. When a new house is built or when a new roof is replaced on an existing house, a ceramic vessel supplied by the godparent of the ceremony is placed on the roof of the house as a kind of "topping off" ceremony.[10] Churches and bulls are the most widely used ceramic shapes for this purpose (figure 6.5), but other vessels used in this way include sheep (figure 6.6), llamas, ducks and flower pots while other ceramic forms (like the *chunchu*, *ukumari* and the double pot) may have also been used in this way in the past. Other objects besides ceramics (such as elaborate iron crosses, plastic flowers and a plastic dish) also occur on the tops of houses either alone or in combination with ceramic flower pots, animals (for example ducks or bulls) or churches. When asked, people in Quinua said that they did not know why they placed ceramic items on the roofs of houses, but that it was their custom to do so. One person believed that such placement indicated that the inhabitants were catholic – a rather surprising statement since in 1967, there were no other religious alternatives except a small pentecostal church down the slope in Muruncancha.[11] Nevertheless, specific symbols of catholicism were important in Quinua. The native religious hierarchy (the *varayuq*) would punish people who did not have a flower cross in their house. Many of the items used on the tops of houses, however, are non-religious symbols (like *tinaqas* and flower pots with plastic flowers) and were said to have no meaning. Litto (1976), however, suggests that the churches on the roofs of houses are a substitute for the crosses on the housetops that occur elsewhere in central and southern Peru and serve as "good luck" symbols to dispel evil.

Another way in which ceramic vessels serve as a channel for the flow of information is their ritual use for drinking ceremonies. By drinking out of a double pot (figure 5.25), for example, a person ritually consumes the content of two cups of a liquid (like *chicha*) and this act expresses and cements ritual godparent (*compadrazgo*) bonds. Drinking is a social ritual with a specific set of rules in which people drink in a sequential series of dyadic acts that moves from person to person

Figure 6.4 Andean peasants dressed as jungle indians (*chunchus*) during the Feast of the Crosses in Luricocha (northwest of Quinua, see figure 3.4). For a ceramic version of this ritual person, see figure 5.23.

around a table or room (Mitchell 1991a). Those who refuse to drink in this way insult others in the group because one has refused the offer of the reciprocal ties of comradeship and warmth (Mitchell 1991b). This pattern, however, is also a form of balanced reciprocity that "binds people into a reciprocal web that permits them to make continuous demands on one another" (Mitchell 1991b: 204).

Because of the importance of this ritual drinking behavior, there are a set of ceramic vessels which are largely used for this purpose. Ceramic bulls are used at fiestas for dispensing maize beer (*chicha*) which is poured through the bull's mouth into individual cups. One informant said that the bull symbolized the "spirit" of the alcohol, but it may also symbolize the *amaru* spirit which causes earthquakes and landslides. Parrot pots are used to serve maize beer (*chicha*) during the ritual activities surrounding the cleaning of the irrigation ditches.[12] Given the importance of drinking maize beer in the recruitment of scarce labor in Quinua, it is not surprising that there are a series of vessels which are largely, if not exclusively, used for drinking ceremonies.

Another ritual use of ceramics is associated with the fiesta of the Virgin of Cocharcas, the patron saint of Quinua. For this celebration, the people of the

Figure 6.5 A ceramic church on the roof of a house in Quinua. Ceramic churches, bulls, sheep, llamas, ducks and flower pots are often placed on the tops of new houses or new roofs of old houses as a kind of "topping off" ceremony.

village hire three orchestras from Ayacucho. After the fiesta is over, the *mayordomo* of the fiesta gives each member of the orchestra an object of pottery in addition to his pay.[13]

Utilitarian pottery may also serve as a channel of ritual information. Although this pottery ordinarily has no ritual use, some of these shapes are occasionally used in ritual contexts. Bowls (*platos*), for example, may be used for service ware during fiestas. During the fiesta for the Virgin of Cocharcas or for the Virgin of Carmen, a fiesta host may make a contract with a potter to make bowls to use as eating vessels for the invited guests. Similarly, small versions of the *puynu* shape may also serve as service vessels for drinking *chicha* at fiestas.[14]

Pottery produced for the artisan market also serves as a channel of information. The content of this information may be no more than a symbol of folk art and life in Peru. But, this folk pottery still conveys an image of a simpler, pristine life in a faraway land untainted by the modern world. Such a symbol creates a demand for Quinua pottery which parallels the demand for twentieth-century redware which is

Figure 6.6 A ceramic version of a sheep made in the black-and-red-on-white painting scheme. Like other animal shapes, it is formed with an opening on the back and may be used for ritual drinking and dispensing of maize beer (*chicha*) at fiestas, or placed on the new and rebuilt roofs of houses.

driven by the nostalgia for the alleged simpler, less complicated "country life" of the American past (Isaacs 1991). This interpretation of the symbolic role of Quinua pottery in the world outside Peru is underscored by the increased proliferation of Quinua pottery into the upscale ethnic and folk art market during the last twenty-five years. In the 1960s and 1970s, Quinua pottery was exported to Japan,[15] Europe, and the USA as an ethnic curio. In late 1965, it was sold in one of Chicago's largest department stores and Spahni (1966) reported that it was sold in Geneva, Switzerland. In the early 1970s, it was sold in the museum shop of the Brooklyn Museum in New York City[16] and in a small boutique selling Peruvian handicrafts in a shopping center on Chicago's "magnificent mile." In the late 1970s, Quinua churches were being offered for sale from a mail order catalogue[17] and used as decoration in a sale catalogue of furniture and linens from a Chicago department store.[18] In the early 1980s, a few pieces of Quinua pottery were offered for sale in a small import boutique in one of Chicago's western suburbs (Naperville) and in Toronto, Canada.[19] In late 1986, Quinua pottery occurred in a shop in the San Diego Zoo and in an ethnic arts boutique (Bazaar del Mundo) in San Diego's "Old Town." More recently, it was offered for sale in the museum shop in the Milwaukee Public Museum, and in Latin American craft boutiques in Dallas, New Orleans, St. Louis,[20] and Bath in England. Although perhaps not a symbol of Peru in all of these cases, Quinua vessels nevertheless serve as a symbol of ethnic folk art and during the last twenty-five years have found their way into the upscale boutique markets throughout much of North America as well as parts of Europe.

Distributing Quinua pottery

The distribution of pottery is crucial for potters because it is the only way that they can turn their ceramic product into food. Potters must have access to a consuming population in order to sustain ceramic production as a supplement or alternative to subsistence agriculture. Distribution of pottery is thus an essential feedback mechanism that can have either a deviation amplifying or regulatory effect on pottery production. In Quinua, a combination of markets, intermediaries and access to transportation networks stimulates and maintains ceramic production by providing a variety of alternatives for potters' output.

The most significant stimulating factor in the distribution of Quinua pottery is its position near a large city and its connection with the road network to and from this city. In 1967, Quinua was only 31 kilometers from the department capital of Ayacucho along a road which connected it with the jungle. This location in a major transportation link within the Department of Ayacucho facilitates access to and from the capital via buses and trucks. In 1974, this road was shortened and paved and made the city of Ayacucho and the remainder of the Republic even more accessible to Quinua potters. This access was relatively unique in the region because as recently as 1988, the paved road between Quinua and Ayacucho was more than half the distance of all the paved roads in the entire Department of Ayacucho (Bonner 1988: 34).

Quinua potters distribute their pottery to two major kinds of consumers: (1) the inhabitants of the Ayacucho Valley who buy pottery for utilitarian and ritual purposes; and (2) populations outside the valley who buy it for an ethnic, artisan or tourist curio. Pottery destined for populations outside the valley is marketed through both local and non-local patterns of distribution.

In order to distribute their pottery to the inhabitants of the Ayacucho Valley, potters utilize the formal markets and itinerant sale in the *puna* (the montane, sub-alpine and alpine zones) above the community. Participants in each of these forms of distribution vary by gender with women selling pottery in the formal markets of the Valley while men exchange it for food on an itinerant basis in the *puna*.

Only a restricted repertoire of shapes is sold in the markets of the valley. These shapes have definite utilitarian purposes and consist exclusively of decorated vessels (the *yukupuynu*, *tachu*, *plato*, *puynu* and *tinaqa*). Undecorated vessels used for carrying or storing liquids, cooking or for making beer (like *tumins*, *mankas*, and *chicha* jars) were not sold in the markets in Ayacucho, Huanta, or Huamanguilla.

Buyers in local markets often critically evaluate pottery before purchase. They first examine the exterior of the vessel sometimes scraping off pieces of fired clay that have adhered to the surface of the vessel and check for hidden holes. Then, they tap the pot with their knuckle in order to discern whether it produces a resonant sound. If satisfied, buyers may tap it around its maximum circumference to insure its integrity. If the vessel has a restricted orifice and the inside of it cannot be seen, buyers may turn it upside down to dump out any remaining ashes and look into the interior of the vessel to check for holes. If the buyers are satisfied that the vessel is undamaged, they may bargain with the seller and purchase it.

Weekly markets in Quinua, Huamanguilla and Huanta are the main markets in the valley in which Quinua pottery appears. The Quinua Sunday market is smaller than those in Huanta and Huamanguilla and has a variety of goods for sale – local produce, fodder for animals and salt. Food is the most abundant item which is sold and exchanged, but some pottery almost always appears in the market, even in the rainy season when little, if any, pottery is made. Most often, vendors will also sell something else besides pottery because the demand for it in Quinua is not as great as the demand in Huanta and Huamanguilla where vendors may sell pottery and nothing else. Most pottery transactions in the Quinua market were for cash, but a seller may accept at least some goods in exchange as well, particularly when she is trying to dispose of her left-over pottery when the market ends about noon.

Quinua pottery is also sold in the Sunday market in Huamanguilla. When I visited the Huamanguilla market in early May, there was a substantial quantity of pottery from Quinua[21] and from Huayhuas (*tumins* and cooking pottery), a pottery-making hamlet near the town of Huanta. This visit co-occurred with the beginning of the pottery-making season at a time when scheduling conflicts with agriculture would preclude much pottery production. William P. Mitchell, however, visited Huamanguilla market on a rainy day in the wet season (when no pottery could be fired) and reported that no pottery was sold there at that time.

In the Huamanguilla market, transactions for pottery were mostly in cash, although occasionally potters exchanged goods for pots. Prior to 1967, subsistence crops were sometimes exchanged for pottery in Huamanguilla. Buyers from the community of Pacaycasa (in the lower montane thorn steppe below Quinua) came to Huamanguilla to exchange maize for pottery using a full vessel of maize as the purchase price for that vessel.[22] This method of exchange is widespread in Peru[23] and was cited by a potter during my 1978 visit as the standard of exchange in maize or grain for a *tachu* sold in the community of Tambo northeast of Quinua. When I visited the Huamanguilla market in May 1967, however, most exchanges for pottery were in cash. Only *coca* leaves were exchanged for ceramic vessels and then only for bowls (*platos*); a bowl full of *coca* leaves was the amount exchanged for that bowl.

In Huamanguilla, as in other markets, haggling about price and close examination of certain shapes constituted critical portions of the buying procedure. Bargaining in the Huamanguilla market was frequently for a price difference of less than 1 United States cent.[24]

Because all local markets occur on Sunday,[25] pottery-making families must use a strategy to successfully distribute their wares to more than one market. This strategy involves dividing saleable pots between members of the family with each member going to a different market. One woman from the hamlet of Huantos, for example, brought her pottery to sell in Quinua while her daughter took vessels to sell in Huamanguilla.

A visit to the Huanta market in early June revealed that few Quinua pots were sold there. In Huanta, Quinua wares compete with pottery made in nearby Huayhuas and Luricocha (figure 3.4). Since Huanta is the closest market to these communities, it is the major market for the utilitarian shapes (such as cooking pottery and liquid-storage and carrying vessels) made in these communities.

Two other factors restrict the occurrence of Quinua pottery in the Huanta market. First, the distance from Quinua to Huanta is greater than that to other markets in the valley. This greater distance tends to prevent Quinua potters from taking their wares to Huanta. Second, the truck and bus connections to Huanta are more complicated than those to other principal markets in the valley. Although the road from Quinua to Ayacucho connects with the road from Ayacucho to Huanta (see figure 3.4), little traffic goes from Quinua to Huanta because all traffic moving into the valley out of Quinua goes to Ayacucho. If Quinua potters want to travel to Huanta, they must either go to Ayacucho first and change vehicles, or travel to the junction of the road to Huanta in the valley bottom and wait until a truck or bus passes that is going to Huanta. Quinua potters could also transport their pots to Huamanguilla or to the junction of the road above Quinua that goes to Huamanguilla in order to get transportation to Huanta. Selling pottery in Huanta thus always necessitates a change of vehicles and increases the susceptibility of the pottery to breakage. All of these factors are probably responsible for the relatively small amount of Quinua pottery in the Huanta market.

The regular truck traffic to Ayacucho makes the market there the most accessible of all the markets in the valley outside of Quinua itself. There is no special market day in Ayacucho and the market remains open every day of the week. But, in contrast to other markets in the valley, less business is transacted on Sunday than on any other day because merchants travel to other markets in the valley. During the six months I was in the Ayacucho Valley, I observed the Ayacucho market twenty-two times. Quinua pottery appeared in the Ayacucho market only seven times between February and June, while Huayhuas pottery was sold there more frequently (table 6.2). Like other markets in the valley, pitchers and liquid receptacles (*puynus, yukupuynus, tachus, tinaqas*) and bowls (*platos*) from Quinua are sold in Ayacucho while Huayhuas potters bring water-carrying jars (*tumins*), cooking pots (*mankas*), beer-brewing jars (*chicha* jars), toasters (*tuqtus*), flower pots and some miscellaneous pottery to sell there (table 6.2).

The distribution of pottery in markets of the valley closely follows the pattern of roads (figures 6.7 and 3.4) and the hierarchical organization of the region into geopolitical units. Pottery produced in individual hamlets is transported to markets at higher level political and transportation nodes (the district, provincial and departmental capitals) of which the hamlet is a part, rather than to other nodes. It appears, then, that district, provincial and departmental capitals are different levels of central places which draw pottery from their respective political territories. Utilitarian pottery is not marketed beyond provincial or departmental capitals while most decorated utilitarian and non-utilitarian pottery from Quinua is sent to Lima.

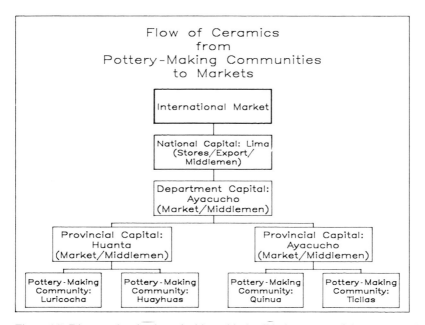

Figure 6.7 Diagram showing how the hierarchical political structure of the pottery-making communities in the Ayacucho Valley corresponds to the movement of pottery. Movement follows the political structure and the pattern of roads (compare with figure 3.4). The smallest political units (districts) occur at the bottom of the diagram with higher, more inclusive political units on each successive level as one moves to the top of the diagram. With few exceptions, pottery moves from the individual districts at the bottom of the diagram towards higher level political units above them to which they are linked by roads. The only exception to this flow of pottery is that Quinua pottery may sometimes be sold in Huanta. Only Quinua pottery moves from the Ayacucho Valley to the national capital (Lima) and into the international market.

Table 6.2. *Sources of vessel shapes in the Ayacucho market, February–June, 1967*

| Date of observation | | Community of origin of pottery | | | | |
Month	Day	Huayhuas	Quinua	Ticllas	Other	Unknown
Feb	18				Huancayo[a]	
	25		*puynu*		Huancayo[a]	
	28	*tumin*				
Mar	7		*puynu*		Huancayo[a]	
	8				Huancayo[a] Andahuaylas or Cuzco[b]	
	14	*tumin* *various*[c]			Andahuaylas or Cuzco[b]	
	15				Huancayo[a]	
	21					X[d]
Apr	13	*tumin* *manka* *tuqtu*				
	30	*tumin* *tuqtu* pitcher				
May	1	*tumin* *various*[e]	*puynu* *tinaqa*			
	2	*tumin*				
	4	*tumin*		*manka*		
	6			*manka*		
	7	*tumin* *florero*	*tachu*[f] *tinaqa*			
	8					X
	20	*tumin* *manka* *tuqtu*				
	22		*puynu* *tachu* *plato* *yuku* *puynu*			
	25					X
	26		*manka*			
Jun	20	*tumin*	*manka*			
	22	*tumin* *florero* *tuqtu* *mediano*				

Besides selling pottery in the local markets of the valley, a second mechanism of distributing pottery to the local populations consists of exchanging pottery for food in the high altitude montane prairie and moist forest zones.[26] In contrast to the females who sell pottery in the markets, males exchange pottery in the *puna*. Potters say that the demand for pottery (*porongos* like *tumin*, *yukupuynu*, *tachu* and *puynu*) in the *puna* is great, and they can exchange pottery for a substantial amount of food (mostly tubers and other agricultural products). One potter said that every two weeks (or whenever he had pottery to sell), he traveled into different areas of the *puna* to exchange his pottery for potatoes to help feed his family. Each *tumin* could be exchanged for half a sack of potatoes. Several potters in Lurinsayuq Pampa were said to regularly distribute their pottery in this way.

Another potter reported that when he was a boy of eight and there was no food in his house, his father took liquid transport vessels (that is *porongos*) to exchange for food in the hamlets of Chilcas, Rumirumi, and Ninabamba – communities which are about 30 kilometers southeast of Quinua. These communities were approximately two and one-half days' (Chilcas and Rumirumi) to three and one-half days' (Ninabamba) walk away and because no pottery was made there, pottery had a high value of exchange. One *porongo*, he said, was exchanged for twice its equivalent volume in maize and a ceramic bull could be exchanged for a chicken. When he was older and whenever his family had no food, he would offer to take *porongos* into

Notes to table 6.2

[a] A variety of pottery from the Huancayo area was sold on these dates. On February 18, cooking pots (*manka*) and toy pots were for sale. On February 25, only toy pots were for sale. On March 7, cooking pots (*manka*), maize toasters (*tuqtu*), toy pots, *canasta* (a ceramic vessel in the shape of a basket) and whistles were being sold. On March 8, cooking pots (*manka*), pitchers (*jara*), ceramic pot covers, flower pots (*florero*), ceramic toys, maize toasters (*tuqtu*) and a canteen were being sold, while on March 15, only ceramic toy pots were offered for sale. Most of these pots came from Aco (glazed ware such as toy vessels), and Concho, Quicha Chico and/or Quicha Grande (cooking pots and toasters) which are northwest of Huancayo (Hagstrum 1989; personal communication).

[b] The vessels sold on this date were pitchers (*jara*) which were reportedly made in either Andahuaylas or Cuzco. It is not likely that the pottery was made in the city of Cuzco, however, because during my residence in Cuzco from August of 1972 to April of 1973, there was no pottery made in the city. The reference that this pottery was made in Cuzco may mean that the pottery was made in the Department of Cuzco.

[c] Other vessel shapes from Huayhuas that were offered for sale on this date included pitchers (*jara*), cooking pots (*manka*), ceramic toasters (*tuqtu*), *tinaqas*, *azugueros* (sugar containers), and *canastas* (ceramic containers made in the form of a basket).

[d] On this date, a cooking pot (*manka*) and a maize toaster (*tuqtu*) from an unknown location were being sold.

[e] Pottery from Huayhuas sold on this date included flower pots (*florero*), cooking pots (*manka*), maize toasters (*tuqtu*), and *chicha* brewing jar (*maqma*).

[f] These vessels were reportedly from Huamanguilla, but because they are identical to Quinua pottery, they are listed as being from Quinua. Furthermore, the strong relationships between the *pago* of Muya in Quinua and the District of Huamanguilla (see chapter 2) also suggest that the same population are involved in their production.

this same area in order to exchange them for food. Pottery which was sold in that area in 1967 was still said to bring a price better than if those vessels were sold locally.

Sometimes intermediaries, rather than potters, sold pottery to *puna* populations. When I visited the market in Huanta, I noticed a man who was repeatedly buying pottery from the pottery vendors there. He only purchased the best quality cooking pots (*mankas*) and liquid transport vessels (*tumins*) taking care to examine each one carefully before purchase. When I asked others in the market what he was doing and why he was so particular about the pots he bought, I was told that he was buying pottery to sell or trade in the *puna*. Pottery, it was reported, was in demand in the *puna* and any vessel could be exchanged for its equivalent volume of tubers. More recently, however, pottery transactions were made in cash.

A different distribution mechanism exists for pottery destined for populations outside the Ayacucho Valley. Quinua pottery sold in this manner is primarily used as an ethnic and tourist curio and is sold to intermediaries (see also Spahni 1966: 85).

The existence of the intermediaries makes the process of selling ceramics relatively easy for the potters in three ways. First, potters do not have to transport their pottery beyond the village, if that far. Second, they can sell all of it at the same time eliminating separate trips to one or more markets. Third, they are frequently paid in advance for their pots.[27] Sometimes, however, a potter may have to wait to be paid. When potters sell their pottery to intermediaries, it may be taken to Lima and the potters are not paid until the buyer returns. Intermediaries may also advance money to potters so that they can buy materials and sometimes they will pay the potters with merchandise such as a radio.

The use of an intermediary for marketing Quinua pottery developed out of the sale of pottery in local stores (see Mitchell 1991a). Originally, many decorated shapes produced in 1967 were only made on contract by local potters. If someone needed a vessel to put on top of the roof of a new house, he would contract with a potter to make one. Long before 1967, a woman store owner from Ayacucho traveled to Quinua to buy pots and she was the first intermediary for selling Quinua pottery.[28] In 1967, however, she was too old to travel and Quinua potters reportedly brought their pots to her in Ayacucho. Once the sale of Quinua pottery moved outside the community, however, the production of Quinua pottery began to expand and to shift away from shapes that had a local utilitarian or ritual use.

In 1967, a single Ayacucho family was the most important intermediary for selling Quinua ceramics (and other craft items). They frequently brought their truck to Quinua and purchased a potter's entire output after firing. Vessels were either taken to Ayacucho to sell in their craft store, or transported to Lima to sell to various shops or exporting agencies. Occasionally, this family asked potters to make specific shapes, but potters said the family bought any type of pottery – traditional or non-traditional, utilitarian or non-utilitarian – provided that it was of "good" quality. They did not purchase "ugly" pottery (see chapter 8). If a potter had "ugly" pottery among his pots for sale, it was separated from the pottery to be purchased and the potter had to sell it elsewhere. If the "ugly" pottery had a utilitarian use, it could be sold in the Quinua Sunday market. If it was not utilitarian, it could be sold to the stores in Quinua.

Potters say that ceramic objects rejected by intermediaries are sold at a cheaper price than pottery that is produced more carefully and is aesthetically pleasing. Vendors who sold this "ugly" pottery in the Sunday market are said to have many local buyers because of its cheapness. In 1978, informants maintained that pottery that was sold locally was still less aesthetically pleasing than that which was made for the tourist market.

The Ayacucho family which was the middleman for Quinua ceramics also owned a hacienda near Ayacucho.[29] During Holy Week festivities of 1967, they sponsored a folklore exposition at the hacienda featuring local artisans such as dancers, musicians, and potters. Local food was served and three Quinua potters were hired to make pottery. Since Ayacucho Holy Week festivities were famous throughout Peru and attracted many tourists, the exposition provided tourists an opportunity to eat local food, drink maize beer, see and hear local musicians and dancers as well as see Quinua potters at work.

Sometimes another level of intermediaries is added to the marketing of tourist ceramics. In 1967, the wife of one potter served as an intermediary between sellers of local crafts and the buyers who came from Ayacucho. She bought pottery, baskets and woven belts from people who needed money and resold them to intermediaries from Ayacucho for a profit of 25–100 percent. Sometimes she advanced money to people to buy materials and frequently asked people to make craft items on special order. Capital is required for such an enterprise and it is likely that she used her husband's monthly wages from the artisan center to support this venture.

One of the Quinua families also served as an intermediary buying ceramics locally and selling them in Lima, but found it more advantageous to transport the potters themselves to Lima to make their ceramics there. So, by 1967, two potters were busily producing Quinua pottery in the capital for the national and international artisan market. All of the clay, sand, and paints were brought from Quinua, but the ceramics were produced and marketed in Lima.

The massive urban migration of rural inhabitants to Lima since the 1950s has greatly stimulated the production of Quinua ceramics in Lima. Rural migrants to the capital continue to have regular contact with their communities of origin, are organized into local "clubs" which return to their community for the annual fiesta and send money to relatives in their home communities.[30] These links and the migration of Quinua potters to Lima have resulted in a massive development of pottery workshops in Lima. This change in the venue of Quinua ceramic production has occurred for largely three reasons. First, production in Lima reduced the risk of damaging the pottery during the trip from Quinua. Secondly, the output from ceramic production is located close to the potters' most significant market. Third, transportation costs were greatly reduced by transporting raw materials rather than the finished product through continuing contact with the rural community (Mitchell 1991a: 115). In the 1980s, the production of Quinua pottery in Lima had grown greatly so that by 1988, some twenty different workshops were producing Quinua pottery with materials brought from Quinua (Mitchell 1991a: 113).

Quinua pottery is also available in local stores in Quinua and Ayacucho. Although some store owners in Ayacucho purchase vessels through intermediaries, others obtain their pottery directly from Quinua potters. Potters also sell their wares to stores in Quinua. Some sell on consignment while others sell pottery directly for cash or in exchange for merchandise. Between 1967 and 1978, the number of stores in Quinua selling local pottery increased dramatically.

Conclusion

From an ecological perspective, pottery consists of a channel for the flow of matter and energy from the environment to human beings. In Quinua, cooking vessels help detoxify Andean crops for human consumption. Several shapes are related to the importance of maize agriculture and consumption. The emphasis upon liquid-carrying vessels in the repertoire of utilitarian shapes reveals the importance of pottery as a channel of the flow of water from the environment for human consumption and reflects the risks involved in carrying liquids from place to place in a variegated mountain environment where breakage may be frequent. Indeed, water-carrying vessels can be viewed as an extension of the irrigation system which constitutes another type of culturally-constructed channel through which water flows from the environment to human beings. Ceramic vessels are also important for the production, storage, transport and consumption of maize beer which is crucial for the recruitment of labor during seasonal labor scarcity.

Quinua pottery also plays a role as a channel of information flow between the members of a society. Some Quinua pottery reflects important mythical themes and pottery holds an important place in certain rituals. This demand for ritual pottery in Quinua is significant for potters' livelihood since they live in such a marginal agricultural area and must depend upon producing ceramics to make a living. The use of ceramics for ritual in Quinua thus helps sustain pottery production because it provides an outlet for the potter's products.

As a channel of matter, energy and information, pottery must conform to a culture's motor habits because it is used and carried by humans. Indeed, the large liquid-carrying vessel is transported in ways that conform to the way loads are carried elsewhere in the Andes.

Potters must also adapt to the social, political and economic environment if they are to turn their pottery into food through sale or exchange. Quinua potters distribute their pottery to local and regional markets which are tied to the road system and political organization of the area. Potters also distribute their pottery in the high altitude *puna* in exchange for food. Intermediaries buy pottery from local potters and then resell it in Ayacucho and Lima.

The widespread distribution of Quinua pottery in Europe and the United States is the result of intermediaries (whether from inside or outside the community) who have access to external markets. The use of such individuals is the only significant means by which pottery is sold and distributed to a variety of artisan markets –

foreign and domestic. It is the only mechanism that channels churches, bulls, and other decorated items of pottery outside of the immediate area. Consequently, the sale of pottery through intermediaries constitutes one of the most important distribution mechanisms in Quinua, and accounts for the movement of most of its pottery outside of the Ayacucho Basin. In the 1980s, a substantial amount of Quinua pottery was produced in Lima using raw materials imported from Quinua.

All of these distribution mechanisms have implications for the distribution of ancient pottery. The conditions of distribution may be different and the type of transportation may have changed, but there are some implications of these data that are relevant to prehistory. The distribution of pottery in the high mountainous zones (the *puna*) above the community is probably an ancient practice and may be an artifact of local ecological complementarity. Potters have also used foot and animal roads in recent times as well as in the past to distribute their pots. Local markets provide a means for potters to sell their pottery by bringing together products of different zones, but demand for pottery would be less with many potters selling simultaneously in the same market. This overcompetitive situation could be mitigated by selling to a specialist trader who knew the markets and could move pottery far enough away in order to obtain a better price for it. Thus, even though modern intermediaries are not strictly analogous to the past, the use of intermediaries is the most effective way to move pottery out of the valley to more distant consumers.

Is it coincidental that modern Quinua potters who produce pottery that is exported all over the world occupy almost the same location as ancient Huari potters whose pottery was distributed widely throughout southern and central Peru? It has already been argued that it is more than coincidental that significant prehistoric and historic events occurred in Quinua. Besides the rise of Huari and the relatively low elevation of the agricultural land in the valley, Quinua was the location of the first Inca and Spanish settlements of the region. On the flat plain (or *pampa*) above Quinua, the decisive battle against colonial Spain (the Battle of Ayacucho) was fought by the army of liberator Simón Bolivar. All of these events suggest that Quinua was in a strategic location along an important prehistoric and historic route of travel and communication through the southern Andes. Today, the main highland road from Lima to Cuzco passes through the valley and Quinua lies along one of the few roads from the highlands to the jungle in the southern Peruvian Andes. It is this access to communication and transportation routes which has provided an important outlet for the ceramics of the region both now and in antiquity.

7

Design correlates of the community

So far, this work has focused on an ecological approach to Quinua ceramic *production*. Previous chapters have described the environment, the adaptation of the potters to that environment, the potters' ceramic products and the relationship of those products to the environment and culture. It has been argued that the community of potters is the unit of adaptation and the relationships of this population to the environment have been elucidated. Following the methodology of cultural ecology, the process of ceramic production was then described and the output from that process was portrayed as channels for the flow of matter, energy and information. The previous chapter outlined the adaptation of the potters to the economic environment of the Ayacucho Valley so that potters can turn their pots into food or some other desirable commodity. Now, the discussion turns to the relationship of an ecological perspective to ceramic design.

If the community of potters is the unit of ecological adaptation, one would hope that there would be some material expression of that unit in the ceramics. By examining the ceramic products of Quinua and identifying the shared design characteristics of those products, one may be able to identify some of the behavioral design correlates (following Schiffer's [1976] definition) of that community. Such correlates would not only link ecological theory and ceramic design, but would provide a basis for constructing a theory for identifying the products of specific communities of potters in ancient as well as modern ceramics.

The sample

The sample analyzed in this chapter consists of 172 vessels of four shapes. These shapes include a low open bowl (figure 7.1) and three globular jars: a wide-necked vessel with a circular mouth (figure 7.2), a narrow-necked vessel with a small circular mouth (figures 7.3 and 7.4), and a narrow-necked vessel with a mouth modeled into a pouring spout (figure 7.5). This data set constitutes every vessel of these shapes that I observed being made and used in Quinua from February through June in 1967. Some of these vessels were being made by Quinua potters or were being sold by them. They include a few cases of multiple vessels of the same shape made by the same potter, but the variation of the designs has been noted.[1] Other vessels were being used in the streets and markets of Quinua. A few vessels were observed being sold or used in the markets of Huanta, Ayacucho and Huamanguilla. In all cases, decoration was copied into field notes, but in a few cases, data on specific design zones were missing because the period of observation was so brief that all of the details of the design could not be noted. Unfortunately, because few pots were made during the rainy season (see the preface), the producer of a vessel is known only for less than 50 percent of the vessels, so there are insufficient data to ascertain how many potters produced the sample. Therefore, there are insufficient data to relate the design to social groups below the level of the community. Nevertheless, the sample consists of all of the vessels observed being made, sold and used in Quinua between February and June, 1967.

These four shapes were selected for a variety of reasons. First, except for pottery churches, these vessels were the most frequently observed shapes in the Quinua area. In 1967, churches were produced almost entirely for the national and international artisan market and therefore had limited utility in the application of these data to archaeology. Second, all of these vessels were decorated in one of the three painting schemes in Quinua and thus were amenable to design analysis. Third, they were all utilitarian vessels that were in daily use by the natives of Quinua. The *tachu*, *puynu*, and *yukupuynu* are all forms of a pitcher used for transporting, storing and dispensing water or other liquids. The *plato* is a general receptacle for food and other

Figure 7.1 The *plato* or low open bowl (N = 36). The scale is in centimeters. For dimensions of vessels of this shape, see figures 5.14–5.16.

items. Fourth, Quinua potters produce these four shapes almost exclusively for local use. Although they occasionally find their way into the artisan market, this outlet for these vessels is a minor one. Potters who produce ceramics for the artisan market made very few, if any, of these vessels. On the other hand, pottery vendors from Quinua were observed selling these four shapes, and almost always these shapes, in the local markets in Quinua and the neighboring communities of Ayacucho, Huanta

Figure 7.2 The *tachu* is a wide-necked globular bottle with a circular mouth (N = 46). The scale is in centimeters. For dimensions of vessels of this shape, see figures 5.14–5.17.

and Huamanguilla. Finally, these shapes are made almost exclusively by Quinua potters and are thus unique among the ceramics produced elsewhere in the valley. Since they are made for utilitarian purposes and their production is aimed at the native population of the valley, they are affected more by the shared decorative tradition of the community than the changing responses of individual potters to the tourist and artisan market.

The design analysis

In order to maximize the archaeological implications of the methodology utilized here, the analysis follows an etic research strategy. An etic strategy emphasizes the objective cross-cultural units of analysis that can apply to any kind of decoration and one which does not rely on the meaning of the design for analysis. Except for glosses in Quechua (the native language of Quinua) used to identify the vessel shapes, no emic data were used in this analysis. Rather, the data were compiled from observations of pottery made and used in Quinua. This analysis thus deals with the formal aspects of design isolated independently of the potters' statements about that design.

Figure 7.3 The *yukupuynu* is a narrow-necked jar with a small circular mouth (N = 44). The match box is included for scale and is 3.4 cm wide. For dimensions of vessels of this shape, see figures 5.14–5.17.

This approach can thus be employed on any group of vessels in the present or the past.

The first step in the analysis was to separate the design data into discontinuous units of observation. Because of the objective nature of these units, another investigator should be able to isolate the same units of observation. The largest such unit is the vessel shape. The next such unit is the "design field" which consists of the portion of a shape that was consistently decorated. The design field is subdivided into smaller units called "design zones" and these zones are the third unit of observation. The final unit of observation consists of the structure of design itself as indicated by the motions of the repetition used to produce it (that is, its symmetry).

Analyses of these units of observation yielded common decorative patterns. In other words, design variation was reduced to a series of consistent behavioral design patterns which have been abstracted from the present sample of vessels and are characteristic of the entire sample. These behavioral patterns suggest that Quinua potters decorate their pottery according to a series of behavioral principles. These principles can be conveniently divided into three categories:

Figure 7.4 A *yukupuynu* painted with different designs from figure 7.3. The match box is included for scale and is 3.4 cm wide. For dimensions of vessels of this shape, see figures 5.14–5.17.

(1) the preparation of the surface of a vessel for decoration;
(2) the selection of the decorative space on the vessel (the design field) and its subdivision into smaller units called "design zones";
(3) the manner in which the designs are painted with regard to their fundamental units and the way in which these units are repeated to form the design (that is, symmetry).[2]

Because the ecological paradigm is synthetic and relational, rather than analytical, it doesn't provide much help with the analysis of ceramic decoration and one must turn to another paradigm for the design description. To be consistent with the presentation of the pottery technology described in chapter 5, the behavioral principles of design are described as choices that potters make when they decorate

Figure 7.5 The *puynu* is a narrow-necked jar with a mouth modeled into a pouring spout (N = 46). The scale is in centimeters. For dimensions of vessels of this shape, see figures 5.14–5.17.

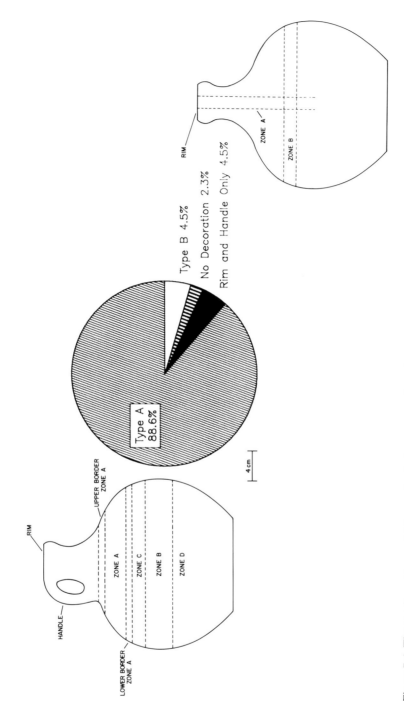

Figure 7.6 The two layout types which organize design space on the *yukupuynu* and their frequency in the sample (N = 44). The layouts of each type occur next to the frequency of that type in the pie chart. Layout type A is thus on the left and layout type B is on the right. Design zone A and its lower boundary are "obligatory design zones" and occur in every vessel of layout type A while both zones A and B occur on every vessel of layout type B. The rim and handle of layout type B may also be decorated.

their pottery. Each of these principles will be discussed in more detail in the sections that follow.

Preparing for decoration

The first principle of decoration involves preparing the vessels for decoration. Several vessel-specific conventions govern the execution of this principle:

(1) For the *tachu*, potters burnish the body clay without applying any slip.
(2) For the *puynu* and *yukupuynu*, potters slip the vessel with red paint before burnishing.
(3) For the *plato*, potters place a red slip on one surface of the vessel before burnishing:
  (a) If the red slip is placed on the exterior of the vessel, the interior is slipped white and burnished.
  (b) If the red slip is placed on the interior of the vessel, the exterior is left unslipped and unburnished.

After the surface has been prepared, the potter can decorate the vessels.

Selecting the field of design

The second design principle for decorating a pot consists of selecting the field of design and subdividing this area into design zones. The resulting organizations of design space are called design layouts and vary from one shape to another. Different ways of allocating design space may also occur on the same shape, and these different organizations of design space are referred to as "layout types." The *tachu* has three types, the *yukupuynu* and *puynu* have two types each, and the *plato* has five types.[3]

While all of the design zones in a particular layout type do not occur on every vessel, there is at least one zone which does occur on every vessel and this zone is called an "obligatory design zone." Those zones which do not occur on every vessel in a particular layout type are "optional zones" and consist of those zones which the potter has the option of using, but may choose not to do so.

The decorated space on the *yukupuynu* usually occurs on the upper part of the vessel between the base of the neck and the vessel's greatest circumference (figure 7.6). The rim and the handle may be decorated with a dotted or solid line.

There are two layout types. On the most frequent type (layout type A, figure 7.6), all of the design zones are horizontal bands which encircle the entire circumference of the vessel.

The less frequent design layout on the *yukupuynu* (layout type B, figure 7.6) consists of a horizontal band located slightly above the point of greatest circumference and a vertical band of identical design placed opposite the handle and intersecting the horizontal band. The rim and handle are not decorated.

On the most frequent *yukupuynu* layout type, the obligatory design zone consists of a wide band (zone A) which covers much of the upper part of

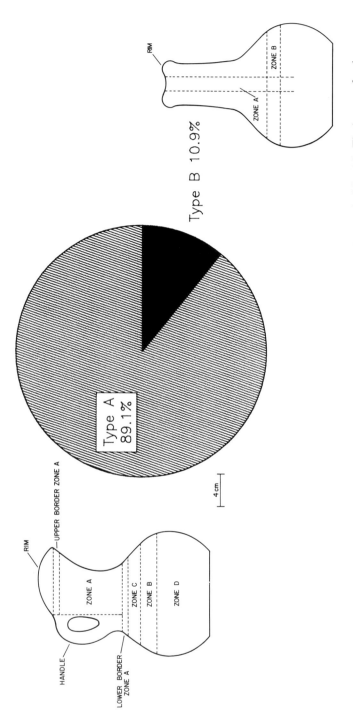

Figure 7.7 The two layout types which organize design space on the *puynu* and their frequency in the sample (N = 46). The layouts of each type occur next to the frequency of that type in the pie chart. Layout type A thus is on the left and layout type B is on the right. Design zone A and its lower boundary are "obligatory design zones" and occur in every vessel of layout type A while both zones A and B occur on every vessel of layout type B. The rim and handle of layout type B may also be decorated.

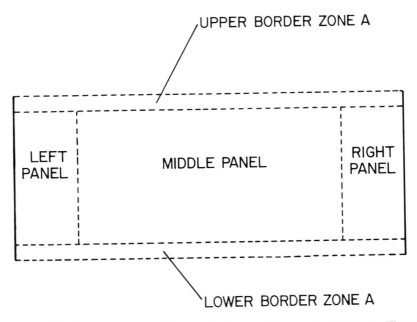

UPPER BORDER ZONE A

LEFT
PANEL

MIDDLE PANEL

RIGHT
PANEL

LOWER BORDER ZONE A

Figure 7.8 The organization of the three design panels in zone A on the *puynu*. The middle panel is opposite the handle.

the body of the vessel (figure 7.6). A small band immediately below this zone marks its lower boundary. The remainder of the design zones on this shape are optional.

The decorative field on the *puynu* extends from the base of the vessel to the rim and includes the rim and handle. There are two design layouts on the *puynu* (figure 7.7). Like the *yukupuynu* (figure 7.6), the pitcher (the *puynu*) also has its vertical space divided into multiple horizontal zones and this layout type represents the most frequent pattern (figure 7.7). A second layout type (type B) is identical to layout type B of the *yukupuynu*.

Like the *yukupuynu*, the most frequent organization of design space (layout type A) for the *puynu* includes a large obligatory zone (zone A). This zone consists of a series of three vertical panels placed around the upper body of the vessel (figure 7.8). The center panel lies directly opposite the handle. This wide zone is bounded on the bottom by an obligatory small band which forms the lower boundary of the zone. The remainder of the zones are optional zones and are usually (but not always) bands which extend around the circumference of the vessel below the lower boundary of the obligatory zone.

Potters organize decorative space on the *tachu* in one of three ways. First, the vessel may be left undecorated. Second, the rim may be painted white with no other decoration. Third, white strips may be placed on the vessel in one of three ways. Most frequently, potters place one strip vertically on the handle and another directly opposite the handle (figure 7.9). Much less frequently, they utilize two other variants to this major pattern:

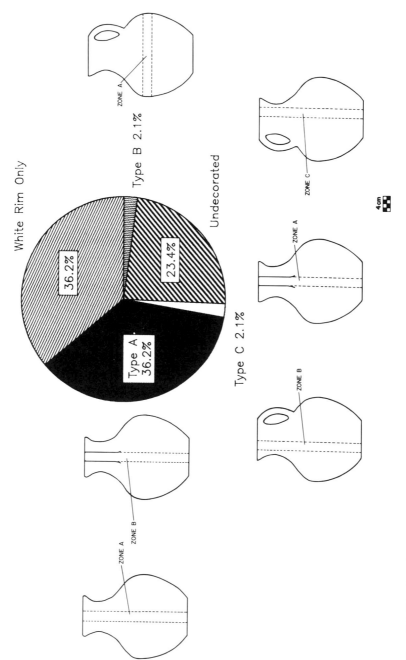
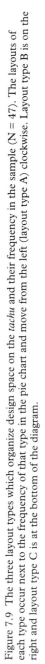

Figure 7.9 The three layout types which organize design space on the *tachu* and their frequency in the sample (N = 47). The layouts of each type occur next to the frequency of that type in the pie chart and move from the left (layout type A) clockwise. Layout type B is on the right and layout type C is at the bottom of the diagram.

(1) A potter may place one white strip horizontally around the vessel at the point of the greatest circumference (layout type B, figure 7.9).
(2) A potter may place the strips vertically in three locations: one on the handle and two others equally spaced from one another so that the strips divide the surface of the vessel into three equal parts (layout type C, figure 7.9).

Further decoration is required, but must be placed along the entire length of these white strips. This decoration consists entirely of bands which combine three straight and/or zigzag lines painted with red and/or black pigments and conforms to the following set of behavioral rules: (1) the band must consist of three lines each painted with red and/or black paint; (2) the center line must be zigzag and be framed by two lines which may be straight (most frequent) or zigzag; (3) the framing lines must mirror one another in color and shape; and (4) all straight lines or axes produced by multiple points of rotation must be parallel.

The decorative space on the *plato* includes the rim and either the outside or the inside of the vessel. Quinua potters have five layout types for organizing and subdividing this space (figure 7.10).

The subdivision of the *plato* design field depends upon the color of the slip used and whether the exterior or interior was chosen as the surface to receive the slip (figure 7.11).

(1) If potters slipped the interior of the *plato* red, then the design field consists of the interior of the vessel. If this alternative is chosen, then the field may be organized in one of three ways:
 (a) On the most frequent type (layout type A), two bands cross at right angles in the center of the vessel (figure 7.10). A third zone lies at the intersection of these bands with a single motif placed within it.
 (b) A second alternative (layout type A1, figure 7.10) consists of a variation of layout type A. The primary difference between type A and type A1, however, lies in the difference in the design space. In type A, two intersecting bands divide the vessel into fourths and the design space is within the bands. In type A1, however, there is no band or line dividing the space into fourths, but the quarter sections form a design of alternating white and red painted sections both in the center zone and the outer zones.
(2) If potters slipped the interior of the *plato* white, then the design field occurs either on the outside or the inside of the vessel. This is a very infrequent pattern, but white interiors tend to occur with red slipped exteriors.
 (a) If the potter chooses the exterior of the vessel for decoration, the field of design will be a circular band on the exterior of the bowl (figure 7.10, layout type B; figure 7.1).
 (b) If, on the other hand, the potters chose the interior of the bowl for decoration, the field of decoration will be a small zone in the center of the interior (figure 7.10, layout type D).

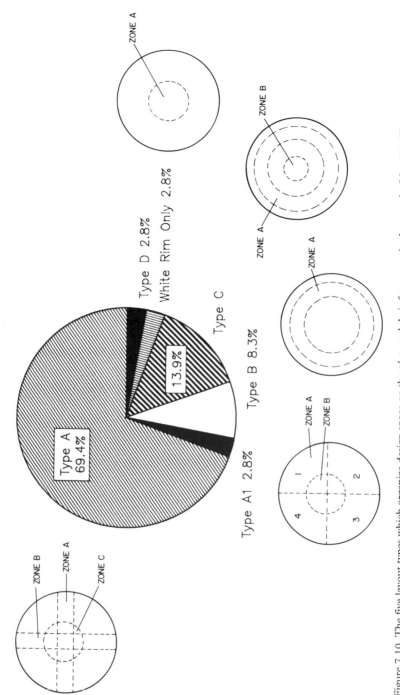

Figure 7.10 The five layout types which organize design space on the *plato* and their frequency in the sample (N = 36). The layouts of each type occur next to the frequency of that type in the pie chart and move from the left (layout type A) counterclockwise.

Symmetry

The final principle of design consists of the internal structure of the designs themselves produced by their patterns of repetition. The analysis of these patterns involves identifying the type of motion inherent in the repeated patterns of design. Although an important part of crystallography and mathematics, symmetry analysis was first applied to ceramic design by Anna O. Shepard (1948, 1956). While Shepard's work on symmetry has been available for more than forty years, it has not received much attention until relatively recently when Dorothy Washburn demonstrated the precision of this important tool.[4] Washburn (1977b) has elaborated Shepard's basic work and, with mathematician Donald Crowe, has refined symmetry analysis and developed flow charts to facilitate its application to archaeology.[5]

In order to understand symmetry analysis and to see its application to the study of ceramic design, one must first understand its basic underlying principles. First, symmetry analysis consists of defining the motions inherent in repeated design. The key here is repeated design; symmetry analysis cannot be used on designs in which there is no pattern or repetition.

Second, the motions of repetition in symmetry patterns always occur at or along one or more of two basic types of loci: a point and/or an axis (that is, a line or vector). Symmetry patterns are thus repeated around a point, along an axis, or along a series of points and/or axes.

The third basic principle of symmetry analysis consists of identifying the fundamental unit of the design.[6] Symmetry analysis must begin with the identification of the fundamental unit of the design. This unit must be an asymmetric unit. That is, it must be an irreducible unit which has no motion of repetition within it (figure 7.12, top). It may be a portion of the design or a segment of a line (Shepard 1956: 268) and must be the unit from which the remainder of the design is generated by one or more repetitive motions. Identification of this unit is absolutely essential

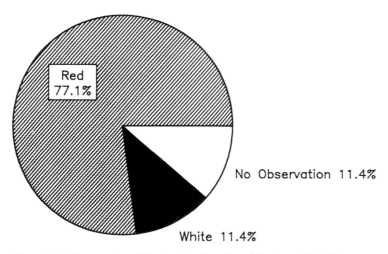

Figure 7.11 Frequencies of the interior slip color of the *platos* (N = 36).

for the analysis and failure to do it properly as an asymmetric unit can lead to ambiguous and imprecise results in the remainder of the analysis.

The "fundamental unit" of a design in symmetry analysis is not the same as the "motif" of a design. A "motif" is usually viewed as a discrete unit of the design which may or may not be repeated. The fundamental unit of a symmetry pattern, however, may or may not be discrete, but must be repeated to form the remainder of the design. A "motif" may be symmetrical or asymmetrical while the fundamental unit of a symmetry pattern must always be asymmetrical and be the smallest possible unit from which the design is generated. A motif in a repeated design could be the fundamental unit of the symmetry pattern (figure 7.12, bottom right) or it could be made up of more than one fundamental unit (figure 7.12, middle, bottom left). The motif is thus a more imprecise unit of design analysis than the "fundamental unit" of symmetry analysis.

The "fundamental unit" of a symmetry pattern is also different from the "element" of a design. Elements are regarded as basic units of the design, but appear to be defined somewhat arbitrarily. These units "make sense" relative to the data set from which they are drawn, but often the method by which they are identified is not specified. The "fundamental unit" of a symmetry pattern, however, always consists of the same precise definition: an asymmetric unit of the design from which the rest of the design can be generated.

A final difference between the fundamental unit of symmetry and a "motif" or an "element" lies in the relationship of these units to the design structure. The identification of an "element" or "motif" in a design does not necessarily involve describing the structural relationship between these units. On the other hand, the process of identifying the fundamental unit in symmetry analysis must also describe the axes (that is vectors) and/or points at, or along, which the fundamental unit is repeated. In this way, one can verify that a unit is indeed one from which the entire design can be generated. Identifying the "fundamental unit" in symmetry analysis thus implicitly involves understanding the structural relationship between such units and how they are linked together to form the design.

A fourth principle of symmetry analysis involves the three basic types of repetitive motion: rotation, translation and reflection (see Crowe and Washburn 1987: 70). Rotation involves the movement of the fundamental unit of the design around a point (figure 7.12, bottom left) so that the design is moved around that point by a given angle.[7] The second basic motion of repetition is translation. In this type, the fundamental unit of the design is moved the same distance in the same direction along an axis or vector (figure 7.12, bottom right). The last basic motion of repetition is reflection which consists of the repetition of the fundamental unit across an axis or vector (figure 7.12, middle right and left). Reflection may be either mirror reflection or slide reflection. In mirror reflection each point of the design is moved to the corresponding point on the other side of the axis (figure 7.12, middle). In "slide" or "glide" reflection (figure 7.13, bottom left), the reflected unit is moved along a vector away from the position of the original unit before it is reflected across an axis. In reality, however, "slide" reflection is really a

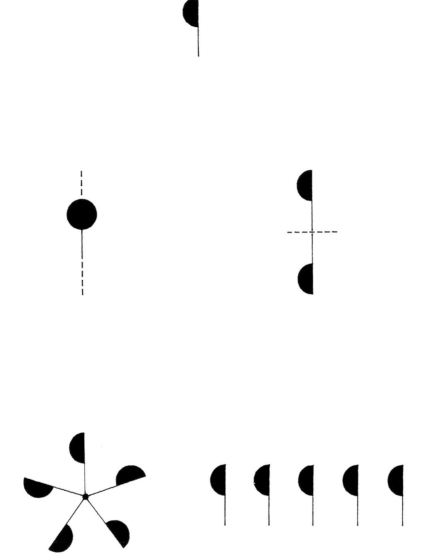

Figure 7.12 The fundamental motions of symmetry analysis using one of the fundamental units in the Quinua designs. In symmetry analysis, the asymmetric fundamental unit (top) must first be isolated as the unit from which the entire design can be generated. In this case, the unit can be repeated by vertical reflection (middle left), horizontal reflection (middle right), rotation (bottom left) and translation (bottom right). All of these designs (except the bottom right) can be motifs or finite designs, but in Quinua, only vertical reflection is used to form motifs using the fundamental unit illustrated here. As is evident from this diagram, one fundamental unit with different motions of repetition can produce considerable variability in designs. This kind of variability, however, does not occur in Quinua because the kinds of motions and repetition appear to both constrain the production of painted designs and influence judgments of acceptability for the sale of painted vessels.

combination of translation (the "glide" or "slide") followed by reflection across a line parallel to the translation vector.

Symmetry patterns that consist of reflection should also specify the orientation of the axis along which the reflection occurs. "Vertical" reflection, for example, is mirror reflection (or mirror image) along a vertical axis while "horizontal" reflection is mirror reflection along a horizontal axis. The axis of reflection may occur at any angle, however, and is not restricted to a vertical or a horizontal vector.

A fifth principle of symmetry analysis involves the classification of the motions of repetition into three broad categories of patterns. The first category consists of designs that utilize motions of rotation and/or mirror reflection. The fundamental

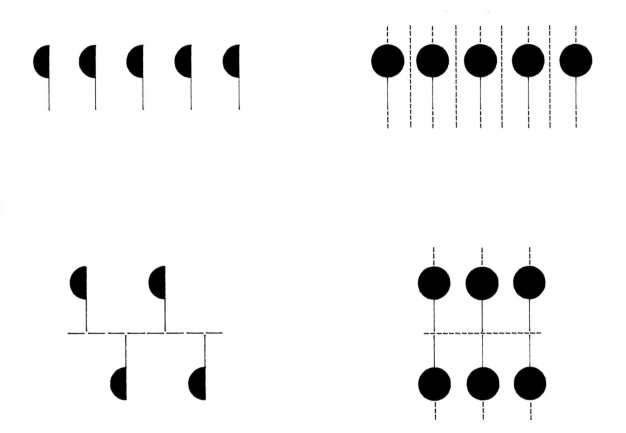

Figure 7.13 The use of the fundamental motions of repetition to produce band patterns (or one-dimensional patterns) using the fundamental unit in figure 7.12 (top). In translation (upper left), all points of the fundamental unit are moved the same distance in one direction. In vertical reflection (upper right), the fundamental unit is reflected as mirror image across a series of vertical axes (dotted lines). Slide reflection (lower left) is a combination of translation and reflection in which the fundamental unit is first moved in one direction and then reflected across an axis. In vertical and horizontal reflection (lower right), the fundamental unit is reflected across a series of vertical axes (see upper right) and then reflected once across a horizontal axis. In this pattern the axes of reflection between the motifs have been removed (see upper right) for simplicity.

unit is thus repeated once along a single axis or a limited amount of times around a point. These kinds of designs are called finite designs because the number of repetitions is small and the design is restricted to a limited area of space (for example figure 7.12, middle and bottom left). Finite designs are thus characterized by the absence of the motions of translation and glide reflection (Crowe and Washburn 1987: 72). A second category of design consists of band patterns in which the fundamental unit is repeated again and again in one direction along an axis (figure 7.13). This category is called a "one dimensional pattern" (Crowe and Washburn 1987: 72) because the fundamental unit can be repeated any number of times in one dimension limited only by the length of the media (figure 7.13). The third category of symmetry patterns involves the repetition of the fundamental unit in two directions to create a pattern that occurs over the entire surface of the media (Crowe and Washburn 1987: 72; figure 7.14). This type of design is called an "all-over" or "two dimensional" pattern.[8] The main difference between "finite" designs, on the one hand, and "band" and "all-over" designs, on the other, consists of the number of motions of repetition. In finite designs, the amount of repetition of the fundamental unit is small and limited whereas in band and two dimensional designs, the repetition is potentially, but not actually, infinite, limited only by the size of the media.

The symmetry of Quinua ceramic design

The greatest advantage of symmetry analysis consists of its precise, unambiguous approach to ceramic design. This advantage, however is predicated on precisely identifying: (1) the fundamental unit of the design (which must always be an asymmetric unit); (2) the axes or points at which the unit is repeated; and (3) the

Figure 7.14 The use of the fundamental unit in figure 7.12 (top) to form a two-dimensional (or "all over") pattern in which a fundamental unit can be repeated infinitely in two dimensions. (This is opposed to band designs in which the fundamental unit can be repeated infinitely in only one dimension.) In this example, translation in the horizontal dimension is combined with horizontal reflection in the vertical dimension. Although the fundamental unit utilized in this illustration occurs in Quinua design, two dimensional patterns are not used. Quinua potters generally restrict the repetitive motions for each fundamental unit to finite motifs and band designs.

motions of repetition. Symmetry analysis can define designs precisely and objectively in a way that can be repeated by another investigator.[9] It also permits great analytical and methodological precision and provides a standardized, comparable and consistent analysis which may not, and often does not, occur with other kinds of analyses that focus on elements or motifs. The methodology is straightforward enough that the process of analysis should be uniform from investigator to investigator and avoids problems of inter-subjectivity that occur with analyses that utilize motifs or elements. Indeed, the mathematical rigor of symmetry analysis is implied in the use of the synonym "pattern mathematics"[10] which expresses its inherent mathematical qualities. Unfortunately, except for the work of Washburn[11] and a few others,[12] the great potential of symmetry analysis in archaeology has not been realized and has been more the domain of mathematicians.

Shepard (1956: 275) points out that although perfectly symmetric designs are straightforward, symmetry may be rendered imperfect because of: (1) the adaptation of a symmetric design to the curved surface of a pot; and (2) the lack of skill or carelessness in the execution. Since all design on ceramic vessels needs to be applied to a curved surface in one way or another, all of the symmetry of ceramic design is imperfect. The design on the Quinua pottery is no exception. While most of the pottery analyzed was neatly painted, sloppiness of design execution obscured motions of perfect symmetry (see figure 7.2). Nevertheless, this analysis treats these designs as if they were neatly painted.

Following the principles enumerated above, the analysis of the symmetry of repeated designs involves several steps. Before one analyzes the symmetry of a particular vessel, one must first analyze the way that the space on the vessel is divided. Then, design fields and design zones need to be identified. Next, one must isolate the fundamental unit of the repeated pattern. After the fundamental unit has been defined, it is necessary to ascertain the motion necessary to produce the finite designs. When a design is repeated again and again along a straight line to form a band pattern, the analysis must also determine the fundamental unit of the band as well as its motion of repetition (see figure 7.15(a)–(c)).

Of the three categories of symmetry patterns (finite designs, band patterns and all-over patterns), Quinua potters only use two: finite designs and band patterns. Although some finite designs occur alone on the four vessels analyzed here, most finite designs are used as a part of band patterns. Some band patterns, on the other hand, have no finite designs and consist only of continuous lines, or less frequently, bands of solid color. The designs on the *tachu* (and a few on the *puynu* and *yukupuynu*) have no individual finite designs (and thus no motif symmetry), but consist only of bands of continuous lines.

Frequencies of various types of symmetry were tabulated and compared for each vessel category, for the total repertoire of designs and for the total number of designs. Bilateral symmetry was the predominant motion of repetition for finite designs (figures 7.16 and 7.17). Almost all of this motion occurs across a vertical axis. As for band patterns, vertical reflection, a combination of vertical reflection and horizontal reflection and a combination of rotation and horizontal reflection were the most frequent patterns of repetitive motion (figures 7.18 and 7.19).

Design structure and the variability of motif patterns

How does the design organization relate to the variation of motifs on the vessels? Does the variation in layout types and design zones affect the variability of the design motifs? In order to answer these questions, motifs were compared with design layouts. On the *puynu* and *yukupuynu*, specific motifs are associated with obligatory zones and these motifs do not occur in any other zone on these vessels nor on the *plato* or *tachu*. On the *yukupuynu*, the predominant motif associated with the obligatory zone (zone A; see figure 7.6) is the "lollipop motif" (figure 7.15(a), motif 1).

The motifs associated with the obligatory zone on the *puynu* (zone A; see figure 7.7) are more complicated. This zone contains one middle panel and is often[13] flanked by a smaller panel on each side of it. The middle panel *almost* always[14] contains a floral motif (figure 7.15(c), motif 20), but this motif has a great deal of variation. No two designs are exactly alike. Almost all of the variation, however, conforms to a series of underlying rules:

(1) The motif must be a plant with three stems. These stems must converge at the base of the plant, and may be either joined or separated.
(2) Individual leaves must be placed on the stems and they are often bilaterally symmetric along an oblique axis.
(3) Flowers may or may not be added to the upper end of each of the three stems on the plant. If they are added, they must be a single large dot or a large dot with smaller dots around it creating a pattern of radial symmetry.
(4) A leaf motif (or less frequently a leaf and a line) that is bilaterally symmetric along a vertical axis may also be placed beside the middle motif in the panel.

Those designs in the middle panel which do not conform to these principles are infrequent in the sample and can be partially explained as the incomplete application of them. One design (figure 7.15(c), motif 21) that appeared in this zone, for example, has no leaves and does not appear to be a plant. But, as a motif, it is still bilaterally symmetric. It appears that Rule 1 above was misapplied, and Rule 2 was not used at all. In two cases, the fern design (figure 7.15(c), motif 23) was used in the middle panel. This variant used a design for the middle panel which should have been used for the left and right panels. Rule 1 was again misapplied by not producing three stems. Rule 2 was applied properly, but Rules 3 and 4 were not used at all.

The flanking panels usually contain one fern-like motif (figure 7.15(c), motif 23) alone[15] or occasionally[16] in combination with another motif such as vertical lines[17] and/or another fern.[18] On rare occasions,[19] a vertical line or leaf is added to either side of the middle panel (figure 7.15(c), motif 22).

There are also rules for decorating the panels to the left and right of the middle

No.	Band Pattern	Finite Motif	Unit of Symmetry — Motif	Unit of Symmetry — Band	Motion — Motif (axis)	Motion — Band (axis)
1.	(band pattern)	•|	A B	Same	B(A)	VR(A+B)
2.	(band pattern)	a. | b.	a. — b. A	B A / B --- A	a. B(A) b. B(A)	VR(A+B)
3.	(band pattern)	a. | b.	a. — b. A	B A	a. B(A) b. B(A)	VR(A+B)
4.	(band pattern)	(motif)	B A --- C	Same	B(A)	HR(C)+ VR(A+B)
5.	(band pattern)	(motif)	B A	Same	B(A)	VR(A+B)
6.	••••••	•	X --- Y P	B A --- C	R(X+Y around P)	HR(C)+ VR(A+B)
7.	4 3 2 7 5 8 aole	None	None	None	None	None
8.	(band pattern)	a. b.	a. A b. A	A B	a. B(A) b. B(A)	VR(A+B)
9.	(band pattern)	4	4	Same	B(A)	VR(A+B)
10.	(band pattern)	a. b. 6a	a. 6a	B A --- C	a. R(X+Y around P) b. R(X+Y around P)	HR(C)+ VR(A+B)

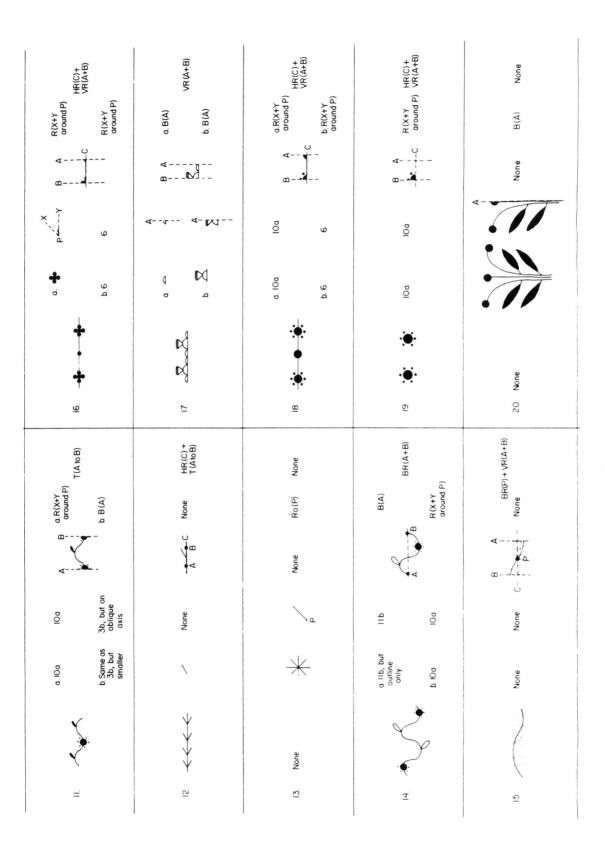

26. None — None — R(X+Y around P) — None

27. IIb — IIb — B(A) — SR(A to B along C)

28. None — None — None — None

29. None — None — None — None

30. IIb — IIb — B(A) — SR(A to B along C)

21. None — None — B(A) — None

22. None — None — B(A) — None

23. None — None — B(A) — None

24. 6a — 6a — R(X+Y around P) — HR(C)+ VR(A+B)

25. 6a — R(X+Y around P) — HR(C)+ VR(A+B)

Figure 7.15(a)–(c) The repertoire of all of the designs used on the *puynu, yukupuynu,* and *plato* shapes in the sample showing an analysis of the repetitive motions (symmetry) of the motif and band patterns. Each design is analyzed showing the fundamental unit of symmetry (the "unit of symmetry") for motif and band patterns and the motions of repetition necessary to generate them from this unit. The designs are numbered so that motifs, bands and their units of symmetry can be cross-referenced for simplicity (for example designs 1, 2, 6a and 9). Dotted lines identified with capital letters (A, B, C, X, and Y) refer to axes of symmetry while a capital "P" refers to a point. Motif symmetry types are bilateral (B), radial (R), and rotational (Ro). Band symmetry types are vertical reflection (VR), horizontal reflection (HR), translation (T), bifold rotation (BR), and slide reflection (SR). (See endnote 7 of chapter 7.) Letters in parentheses in symmetry columns refer to axes (A, B, C, X and Y) and points (P) at which units of symmetry in the previous columns are repeated. A plus ("+") is a simple concatenation symbol that means "and". Thus, for design no. 1, the motion indicated as "B(A)" in the motif column means "bilateral symmetry along axis 'A'." For the motion of band pattern for design no. 1, the designation "VR(A+B)" in the band column means "vertical reflection along axes 'A' and 'B'." Bands of solid color and straight or wavy lines were not included in this analysis (from Arnold 1983: 151–153, reprinted with permission of the UCLA Institute of Archaeology.

panel (figure 7.8). If these panels have designs placed in them, the following rules appear to govern their creation:

(1) The fern motif (figure 7.15(c), motif 23) must be placed in each panel.
(2) If additional designs (parallel lines or fern motifs) are added on each side, they must be bilaterally symmetric along a vertical axis passing through the center of each panel (figure 7.15(c), motif 23).
(3) Designs in each panel must be identical in content and symmetry.

Each panel is bilaterally symmetric along a vertical axis both with regard to the symmetry of motifs within them and with regard to the overall design composition of the panel. In allocating the designs in this zone, an axis of symmetry directly

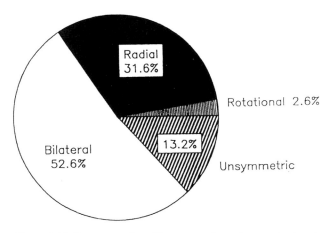

Figure 7.16 Summary of motif symmetry from the sample showing the percent of each motif symmetry type found in the total repertoire of motifs (N = 39).

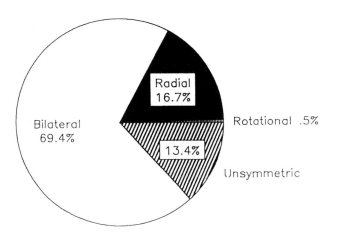

Figure 7.17 Summary of motif symmetry in the sample showing the percent of each motif symmetry type found in the total sample of motifs (N = 209).

opposite the handle bisects the zone into two halves. The zone and the designs within it are mirror images of one another across the axis. This same axis serves as an axis of bilateral symmetry for the floral motif in the middle panel of the zone. The obligatory zone on the *puynu* thus has only finite designs and these designs are characterized by only one symmetry pattern: bilateral symmetry.

Community patterns of design

After describing the design space and the symmetry patterns, it is now possible to derive the design correlates of the community (table 7.1). These correlates are the predominant decorative patterns of design in the sample and are believed to be community-wide design conventions.

The first such correlate involves surface treatment. Surface preparation, slip and paint colors tend to be consistently similar on each vessel shape. On the *puynu*, *yukupuynu*, and *plato*, potters utilize white painted design on a burnished red slip. The *tachu* has an unslipped, but burnished surface with white bands which are used as a base for red and/or black painted designs.

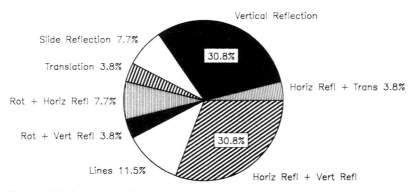

Figure 7.18 Summary of band symmetry in the sample showing the percent of each type of band symmetry found in the total repertoire of bands (N = 26).

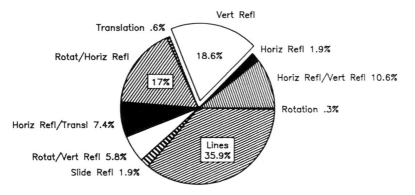

Figure 7.19 Summary of band symmetry in the sample showing percent of each type of band symmetry found in the total sample of bands (N = 312).

Table 7.1. *Summary of predominant design patterns in Quinua (the design correlates of the community)*

| | Vessel shape | | | |
Design pattern	*yukupuynu*	*puynu*	*tachu*	*plato*
Slip color	red	red	unslipped	red
Surface preparation	burnishing	burnishing	burnishing	burnishing
Paint color	white	white	white zone	white
Organization of design	type A[a]	type A[b]	—	type A[c]
Obligatory zones	zone A, lower border zone A[a]	middle panel zone A, lower border zone A[a]	all zones	zones A and B[c]
Design associated with particular zones	lollipop motif (zone A)	three-stemmed plant (middle panel, zone A)	three lines of red and/or black	—
Band symmetry	vertical reflection[d]	translation and horizontal reflection[e]	rotation and horizontal reflection[f]	horizontal reflection and vertical reflection[g]
Motif symmetry	bilateral[h]	bilateral[i]	—	—
Zones with least variability in designs and symmetry	zone A, lower border zone A[a]	zone A, lower border zone A[b]	—	—

[a] Patterns are keyed (with footnotes) to figures with quantitative support. For example, the evidence for this pattern comes from Figure 7.6.
[b] Figure 7.7.
[c] Figure 7.10.
[d] Figure 7.26.
[e] Figure 7.25.
[f] Figure 7.27.
[g] Figure 7.28.
[h] Figure 7.21
[i] Figure 7.20.

A second design correlate consists of the organization of design space on the vessels. Each vessel shape has a predominant organization of design space. On the *yukupuynu* and the *puynu*, the organization of the design space into a series of horizontal bands (layout type A) had a high frequency in the sample. The *plato* and the *tachu* also have a predominant pattern of design layout (layout type A), but the frequencies are not as high as the predominant patterns of the *yukupuynu* and the *puynu*.

A third community pattern of design consists of design zones which are always present (that is the "obligatory zones") on the most frequent spatial layouts for each vessel (table 7.1). On the *yukupuynu*, a wide band and its lower border always occur in layout type A on this shape. On the *puynu*, the middle panel (figure 7.8) and its lower border are always present even though the left and right panels of this zone are usually present as well. On the *plato*, there are also certain zones which always occur on each layout type, but because the predominant layout type is much less frequent than on the *yukupuynu* and *puynu*, they are not reiterated here.

A fourth community pattern consists of the co-occurrence of certain motifs with specific design zones. The least variation in design repertoire occurs in obligatory design zones which are those zones which occur on all vessels of a specific layout type. Conversely, the design repertoire for the optional zones is much greater. On the *puynu* shape, the obligatory zone is divided into three panels. The designs for each of these panels consist mainly of a floral motif and a fern motif and these designs are not placed in any other zone on the vessel. On the *yukupuynu*, the lollipop motif (figures 7.4 and 7.15(a), motif 1) occurs in only one zone (zone A). For the *tachu*, the three line band of red and/or black paint never occurs in these colors on any other vessel. Finally, although some designs are associated with particular design zones on the *plato*, there is so much variability in the design layouts that it is difficult to ascertain whether or not the designs in particular zones represent community patterns.

A fifth community pattern of design consists of high frequencies of certain types of motif symmetry. Bilateral symmetry (most often along a vertical axis) was the repetitive motion of the highest frequency in the total repertoire and the total sample of design motifs (figures 7.16 and 7.17). It occurs most often on the *puynu* (figure 7.20) and *yukupuynu* (figure 7.21) with the *plato* (figure 7.22) having relatively equal percentages of bilateral and radial symmetries. These patterns are highlighted when the frequencies of motif symmetry in the entire sample of motifs are plotted according to vessel shape (figure 7.23).

A sixth community pattern of design consists of specific patterns of band symmetry, but the patterns are not as frequent as the patterns of motif symmetry. Vertical reflection and a combination of vertical reflection and horizontal reflection provide the predominant motions in the formation of bands in the total repertoire of band patterns (figure 7.18). When the frequencies of the symmetry patterns are tabulated according to the total sample of bands present (figure 7.19), these patterns change slightly; vertical reflection and a combination of rotation and horizontal reflection are the predominant type of repetitive motion.

There is, however, a great deal of variation in the motions used in the formation of band patterns. When these patterns are plotted by vessel shape, a different picture emerges (figure 7.24) and each shape has a different pattern of band symmetry. A combination of horizontal reflection and translation was the predominant motion on the *puynu* (figure 7.25) while vertical reflection was the predominant motion on the *yukupuynu* (figure 7.26). Rotation and horizontal reflection predominated on the *tachu* (figure 7.27). A combination of horizontal reflection and vertical

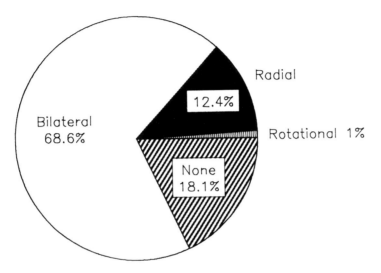

Figure 7.20 Frequency (in percent) of motif symmetry classes on the *puynu* for layout type A (N = 105). Layout type B (see figure 7.6) has no motif symmetry; all designs are bands.

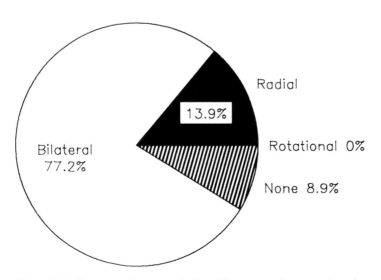

Figure 7.21 Frequency (in percent) of motif symmetry classes on the *yukupuynu* for layout type A (N = 79). The second layout type for this shape (layout type B) has no motif symmetry.

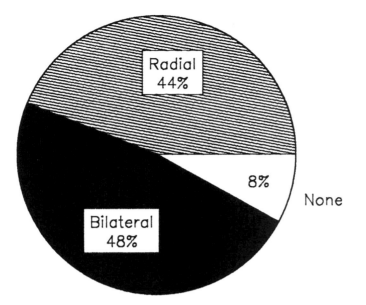

Figure 7.22 Frequency of motif symmetry types on the *plato* based on the total number of motifs (N = 25).

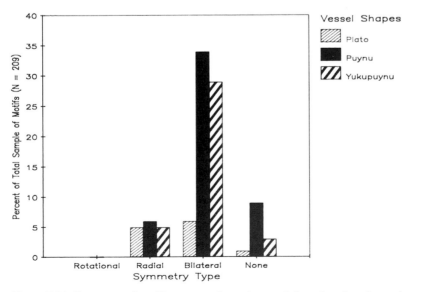

Figure 7.23 Frequency of motif symmetry classes by vessel shape based on the total sample of all motifs. The designs with no motif symmetry (that is those in the "None" category in the graph) are band patterns without motif symmetry and include straight lines and bands of solid color. The designs on the *tachu* have no motif symmetry and thus are not included on the graph.

reflection was the predominant band motion on the *plato* (figure 7.28), but five other symmetry patterns had roughly equal frequencies (around 10 percent each). When the frequencies of band symmetries are analyzed by single (rather than compound) motion, vertical reflection and horizontal reflection predominate (figure 7.29).

A final community pattern consists of the location of the design variability on the

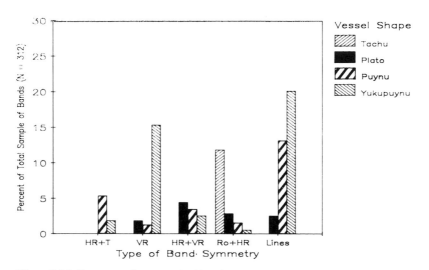

Figure 7.24 Frequency (in percent) of band symmetry types by vessel shape. For simplicity, frequencies of any symmetry type of less than 3 percent of the sample were not graphed. The "lines" category includes bands of straight lines and those of solid color. Band symmetry that is a combination of two basic symmetry types is indicated by a "+" (which means "and" or "combination of"). These types are abbreviated according to the following key: HR is horizontal reflection, T is translation, VR is vertical reflection, and Ro is rotation.

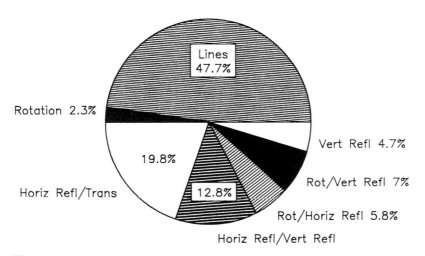

Figure 7.25 Frequency of band symmetry types on the *puynu* (all layout types) based on the total percent of bands used on the vessel (N = 86).

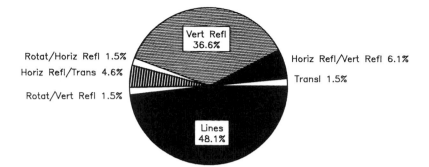

Figure 7.26 Frequency of band symmetry types on the *yukupuynu* (both layout types) based on the total number of bands (N = 131) used on this vessel in the sample.

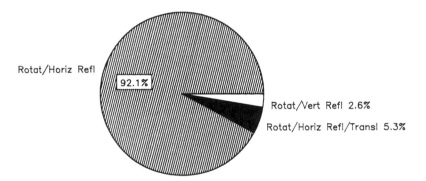

Figure 7.27 Frequency of band symmetry types on the *tachu* for all layout types based on the total number of bands (N = 38) used on this vessel in the sample.

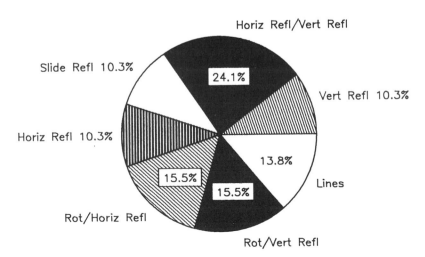

Figure 7.28 Frequency of band symmetry types on the *plato* for all layout types based on the total number of bands (N = 58) used on this vessel in the sample.

vessels. Does variation occur equally in all of the spatial units of the design like layout types and design zones? Or, are there spatial areas that have less variation than others? The design data shows that most of the variability in the sample occurs outside of the units of design space with the highest frequencies. This is contrary to expectation because one would expect more variability in the more frequent patterns in the sample. There are two kinds of co-occurrence of variability in the design sample.

First, the most frequent symmetry classes tend to co-occur with the most frequent layout types and conversely, infrequent symmetry classes are associated with infrequent design layouts. When the frequencies of motif symmetry are plotted with layout types, infrequent layout types are associated with non-typical motif symmetry. For the *puynu* and *yukupuynu*, the most frequent layout type (type A) is associated with bilateral symmetry in motif patterns (figures 7.20 and 7.21), while the less frequent layout type (type B) has only bands and thus no motifs, nor motif symmetry. On the *plato*, the most frequent layout type is associated with radial symmetry, rather than bilateral symmetry in the total sample of motifs (figure 7.30).

When band symmetry is plotted with the layout types, vertical reflection is associated with the high frequency layout type (layout type A) on the *yukupuynu* (figure 7.31), and a combination of horizontal reflection and translation is associated with the high frequency layout type (layout type A) on the *puynu* (figure 7.32). A totally opposite pattern occurs on the *plato* with greater variability in band symmetry in the most frequent design layouts than in the less frequent layouts. The most frequent layout type on the *plato* (layout type A) has no clear dominant repetitive motion (figure 7.33).

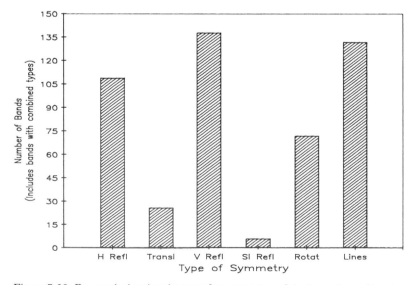

Figure 7.29 Bar graph showing the most frequent types of single motions of band symmetry patterns. Raw frequencies (rather than percentages) were used because one band may consist of two motions and the same band would have to be counted twice. The "lines" category consists of bands of straight lines or solid color.

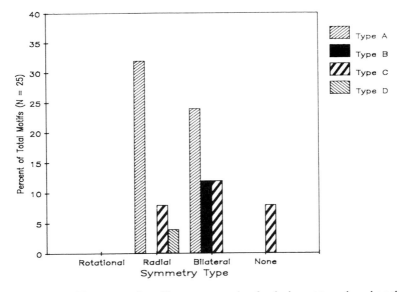

Figure 7.30 Frequency of motif symmetry on the *plato* by layout types based on the percent of total motifs (N = 25) used on this vessel.

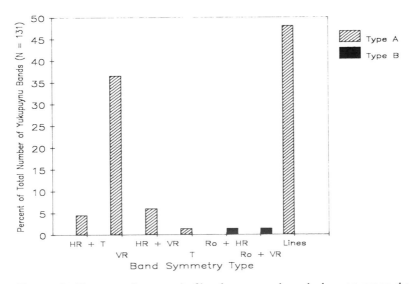

Figure 7.31 Frequency (in percent) of band symmetry classes by layout types on the *yukupuynu* based on the number of bands used on that vessel. Abbreviations refer to combinations of the basic symmetry types according to the following key: HR is horizontal reflection, T is translation, VR is vertical reflection, and Ro is rotation.

A different kind of band symmetry is present on the *tachu* perhaps because the vessels consist of a different painting scheme than the *puynu, yukupuynu* and *plato*. The *tachu* design has no motifs, only band patterns. Nevertheless, less variation in symmetry pattern still co-occurs with the most frequent layout type on the *tachu* (figure 7.34).

The co-occurrence of less variability of symmetry classes with more frequent layout types suggests that community patterns of band symmetry, like motif

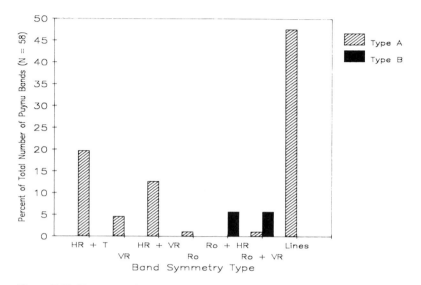

Figure 7.32 Frequency (in percent) of band symmetry classes by layout types on the *puynu* based on the total number of bands used on that vessel. For key to abbreviations see figure 7.31.

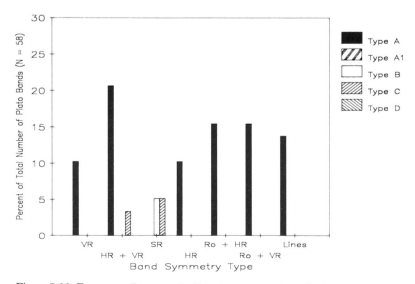

Figure 7.33 Frequency (in percent) of band symmetry classes by layout types on the *plato* based on the total numbers of bands used on that vessel. HR is horizontal reflection, T is translation, VR is vertical reflection, SR is slide reflection and Ro is rotation.

symmetry, are tied to definite layout types. Variation from these high frequency layout types also involves a variation from the associated symmetry class.

Second, there is a tendency toward greater variability in designs and symmetry classes in the optional zones on a vessel than in the obligatory zones. The variation in symmetry occurs with both motif and band patterns and is related to the variability of the designs in the optional zones. When the number of designs in the optional and obligatory zones are compared (figure 7.35), there is less variation in the number of designs in the obligatory zones on the *puynu* and *yukupuynu* than on the other vessels. On the *plato*, however, the pattern is reversed with greater variation in the obligatory zones than in the optional zones. This pattern may be related to the greater variety of *plato* layout types. For motif symmetry (figure 7.36), only the *puynu* has more variation in the optional zones than the obligatory zones and the *plato* has the reverse pattern. The *yukupuynu* has an equal number of types of motif symmetry in each type of zone. The *tachu* has no motifs, only band symmetry. For band symmetry, both the *puynu* and *yukupuynu* show more variability in the optional design zones than the obligatory design zones (figure 7.37). There are no band patterns in the optional zones on the *plato* and there are no optional zones on the *tachu*.

A summary of design variability

While the community patterns of design tend to have consistently high frequencies in the sample, these frequencies do not approach one hundred percent and there is still great variability in the design patterns. Variability outside these community patterns, however, is far greater than that within them; one kind of variability

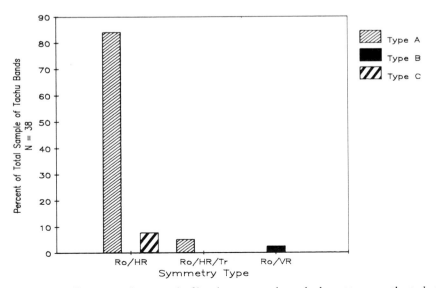

Figure 7.34 Frequency (in percent) of band symmetry classes by layout types on the *tachu* based on the total number of bands used on that vessel. The band symmetry motions use combinations (indicated here by "/" for economy of space) of basic symmetry types according to the following key: Ro is rotational symmetry, HR is horizontal reflection, Tr is translation and VR is vertical reflection.

co-occurs with other kinds of variability. Some kinds of this variability co-occur with different vessel shapes; other kinds of variability co-occur with different layout types and non-obligatory design zones. Most remarkable is the fact that the most frequently occurring design zones in the sample tend to have the least variability of motif and symmetry patterns while the less frequent design zones tend to have the most variability.

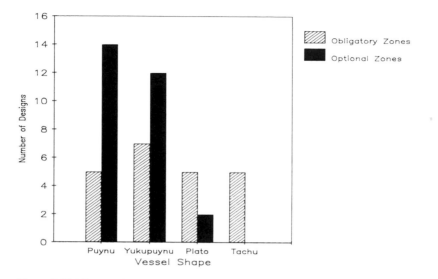

Figure 7.35 The number of different designs (bands/motifs/lines) in the obligatory zones on each vessel shape compared with those in the optional zones. The *tachu* has no optional design zones.

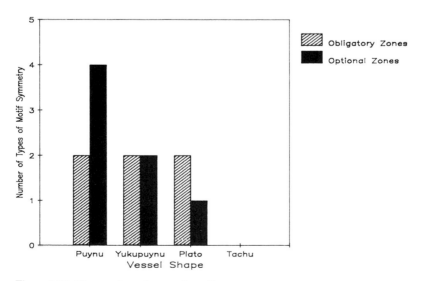

Figure 7.36 The number of types of motif symmetry in the obligatory zones on each vessel shape compared with those in the optional zones. (The *tachu* has no optional design zones. *Tachu* designs are bands and thus have no motif symmetry.)

Most of the variability in the sample generally occurs within the community-defined ways of allocating decorative space, but outside of the high frequency design zones, motifs and symmetry classes. For example, infrequent design layouts are associated with infrequent symmetry classes. When the frequencies of motif symmetry classes are plotted with different layout types, infrequent layout types are associated with infrequent classes of motif symmetry. In a similar way, there is a tendency toward less variation in designs and their symmetry classes in those design zones which always occur on a particular shape (obligatory zones) than on those which are not always present (optional zones). This variation occurs with both motif and band patterns and is related to the variability of the designs in the optional zones.

Other pottery-making communities

In order to further demonstrate the co-occurrence of stylistic correlates with a particular social unit, one should compare the design correlates of the community of potters in Quinua with pottery made in other communities in the valley. Do these correlates just apply to Quinua or do they represent a social and spatial unit larger than the local community of potters defined here? Five other communities in the Ayacucho Valley produce pottery. Although this pottery was not studied as intensively as that from Quinua, some general comparisons are possible.

Some potters live in the *barrio* of Santa Ana within the city of Ayacucho (see figure 3.4).[20] Six potters (including both males and females) practiced the craft in four households and two visits were made to three of these households. The first visit occurred during the rainy season in mid-February. Pottery production was a part-time activity that was strongly affected by the limiting factors of adverse weather and scheduling conflicts with subsistence activities. No pottery was being made at the

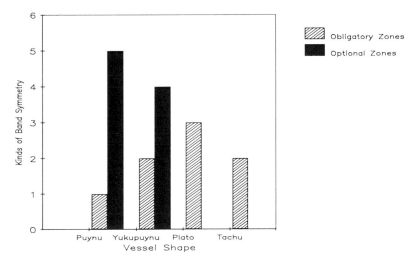

Figure 7.37 The number of types of band symmetry in the obligatory zones of each vessel shape compared with those in the optional zones. The *tachu* has no optional design zones.

time, but potters said that they would begin production in April when the rainy season ended. Returning in May in hopes of observing the craft in progress revealed that potters were still not making pots because the harvest was still underway and pottery making would not begin until it was completed.

Santa Ana potters said that they use a mixture of sand and two kinds of clay (black and red) to make pottery. One kind of clay came from a location called Marcapata near the hamlet of Rancha along the road to the coastal city of Pisco. Potters travel to this source themselves, obtaining the clay 3 to 5 meters inside a small mine. They pay either by the load (US $0.44) or a one-time fee (US $21.75) for the right to mine the clay. The other clay comes from a source called Cabrapata located on a mountain high above the *barrio*. The two clays are ground and then mixed with sand to form the paste.

Ayacucho potters make pottery on a forming device that is identical to that used in Quinua (see figure 5.7) and produce large jars for maize beer, flower pots (*maseteros*), cooking pots, wash basins, pitchers and water-carrying jars (*tumins*). Three potters have abandoned making large vessels, however, and have begun to make miniature vessels for tourists. Potters fire their vessels in the open air inside a low wall (20–30 centimeters high) that is arranged in a circle and use any combustible substance (such as cow dung) for fuel.

No more than a few vessels were observed in Santa Ana at the time of my visit. Although most shapes had the same Quechua and Spanish gloss as the Quinua shapes, none were decorated. It was thus impossible to precisely identify the similarities or differences between the undecorated Ayacucho shapes and the undecorated Quinua shapes. The miniature pots made there, however, were completely different from Quinua vessels because no miniature pots were made in Quinua in 1967. The main similarity between Quinua and Ayacucho pottery was the forming technology and the main differences were the resource locations and the firing and paste preparation techniques.

Potters are also located in the community of Ticllas and in the nearby hamlet of Atacocha on the western edge of the valley directly north of the city of Ayacucho (see figure 3.4). Potters practice their craft primarily in June and July after the harvest is completed, but Ticllas pottery was observed for sale in the Ayacucho market on two occasions in May. Potters also are said to make and sell their pottery whenever they need to obtain grain for food. Potters use a micaceous clay to produce cooking vessels with no decoration (figure 7.38) and are said to use a turn-table device for fabrication like that used in Quinua and in Santa Ana. Liquid-carrying vessels (*porongos*) are also reportedly made in Ticllas, but only the cooking pots were observed in the Ayacucho market. Vessels are fired in the open with a special kind of wood.

Since the Ticllas pottery is undecorated, it is distinct from the decorated pottery made in Quinua. Since no cooking pottery was made in Quinua while I was there, comparisons of cooking pottery from Quinua and that of Ticllas were not possible. Superficially, at least, the cooking vessels from each community appear to be identical.

Pottery-making households also occur northwest of the village of Luricocha in the northern part of the Ayacucho Valley (see figure 3.4). Informants report as many as five or six hamlets produce pottery in this area. A visit to two of these hamlets confirmed that pottery is made at least in one hamlet (Llanza) located 3 kilometers northwest of Luricocha and another (Pampay) located 4 kilometers northwest. Other pottery-making hamlets reportedly occur in the mountains above Luricocha (San Pedro de Curis, Ukana, Allpanqa [Champana]) and another is said to occur near the Rio Cachi below the village (Cangalla). Pottery made in Allpanqa reportedly consisted of cooking vessels (*ollas*), toasting vessels, bowls (*platos*), water-carrying vessels (*porongos*), and *tinaqas*.

Three potters were identified in the hamlet of Pampay (see figure 3.4). Ceramics are produced in the latter part of May after the harvest is completed and production continues through June and July. Potters obtain a clay from three mines in a location called Allpaniuq[21] in the nearby mountains which requires no tempering. They produce utilitarian vessels in relatively few shape categories[22] with limited plastic decoration (figure 7.39).

Although not all the shapes produced in Pampay were observed, only decorated *tinaqas* were observed and decorative techniques consisted of stamping. Decoration is placed above the handles around the circumference of the vessel and consists of pointed marks or stamping with the end of a reed. The rim on some vessels was impressed diagonally with the side of a small rounded object in a closely-spaced sequence. Like those made in Quinua, *tinaqas* in Pampay and Llanza had two

Figure 7.38 Ticllas cooking pots being sold in the Ayacucho market. These cooking pots appear to be indistinguishable from those made and used in Quinua.

handles on opposite sides of the vessel. Some vessels also had lugs consisting of a 5 centimeter strip of clay placed in a semi-circular position in the same horizontal plane as the handles, but at right angles to them.

Cooking pots made in Pampay were much like Quinua cooking vessels and had either two or four handles attached from the rim to the upper body. Some cooking vessels had three handles placed equidistantly around the vessel.[23]

Pampay potters do not fire their pottery using a kiln, but dig a hole in the ground that is 10–15 centimeters deep and a meter in diameter. They use dried cow dung as fuel, but it is not separated from the pottery as in the Quinua kilns, but is piled on top of the vessels before firing.

The pottery made in the Luricocha area was very different from that made in Quinua. Of the few vessels observed, *tinaqas* were predominant, but their shape was slightly different than those from Quinua. Quinua *tinaqas* tended to have straight sides which tilt inward from the point of greatest circumference toward the rim. Luricocha *tinaqas*, however, have a more rounded upper body. Unlike Quinua vessels, Luricocha vessels are decorated with a stamping technique on the rim and upper body. Motifs tend to be circular and placed around the upper body of the vessel in a band which is characterized by a combination of vertical and horizontal reflection.

Figure 7.39 A *tinaqa* made in the hamlet of Pampay near the village of Luricocha (see map in figure 3.4). Pottery from this hamlet has stamped decoration above the shoulder of the pot unlike the painted decoration of Quinua pottery. The scale is in centimeters.

Pottery is also made in the community of Huayhuas southeast of Huanta (see figure 3.4). Potters reportedly live in the nucleated settlement rather than in rural hamlets and produce exclusively utilitarian ware with limited plastic or painted decoration (figures 7.40 and 7.41). Huayhuas was not visited, but O'Neale (1977) visited the community in the 1940s and has described pottery production there. Some of the potters reportedly fire their pottery using kilns while others fire in the

Figure 7.40 A Huayhuas *canasta* in the Ayacucho market. Huayhuas potters generally fabricate different shapes, use wider lines for different motifs, and organize their designs in a different design structure from Quinua potters even though both communities decorate their pots using a white-on-red painting scheme. The scale is in centimeters.

Figure 7.41 Huayhuas flower pots (*floreros*) being sold in the Ayacucho market. The scale is in centimeters.

open with cattle dung. Pottery from Huayhuas is sold in Ayacucho, Huanta and Huamanguilla. Descriptions of Huayhuas pottery elaborated below are based on observations of the vessels sold in Ayacucho (see table 6.2).

The vessel shapes produced in Huayhuas tend to be different from those made in Quinua. Huayhuas produces some of the same repertoire of vessels that Quinua potters can fabricate,[24] but Quinua potters tend to produce few, if any, of the vessels that Huayhuas potters produce. Huayhuas potters make pitchers (*jara*), *tinaqas*, ceramic toasters (*tuqtu*), basins (*mediano*), flower pots (*florero*, figure 7.41), sugar bowls (*azugueros*), chamber pots (*vasinika*) and basket-shaped pots (*canasta*, figure 7.40). Of these shapes, however, Quinua potters make only pitchers, chamber pots and *tinaqas*.

Plastic decoration on Huayhuas vessels only occurs on toasters (*tuqtu*) and consists of three parallel incised lines around the circumference of the vessel about one centimeter below the rim. On a few vessels, the design consisted of two parallel lines with a wavy line in between them. Vessels that did not have these incised lines were either red-slipped or had the rim painted red.

Tumins from Huayhuas are largely undecorated, but some potters produce red-slipped vessels with white decoration. While Quinua potters also produce a white-on-red pottery, Huayhuas pottery is different from Quinua pottery in a number of ways. The vessels painted in Huayhuas are not the same as those painted in Quinua. In Huayhuas, painted vessels include *tinaqas*, flower pots (*florero*), toasters (*tuqtu*), small cooking pots (*manka*), sugar bowls (*azugueros*) and basket-shaped pots (*canasta*, see figure 7.40). Of these vessels, only toasters, sugar bowls, and basket pots were not made in Quinua, and Quinua potters paint only *tinaqas*, pitchers and flower pots. Nevertheless, the number of shapes painted in Quinua was greater than those painted in Huayhuas (see chapter 5).

Another difference between the Quinua and Huayhuas vessels involves slipping patterns. Huayhuas potters do not always place a red slip on their decorated vessels. When they do, the slip may be sloppily applied, may not be burnished, or it may only occur inside and outside the rim of the vessel (for example on some toasters, *tumins*, flower pots, small cooking pots and pitchers). In Quinua, on the other hand, the red slip is almost always neatly applied, burnished and covers the entire vessel. Sometimes the Huayhuas vessels (like pitcher, *tinaqa*, chamber pot) may have a band of white paint applied around the neck of the vessel.

The line width of the white decoration in Huayhuas is greater than that in Quinua (compare figures 7.40 and 7.41 with figures 7.1, 7.2 and 7.5). Huayhuas potters use a brush that creates a line width of one half to one centimeter, while Quinua potters use a feather or small brush which creates a line less than one quarter centimeter (figures 7.3–7.5). In contrast to Quinua where potters elaborately subdivide the field of decoration into smaller zones (see figures 7.6–7.10), the decorative field on most Huayhuas pottery consists of only one zone (figure 7.41). On the *canasta* shape from Huayhuas, however, there were two vessels that had subdivisions of the decorative field into smaller zones (figure 7.40), but these were rare in the sample. In comparison to the Quinua vessels, Huayhuas vessels have greater variability in the composition of the design fields with no duplicates in the designs in the small number of vessels examined (figure 7.41). The motifs from Quinua (figures 7.15(a)–(c)) also tend to be different than the motifs from Huayhuas (figure 7.42) although some similarity exists. Finally, motif and band symmetry patterns were similar to Quinua with bilateral symmetry as the predominant motif symmetry pattern (figure 7.43), and vertical reflection as the predominant pattern of band symmetry (figure 7.44). Unlike Quinua, however, there was no co-variation of vessel shape, design zones or symmetry pattern (figures 7.45 and 7.46).

In summary, the most striking characteristics of Huayhuas pottery in comparison to Quinua pottery were its lack of care and precision in slipping and painting, the greater line width of its designs and its greater design variability. There was also a lack of association between specific shapes and patterns of slipping, painting, designs, and types of symmetry. These observations suggested that the potters who produced the vessels were engaging in considerable experimentation with a range of variability that was much greater than that in Quinua.

From the incomplete data from other communities of potters in the valley, it appears that there are both similarities and differences between the pottery made in these communities and that of Quinua. Great differences exist between the decorated pottery of Quinua and that from other communities and it appears that the specific design correlates for the community of potters in Quinua are indeed unique.

When one focuses on the undecorated pottery, however, the picture is less clear. The production of certain undecorated shapes[25] is widespread in the valley and the design correlates of each producing community for these vessels are difficult, if not impossible, to identify.

Summary of the community patterns

Quinua potters produce a wide variety of ceramics with a complex technology which is unique within the Ayacucho Valley. In contrast to the potters in the *barrio* of Santa Ana in the city of Ayacucho and the potters in Huayhuas, Luricocha and Ticllas, Quinua potters utilize two paste types to make many more vessel shapes than any of the other potters in the valley. One paste is untempered and used for undecorated pottery and the other is tempered and used to make the decorated pottery. Quinua potters use a variety of vessel-forming techniques (modeling, modified coiling and molding) to produce a repertoire of approximately forty shapes which originally were used for utilitarian, decorative and ceremonial purposes. They also utilize more decorative techniques than any of the other potters in the valley. They decorate their pottery in three painting schemes. Each of these schemes occurs on certain vessel shapes and each utilizes its own paint, burnish and slip combinations. Furthermore,

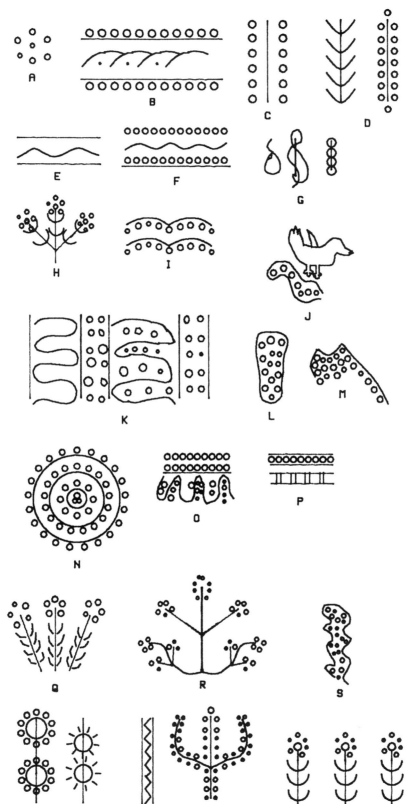

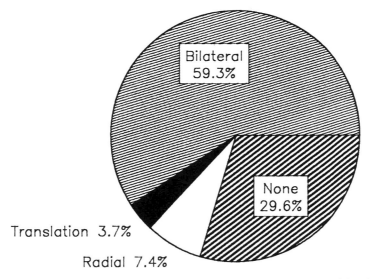

Figure 7.43 The frequencies of motif symmetry used on four shapes of Huayhuas pottery (N = 27).

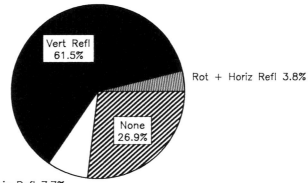

Figure 7.44 Frequencies of band symmetry used on four shapes of pottery made in Huayhuas (N = 26 because a photograph of one vessel used in figure 7.43 was not clearly visible).

Figure 7.42 (*opposite*) Repertoire of white designs painted on Huayhuas vessels being sold in the Ayacucho market. Although a few of these designs are similar to Quinua designs (for example motifs and bands in items A, B, E, T and U), most of these designs are different from those used in Quinua (see figure 7.15(a)–(c)). Even the ones that are similar are painted with greater line widths, and are placed in a different design structure from Quinua designs.

Quinua potters use a variety of plastic techniques for decoration like molding, modeling and stamping.

Finally, the technology and decoration of Quinua pottery is not only unique in the Basin, but the community of potters in Quinua has a definite set of objective design correlates which are unique to it (table 7.1):

(1) Surface preparation and slip and paint colors tend to be consistently similar on each vessel shape.
(2) Certain ways of allocating and sub-dividing the design space on each vessel shape have a very high frequency in the sample.
(3) There are certain design zones which are always present within the predominant way of allocating design space on each vessel.
(4) Certain designs are always associated with the obligatory design zones on each shape.
(5) High frequencies of bilateral symmetry are used to form the motifs in the design. Frequencies of band symmetry are much lower and do not reveal a predominant pattern as pronounced as the bilateral symmetry for the motifs. Vertical reflection and a combination of vertical and horizontal reflection are the most frequent types of motion used in forming the bands in the total repertoire of band designs. For the total sample of band designs, however, the predominant patterns are vertical reflection and a combination of rotation and horizontal reflection.

When these correlates are examined relative to each of the different painting schemes used in Quinua, a more complex picture emerges. Each of these schemes occurs on certain vessel shapes and each has its own set of designs and paint, burnish, and slip combinations. Furthermore, each vessel shape in each scheme generally has more than one layout of design space. These layouts utilize a variety of design zones and often have a wide range of designs and symmetry classes.

The design correlates of Quinua potters are thus not so much in the design itself or its elements, but rather in its structure. The community design patterns do not just occur in a highly restricted repertoire of designs, but rather are manifested in almost all levels of design structure from the layout of the design field and its subdivision into zones to the use of motif and band symmetry. These results provide empirical support for the conclusion of Hardin (Friedrich 1970) who found that the patterns of interaction in a Tarascan community of potters did not occur in the design elements or in the motifs, but rather in the design structure. Washburn's (1990) work with Bakuba textiles in Zaire has also shown that symmetry used by each ethnic subgroup of the Bakuba shows a common pattern.

The community of potters thus is not only the unit of adaptation and evolution, but it has definite technological and design correlates in the ceramics themselves. These correlates are unique to the community of Quinua and are different or non-existent in other communities in the valley.

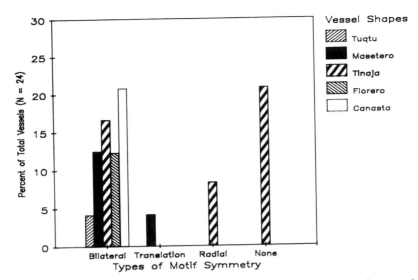

Figure 7.45 Frequencies of vessels painted with each motif symmetry type in a sample of Huayhuas pottery. Only one motif symmetry type occurs on each vessel.

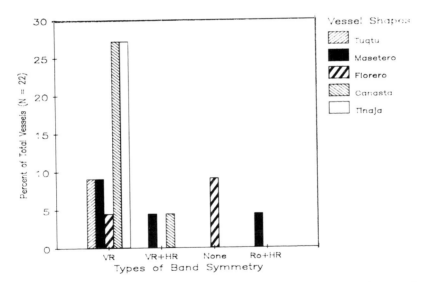

Figure 7.46 Frequencies of vessels painted with each band symmetry type in a sample of Huayhuas pottery. One band symmetry type occurs on each vessel. VR is vertical reflection, HR is horizontal reflection, and Ro is rotation.

8

Design and society

This work has taken an ecological approach to ceramic production and utilized the population of potters as the unit of adaptation. So far, this population and its ceramic products have been related to the environment, and to the technology, social organization and to a lesser extent, the beliefs of Quinua. In the previous chapter, the unit of adaptation became the unit of design analysis and a set of design features common to the population were derived. These design "correlates" consisted of the predominant choices that potters made in decorating their pottery. It was argued that these correlates are unique to Quinua and are different from the decoration on pottery produced elsewhere in the valley.

While an ecological approach to ceramics must focus on the relationship of potters and their products to society and the environment, it should also examine the relationship of ceramic design to the society. This chapter thus explores how the design "correlates" derived in the last chapter relate to the social behavior in the community.

Models of style and Quinua ceramic design

The concern with relating ceramic design to the society that produced it corresponds to some of the concerns with the concept of style in archaeology. Discussions of style have experienced a resurgence in recent years with debate considering whether "style" and "function" are separate, whether stylistic units have social significance and whether styles contain messages deliberately encoded by the producer.[1]

One of the key issues in the study of style concerns the relationship of style to the society which produced it. The pioneering work of Deetz (1965), Longacre (1970), and Hill (1970) showed the kind of social inferences that could be made from the analyses of ceramic design. In the intervening years since these seminal studies were published, archaeologists have proposed several models relating ceramic style to social behavior: the transmission model, the interaction model and the "style is symbol" model.

The first of these models involves the transmission of style from generation to generation following the society's pattern of descent and post-nuptial residence.[2] Allen and Richardson (1971), however, have shown that archaeologists' views of descent and residence are founded upon "ideal" statements of what kin-based patterns should be rather than what they actually are. This model also has been challenged by ethnoarchaeological research. Studies among the Hopi have demonstrated that learning patterns do not correspond to a single social structural pattern such as descent, family or clan.[3] Ethnographic research in Ticul, Yucatan, on the other hand, has produced a contrary result. When the actual residence locations of potters were used in the analysis of learning patterns, a model based on patrilineal land inheritance and virilocal post-nuptial residence accounted for most of the learning of the craft (Arnold 1989). Variations from this pattern can be explained by a more comprehensive model which includes the behavioral rules governing household composition. Since learning of the craft always occurs in a household, one can learn to make pots from any member of the household even though most potters learned from their fathers. Learning pottery making in Ticul thus is not just the product of an inheritance and post-nuptial residence pattern, but is the result of behavioral rules (and culturally acceptable variants of those rules) which govern household composition.

How does the transmission model relate to the Quinua data? Quinua potters are men and learn to make pottery from their fathers. Designs are passed down patrilineally and this pattern is reinforced by a virilocal post-nuptial residence pattern. Even though a potter's wife may also paint pottery, the potter himself exerts complete control over the designs that his wife uses. If a potter's wife knows nothing about painting, then her husband teaches her to paint his designs. If, on the other hand, a potter's wife is the daughter of a potter and already knows how to decorate pottery, then her husband may allow her to paint her own designs for a short time after marriage. If her husband likes the designs, he may allow her to continue to use them. If, however, her husband does not like her designs, he will teach her to paint his own designs so that hers will not embarrass him. He does not want others to think that he is a new and inexperienced potter.

How does this explanation relate to the design correlates of the population of Quinua potters? Even though this explanation accounts for the transmission of the craft from generation to generation and comes from the potters themselves, it does not explain the existence of design correlates in the community. It does help understand the relationship of design to the society, but it only explains patterning below the level of the community.

A second model relating ceramic design and society is the interaction model.[4] This model posits that the pattern and intensity of potters' social interaction is responsible for the similarity of the design structure in a community rather than the design elements.[5] Elements do not reflect this interaction in the same way, but rather appear to diffuse through a community quickly with very little interaction (Friedrich 1970).

How does the interaction model contribute to understanding the relationship of design to society in Quinua? This model suggests that the community design correlates are a product of the social interaction of the population of potters. Quinua potters all live within the District of Quinua in the *barrio* of Lurinsayuq. Although most of the potters are dispersed in the rural hamlets of the *barrio*, they are tied together politically, socially and spatially. Even the most distant potters interact with others at least several times a year during the rituals surrounding the cleaning of the irrigation canals, the fiesta for the Virgin of Carmen (p. 129), and the *fiesta* for the patron saint of the community (the Virgin of Cocharcas). Furthermore, potters come to the village for other religious observances, to conduct business at the district offices, to attend the weekly market, and to make purchases at village stores. Potters may not verbally interact about their craft during these social, political and economic events, but they may see the work of other potters and may be influenced by it. Furthermore, some marriages occur between potters, and the bilateral kin group (that is the *ayllu*, see chapter 2) that results from such intermarriages provides kin-based interaction that extends learning experiences beyond that gained from one's father.

There is a greater degree of social interaction among Quinua potters than between Quinua potters and other potters in the valley. Interaction with potters elsewhere is minimal (if it exists at all) because there is no social unit and associated activities that bring disparate populations of potters in the valley together for interaction. Contact with other potters occurs only if Quinua potters see the wares from other communities in local markets. Since women sell the pottery and the men control the designs on the vessels, no significant influence is likely between the male potters of Quinua and pottery from elsewhere. This explanation partially accounts for the differences between the Quinua design correlates and the ceramic decoration from elsewhere in the Ayacucho Valley.

Seeing the Quinua design correlates as simply the product of learning in a patrilineal line, post-nuptial residence rules and patterns of social interaction, however, precludes finding relationships with the rest of the cultural system. How else do the design correlates of the population of potters relate to social patterns in the community? Why do Quinua potters choose some designs rather than others?

These questions bring us to the third model relating style and society, the "style is symbol" (or "information transfer") model.[6] This model posits that style serves as a symbol of some other dimension of the society and that this meaning has been deliberately encoded into the style. In this model, style is also seen as a channel of information that flows between individuals in the society and serves to identify group affiliation.[7]

How does the "style is symbol" model relate to Quinua ceramic design? If all of the aspects of design deliberately encoded social information, one could presumably ask Quinua potters the messages that they encoded in their designs. Unfortunately, this approach was not possible. While some potters provided information about the meaning of some of the more realistic motifs that they painted such as maize, a flower, a rose, or eucalyptus, potters were not asked to provide detailed meanings for their designs.[8] The main reason for this methodological oversight was that the "style is symbol" group of models began about ten years after field research in Quinua was completed (see the preface). Even if potters could have been asked about the meaning of their designs, my lack of facility in Quechua and potters' limited knowledge of Spanish would have severely limited the amount and quality of the data collected. Even if it were possible to ask potters about their designs, there is serious doubt whether potters could explain the meaning and underlying structure of all the designs. There are several reasons for this, but humans, in general, are often not aware of the meaning of their own behavior whether that behavior concerns "style" or not.

These models do not explain one very important fact about Quinua ceramic design: its great variability (see chapter 7). While design correlates of the community appear to represent general patterns in the community, there is also a great amount of design variability even in the four vessels described here.

How are the design correlates maintained in light of so much variability? The answer to this question lies in the aesthetic standards of the population which provide a selective force for the surface structure of the design. This selective force is related to the acceptability of the design and consists of the principles which are used to evaluate it. These principles were not explicit, but expressed generally in negative form; vessels which were inappropriately painted were considered to be "ugly."

In order to identify the aesthetic principles which were violated by vessels judged to be "ugly," the designs on these vessels were analyzed to isolate those features which might be the standard against which pottery design was evaluated.

One set of "ugly" vessels were identified by an informant in the Quinua Sunday market. These vessels were *puynus* and *yukupuynus* which were decorated with layout type B (figures 7.6 and 7.7). Although the reason for the "ugliness" was not provided, observation suggested that several factors may have been responsible for this judgment. First, although these vessels conformed to the basic white-on-red painting scheme, they did not conform to any of the high frequency patterns of design layout, motifs, bands, motif symmetry and band symmetry used on these shapes. Rather, the vessels were painted with designs and a design configuration similar to those used on *tachus* that were decorated with the black-and-red-on-white painting scheme (see p. 100). *Puynus* and *yukupuynus* painted with the white-on-red scheme have horizontal bands around the vessel. Within this configuration is a wide, dominant zone which contains specific motifs. On both shapes, bilateral symmetry tends to be the predominant symmetry pattern for motifs in this zone (figures 7.20 and 7.21). Vertical reflection also tends to be the repetitive pattern for bands on the *yukupuynu* (figures 7.24 and 7.25) and vertical reflection and translation tends to be the predominant pattern of band for the *puynu* (figures 7.24 and 7.25). The "ugly" vessels, however, did not utilize any of these patterns. Rather, they were painted with a different design organization, had no motif symmetry, and used a combination of rotation and vertical reflection, and rotation and horizontal reflection to produce the band designs. None of these patterns occur generally on other *puynus* and *yukupuynus*. Finally, the "ugly" vessels were painted sloppily with careless application of both the slip and designs.

Two other vessels judged to be "ugly" were observed in Quinua stores. These vessels were pitchers (*puynus*) decorated with red and black lines on an unslipped, but burnished body. The designs themselves were identical to those that occurred on other *puynus* in the white-on-red color scheme except that the red slip had been omitted and the designs had been applied with red and black paint rather than white paint. The resulting vessel was a hybrid of the black-and-red-on-white and the black-and-white-on-buff painting schemes (see p. 100). Potters were using conventions for one shape that were more appropriate for another shape.

The "ugly" pottery of Quinua is thus characterized by one or more of the following features. First, "ugly" vessels lack slips that are typical of other vessels of a particular shape. Second, they have atypical and infrequent design layouts. Third, they use designs in one painting scheme which were more typically associated with another painting scheme (see chapters 5 and 7). Fourth, they have symmetry patterns that are inappropriate for a particular shape. Finally, the execution of painted design on "ugly" vessels lacks care and precision. All of these features suggest that vessels which potters judge to be "ugly" violate some of the community-wide design correlates (of layout, motif, motif symmetry and band symmetry) that were laid out in the last chapter. The design "correlates" of the community are thus not just a collective community design pattern, but are also an expression of an aesthetic standard for the designs.

The models of style just elaborated are not competing explanations, but complementary ones. Each emphasizes a particular dimension of the production and transmission of ceramic design and thus all are interdependent components of any theory of style. Design is passed down from generation to generation, is reinforced by post-nuptial residence patterns and by social interaction. Decorated vessels are judged appropriate or inappropriate by aesthetic standards of beauty and ugliness. While all of these models of style make a contribution to understanding ceramic design in Quinua and to explaining the community-wide correlates of design, none of them account for, nor explain, the great amount of variability in Quinua design. In many respects, the variability in the Quinua ceramic design is just as interesting as the design correlates of the community.

Design models and variability

Why is there so much design variability in the four shapes analyzed here in spite of the existence of patterns that are predominant in the community? There is no single cause of this variability and it comes from several sources. The first source is individual creativity. Such creativity is not random, but most often it appears to occur within the boundaries of community-defined structures of design space and symmetry. On the other hand, individual motifs and band designs are much more variable and appear to be the channels of individual creativity. Most variation in design and symmetry patterns occurs outside of obligatory design zones and the relatively fixed motifs within them.

In some cases, individual creativity is expressed within specific structures of motif composition. The flower motif that occurs in the main design zone of the *puynu*, for example, is painted using a relatively fixed set of rules which govern the structure of the plant (see chapter 7, p. 159). The way in which the individual flowers and leaves are painted on this motif, however, varies greatly within these rules. Some motifs, for example, have a flower which is a single large dot, while other flowers consist of large dots surrounded by smaller dots. The leaves on one variant of this motif are attached to the stem of the plant while the leaves on other variants are attached to the base of the plant.

Handle decoration on *yukupuynus* and *puynus* is also highly variable and appears to vary from potter to potter. Like the painting of the flowers on the *puynu*, however, this variability also appears to exist within a particular structure which is common to the community. Handle decoration may be solid or it may consist of horizontal lines. If horizontal lines are used, they vary in thickness and are grouped together in a variety of ways much like the bar codes on items in a modern supermarket.

These data suggest that information on individual potters may be encoded within the design. Each Quinua potter is said to have his own designs, and a potter can identify the creator of a pot from its decoration. One potter explained this relationship by using the metaphor of handwriting. If someone knows another's handwriting, he said, one could always identify the author of a handwritten text. But, without knowing the person to whom a writing style belonged, identification would be impossible.

A second source of design variability in Quinua comes from social units below the level of the community such as the *pago* and hamlet (see chapter 2). Potters say that the design on pottery from the *pago* of Muya is distinct from pottery made in the rest of Quinua. The black-and-white-on-buff painting scheme, for example, may be exclusively produced in Muya. The few examples of this painting scheme used in the analysis presented in chapter 5 came from Muya and from a hamlet adjacent to it (Patampampa). Furthermore, sources for all of the raw materials used in this scheme occur in Muya. Since potters in Muya were not visited and no vessels of this style were observed being made in the rest of Quinua, it is quite likely that the black-and-white-on-buff painting scheme is indeed restricted to Muya.

The existence of design correlates for social units below the level of the community may be one reason why the frequency of layout types on some shapes in this sample is not as high as that of other shapes. One of the design layouts for the *tachu*, for example, consisted of an undecorated body and a white rim (see figures 7.9 and 5.11). These vessels are said to be made only in the *pago* of Muya. *Tachus* decorated with a different design layout (type A), on the other hand, were said to have been made in the *pagos* of Lurinsayuq and Llamahuilca (see chapter 2).

It is also likely that there are stylistic correlates for hamlets (*sitios*) below the level of the *pago*. One potter said that all Quinua potters produce the same vessel shapes, but potters in each hamlet (*sitio*) use a different painted design. The designs produced in Utkuchuku, for example, were said to be different from the designs produced in Añaqata. Similarly, the lollipop motif painted in the main design zone on the *yukupuynu* was made in the *pago* of Lurinsayuq and in Wayuniuq (a *sitio* in the *pago* of Llamahuilca), but was not placed on vessels produced in other hamlets (compare figures 5.12 and 7.14 with figure 7.3). Potters may not be able to identify the hamlet of origin of all pottery, but they can recognize pottery from hamlets familiar to them.

Since the designs of each hamlet are dependent upon the person from whom the potter learned the craft (usually the father), and each hamlet includes only a few households, it may be difficult to separate individual variability from inter-hamlet and inter-lineal variability. The only deviation from the predominant layout type on the *puynu* and *yukupuynu* (layout type B, see figures 7.6 and 7.7), for example, consisted of vessels produced in the hamlet of Huantos. Although these vessels were said to be made by two sisters, the "style" of the vessels was recognized by an informant as coming from the hamlet of Huantos. The fact that these vessels were also considered to be "ugly" meant that multiple sources of variability may intersect simultaneously on the same pot.

Culture change is a third source of design variability in Quinua and it may explain the great variation of design space, designs, and symmetry patterns on the bowl (the *plato*) compared to the *puynu* and *yukupuynu*. The *plato* is the only shape of the four described in this study which has no Quechua name. It is the same shape as a gourd bowl, but gourds have been more traditionally used as food bowls than ceramic ones. These factors suggest that the bowl is relatively new in Quinua and may have been produced for a shorter time than the *puynu*, *yukupuynu*, and *tachu*. Its decoration probably has not been integrated into the decorative tradition of Quinua like that of the other shapes and therefore is the source of design experimentation. There is also some evidence that design variability on bowls may be due to the existence of design correlates of social units below the level of community.

Culture change affects the design variability of Quinua pottery mainly through the artisan demand for pottery. Although it was not evident at the time, the hindsight of twenty-five years has revealed that Quinua ceramic production described here was on the threshold of great change. The effect of the artisan demand was evident in 1967, but every effort was made to focus on those aspects of production and design for which this influence was minimal. The vessels used for the design analysis in this study, for example, were those shapes which were observed the most frequently in Quinua. They were shapes used the most frequently by local peasants and were those which were sold to the local populations of the valley (see chapters 5 and 6). Some vessels analyzed were newly made and ended up in the artisan market, others were old and may have been used by local inhabitants for years. A few vessels analyzed, however, were rejected by the merchants who bought local pottery to sell to tourists. It is impossible to totally filter out such non-standard ceramic designs because cultures are constantly changing, but great care has been taken to distinguish between traditional Quinua pottery and that which is being produced largely for a market external to the Ayacucho Valley.

The artisan demand for pottery primarily affects design variability in two inter-related ways: the selection of certain vessels for export and the response of potters and local buyers to this selection. In 1967, the strongest selective force was one Ayacucho family who bought Quinua pottery and then transported it to Lima. Although pottery occasionally reached the artisan market in more diffuse ways, this family was the primary source of pottery marketed outside of the valley. The artisan center was also important in publicizing Quinua ceramics in Peru, and in intro-ducing new ideas and forms, but in 1967, it had only been established for two years. It was thus too new to significantly affect local ceramic production. Since then, however, there have been a variety of selective factors which have affected the development of Quinua ceramics, but they are outside the scope of this study.

In 1967, the selective force of the market for artisan pottery had affected the shape and design of Quinua pottery (rather than the technology). When the Ayacucho merchant-family came to Quinua to buy pottery, they bought everything that a potter made except "ugly" vessels. These were left behind and were sold in the Sunday market if they were utilitarian vessels. If the vessels were not utilitarian, they were sold to local stores. This practice made the Quinua stores a "dumping ground" for unwanted pottery and this was apparent from the repertoire of ceramics found in these stores. Much of it consisted of unusual, and infrequently produced shapes that were technically poor or carelessly decorated. The amount of dust on some vessels suggested that they had been in the store a long time. It is hard to generalize about this pottery, however, because some of the finest workmanship seen on Quinua pottery occurred on vessels sold in these stores.

The effects of the selection process of the pottery merchants on the sale of local pottery can be illustrated by an observation in the Quinua market. On one market day, several women were selling pottery. One was selling bowls (*platos*), another was selling *tachus* and a third was selling what was considered to be "ugly" pottery. The bowls and the *tachus* were neatly painted and conformed to the design correlates of Quinua described in the last chapter. During my observation, however, the sellers of the culturally acceptable pottery completed no sales even though several buyers had examined the *tachus*. During this same period, however, the woman selling "ugly" pottery had sold four vessels. It appeared, then, that those potters who make more desirable vessels may not be able to obtain the price that they want for their vessels from the local population. On the other hand, the potters who make "ugly" vessels cannot sell them to the intermediaries and must sell them in the market and local stores for a cheaper price. This undercuts the local market for aesthetically appropriate vessels.

The selection of artisan pottery by outside merchants can have a profound effect on pottery left behind in Quinua. First, such a process could increase the frequency of technically poor vessels in a community and those that are outside of the aesthetic standards of most potters. Second, this practice would have a profound effect on experimental pottery produced for the artisan market. If a potter experimented by making new forms and designs and these vessels were not purchased by a pottery merchant, experimental pottery would accumulate in the community at a rate far out of proportion to that which was actually produced. It appears then that during a time of experimentation, exported pottery may be more uniform than that pottery remaining within the community at the source of the production.

Summary
Within the great amount of variability in the Quinua ceramic design, certain patterns of design structure and organization occur very frequently. These patterns consist of the organization of decorative space, the presence of certain design zones, certain types of motif and band symmetry, and the low variability of the motif, band and

symmetry patterns that occur within the high frequency design zones. The previous chapter argued that these patterns were the design correlates of the community of potters in Quinua. This chapter has suggested that there are a number of reasons why these design correlates exist. First, designs tend to be passed down from generation to generation in the male line, and this pattern is reinforced by virilocal post-nuptial residence and by the control that the male potter exerts over the painting process. Second, the design correlates tend to be consistent because of the sustained social interaction between members of the community and the lack of interaction between Quinua potters and other potters in the valley. Third, the design correlates are reinforced by an aesthetic standard which defines what is unacceptable while apparently allowing great latitude in what is appropriate. It is not likely that potters consciously recognize these evaluative principles, but rather, they appear to operate on an unconscious level much like the grammars of language. Quinua designs that do not conform to the major design correlates of the community are evaluated by potters as being "ugly."

The major problem with all of these explanations of the design correlates of Quinua potters is that they do not account for the great amount of variability in the decoration. Some of this variability is the result of individual creativity, while some can be attributed to the existence of design correlates of social units below the level of the community. Other variability is the result of culture change and the effect of artisan demand on a traditional craft.

This chapter closes the ecological approach to Quinua ceramic production. The next chapter will apply the results of the ecological approach to the archaeology of the Ayacucho Valley and to the Peruvian Andes as a whole.

9

Archaeological implications: the Ayacucho Valley

So far, this book has focused on a multi-faceted ecological approach to ceramic production in Quinua. The environment of the region has been described (chapter 2) along with the contribution that the culture history makes towards understanding that environment (chapter 3). The unit of ecological analysis has been defined as the local community of potters (chapter 4) and the relationships of that population to the environment have been described (chapter 4). The process of production has been detailed (chapter 5) and its outcomes have been related to the community as channels of matter, energy and information (chapter 6). The means by which potters turn these products into food were presented as an adaptation to the political and economic realities in the valley (chapter 6). Finally, the material expression of the adaptive unit (the community of potters) was worked out as a set of design conventions common to the community (chapter 7) and in the previous chapter, the relationship of these conventions to the society in Quinua was suggested.

It is now time to apply the results of this ecological approach to the past. This application will be divided into two parts. This chapter focuses on the contribution of this study to the archaeology of the Ayacucho Valley and that of the rest of the Central Andes while the next chapter explains the implications of this ecological approach to archaeology in general.

How does the ecological approach developed in this book relate to the archaeology of the Ayacucho Valley? Can the study of present-day ceramic production in Quinua be linked to the archaeology of the region even after 1,200 years have elapsed? One of the obvious ways of relating the present to the past consists of linking them in a direct historical way. To do so, one must argue that the present society is a historical descendant of an ancient one and then provide evidence to support this assertion. Unfortunately, this approach is inappropriate in this case because there is no stratigraphic or historical evidence linking contemporary ceramic production in Quinua with any ancient ceramic complex in the valley. Nevertheless, the culture history of the valley does suggest several hypotheses which may link ancient and modern ceramic production.

One hypothesis suggests that Quinua ceramic production has its roots in the Colonial Period and thus represents the modern descendant of a technology originally introduced during Peru's 300 years of Spanish domination. Most Quinua vessels, however, are totally unlike colonial Spanish vessels,[1] have Quechua names, and are not made with a Hispanic technology (such as glazing). Since some Quinua shapes[2] have clear antecedents in the pre-Hispanic period rather than the historic period, it is probable that Quinua ceramic technology does not stem from Hispanic influence, but rather antedates contact with Spain. One of the earliest historical sources for the Ayacucho region indicates that potters were already plying their craft in the Province of Huamanga in the sixteenth century.[3] It is not known, however, whether these potters were in Quinua or elsewhere in the Province (perhaps in Ayacucho and Ticllas) or whether they were making pottery with an indigenous or a Hispanic technology. Since the craft was geared to fabricating vessels for the indigenous practice of beer (*chicha*) production in 1557,[4] it was almost certainly present in the area before the Spanish established their first settlement in the valley fifteen years earlier.

A second hypothesis for the origin of the craft in Quinua is that the Incas brought potters to the area as exiled colonists from the village of Acos southeast of Cuzco (see chapter 3). Relocated potters could have provided pottery for the local inhabitants as well as for tribute to the Inca state. If potters were among the colonists transported from Acos, however, one would also expect to find potters throughout the area in which the Acos Indians were relocated,[5] not just in the area around Quinua. Moreover, one would expect that Quinua pottery would be similar to pottery of Acos before the Inca conquest. Unfortunately, the pottery used in Acos at the time of the Inca conquest does not appear to be similar in any way to pottery made in Quinua today. Rather, Acos pottery is a Killke-related style which consists of red (and sometimes black) parallel lines and red pendant triangles from the rim of bowls on a burnished body clay.[6] The style is very different from most of the modern Quinua pottery and those similarities that do exist are superficial. The Killke-related styles of Acos thus probably do not represent the origin of the craft in Quinua.

Little similarity also exists between modern Quinua pottery and that from the Inca Period. Two similar motifs occur on both styles,[7] but these similarities are superficial and could also result from modern potters copying Inca designs. Inca shapes are also vastly different from modern Quinua shapes.[8]

The origin of Quinua ceramic production may also date back to the Middle Horizon Period (A.D. 600–800) long before the Inca conquest. Certainly, the closeness of modern Quinua potters to the great urban center of Huari suggests that modern potters may be descendants of those who abandoned the city during the later part of the Middle Horizon. Huari pottery does share several characteristics with Quinua pottery such as modeling, multi-colored slips and paints, and multiple painted styles. Furthermore, Huari vessels, like those of modern Quinua, were expressions of mythology and were widely used in ritual.[9] Some of the Quinua shapes are similar to Huari shapes[10] and similar to shapes found at the Middle Horizon center of Tiahuanaco in Bolivia.[11] Some Quinua vessels, for example, are shaped like animals, are used for pouring maize beer (see figure 6.6) and look remarkably similar to some Middle Horizon vessels (figure 3.2). Nevertheless, the similarities between the Middle Horizon pottery and that of modern Quinua are still relatively superficial and general.

The problem with all of these explanations is that there is no archaeological evidence linking Quinua ceramics to any ancient pottery in the area. Without intensive survey and excavation around Quinua and the development of a strati-graphic sequence that connects modern Quinua with the archaeology in the region, it is impossible to ascertain whether the similarity between modern and ancient pottery means technological and demographic continuity between the present and the past, or if it is simply the result of modern potters replicating ancient shapes and copying the designs from ancient sherds. Even though there is no straightforward evidence linking Quinua ceramics and the ancient site of Huari, there is some indirect evidence: the closeness of modern Quinua potters to ancient Huari and some general technological similarities of the modern pottery to that of the Middle Horizon (for example modeling).

The focus on culture historical explanations for the origin of Quinua pottery may give the mistaken impression that because it is not possible to use a direct historical approach to the archaeology of the region, little can be known about the ancient ceramic production of the valley. Nothing could be more misleading. Although culture historical explanations may be interesting and may appear to account for the origin of Quinua ceramics, they reveal nothing about the relationship between ceramic production and its environmental and cultural context. Culture historical explanations do not explain why ceramic production has been viable in the Quinua area and why it may have persisted over time. Furthermore, such explanations reflect untested assumptions about the relationship of ceramics, society and history.

While Andeanists may want to know when pottery making began in the Quinua area, and if modern Quinua ceramics can be linked to the Middle Horizon, the answer to these questions has little relevance to pottery production elsewhere in the world. From an ecological perspective developed in this work, the important question is not *when* ceramic production began in the Quinua area, or *if* it can be related to the Huari ceramics, but rather *how* and *why* ceramic production was maintained in Quinua relative to the physical and social environment of the community.

From the discussion already developed in this work (chapter 1), it is possible to utilize some theoretical generalizations to understand ancient ceramic production in the Ayacucho Valley as well as that of the rest of the Central Andes. An explanation of this approach was detailed in an earlier publication (Arnold 1985) and was briefly summarized in the introduction to this book. It will be reiterated here in a slightly different way in order to emphasize the value of the ecological approach for under-standing ceramic production in antiquity.

Applying the present to the past

One of the problems with applying ethnoarchaeological data to the past concerns the limitation of the use of analogy. Archaeologists are acutely aware that the present may not be a good model for the past. Cultures change and the conditions of the twentieth century are not the same as those hundreds of years ago. Few modern societies can be related to ancient societies in a direct historical way and it is often difficult, if not impossible, to factor out the influence of a modern industrial cash economy that has created a demand for traditional pottery.

One of the ways to get around the limitation of analogy and the lack of data for a direct historical approach to the past is to build a ceramic theory based upon the unique physical and chemical characteristics of the ceramics themselves. Such a theory is based on fundamental relationships between ceramics, the environment and culture that are isomorphic from society to society and are thus universal in all human societies that make pottery. These isomorphic relationships have their foundation in the physical and chemical characteristics of the clays themselves.

Clays have common properties which require water, a forming process, drying and a substantial amount of heat to produce a fixed form that will not revert again to an amorphous mass. If populations want to produce ceramics, and do it successfully, then they must respond to these characteristics in similar ways and develop processes that take into account the unique characteristics of clays. These processes are linked to certain environmental conditions and to certain cultural patterns that are widespread among societies that make pottery both in the present and in the past (see Arnold 1985).

These links do not just consist of the characteristics of raw materials themselves, nor in the way they are used, nor in the complex technological processes *per se* for making the pottery. Rather, they focus on the relationships between the raw materials and technological processes on the one hand, and their cultural and environmental context on the other. Because these relationships are tied to the fundamental processes of ceramic production itself, they can help explain the development and maintenance of ceramic production in the present as well as in antiquity without recourse to direct historical analogies or ethnographic homologies. These isomorphisms are thus analogies of process, not of form; they are "processual" analogies.

Processual analogies in ceramic production

The most obvious relationship of ceramics with the environment occurs with the resources used to make them. Not all clays are equally suitable to make pottery, but their availability can be measured in distance (in kilometers and time) that potters must travel to obtain them when they use their own bodies for transport.[12] When the frequencies of a worldwide sample of distances to clays and tempers are plotted on a log scale, three distinct changes emerge in the slope of the curve (figures 9.1 and 9.2). These slope changes appear to be different thresholds of energy and distance that potters must travel to obtain these resources. The first such threshold occurs at 1 kilometer and consists of the single highest percentage of the distances in the sample. Since the frequency drops steeply after this distance, 1 kilometer is inferred to be a "threshold" of energy expenditure which is the "preferred" distance of procurement. The second threshold occurs at the first change in slope of the curve and lies at 3 kilometers for temper sources and at 4 kilometers for clay sources (figures 9.1 and 9.2). The third threshold occurs at the last change in the slope of the curve and lies at 30 kilometers for both clays and temper. This last threshold includes 86 cumulative percent of the distances to clay sources and 91 cumulative percent of the distances to temper sources (tables 9.1 and 9.2). The few distances in the sample beyond the last threshold are so infrequent that the probability of their occurrence in the societies of the world is very small. These threshold distances reveal an isomorphic relationship between pottery production and distance to

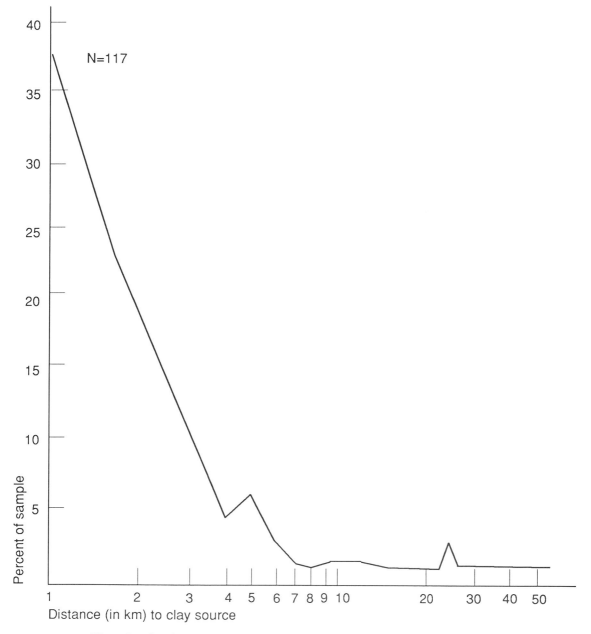

Figure 9.1 Graph showing the percent of the sample of distances to clay sources in the ethnographic literature plotted on a log scale of those distances (from data in Arnold 1985: 34–49; 1988).

Table 9.1. *The threshold distances to clay sources and the cumulative percent of the sample occurring at those distances*

Threshold[a]	Distance in kilometers	Cumulative percent of sample
Preferred	1	36.8
Second	4	70.9
Third	7	85.5

[a]Thresholds were inferred from the line graph (figure 9.1) as those distances at which dramatic changes in downward slope of the curve occurred. The "preferred" threshold indicates the distance with the largest percent of the sample. For a fuller discussion of the relationship of energy costs and distances to ceramic resources see Arnold 1985: 32–57.

Table 9.2. *The threshold distances to temper sources and the cumulative percent of the sample occurring at those distances*

Threshold[a]	Distance in kilometers	Cumulative percent of sample
Preferred	1	48.6
Second	3	74.3
Third	7	91.4

[a]Thresholds were inferred from the line graph (figure 9.2) as those distances at which dramatic changes in downward slope of the curve occurred. The "preferred" threshold indicates the distance with the largest percent of the sample. For a fuller discussion of the relationship of energy costs and distances to ceramic resources see Arnold 1985: 32–57.

sources of raw materials in a wide variety of societies in the ethnographic present. They can thus be seen as crude probabilities that can help retrodict distances from ancient ceramic production sites to their resources (Arnold 1985: 35–57; 1988).

Weather and climate also have a relationship with pottery making – either limiting or stimulating the development of the craft (Arnold 1985: 61–98). In order to make pottery, the potter not only needs raw materials, but also needs specific environmental conditions to facilitate the drying of raw materials, fuel and pottery and to fire the vessels without damage. The physical and chemical characteristics of clays require drying before firing and this relationship helps explain why weather and climate affects ceramic production. The link between ceramic production and climate can thus enable an archaeologist to infer the seasonality, presence, absence, intensity and relative scale of ceramic production that occurred in the past using paleo-climatic data. Without capital investment in workshops and drying facilities, climate constraints can prevent ceramic production from being economically viable and in some cases may create total deviation counteracting feedback by preventing the emergence of any significant ceramic output (see Arnold 1985: 61–98).

A third relationship between ceramic production, environment and culture involves scheduling conflicts with subsistence activities. Since many potters are part-time specialists, they require subsistence activities in order to live. Because of the environmental limits on making pottery, however, the craft has to be scheduled so as not to interfere with these activities. The primary way scheduling conflicts have been avoided is to assign conflicting activities to different sexes (Arnold 1985: 99–108). Because of the compatibility of pottery making with nursing children, child care and domestic responsibilities, household potters are most frequently women, but may also be men when there are no scheduling conflicts with subsistence. Once pottery production becomes a full-time specialty and moves into workshops outside of the home, women cease being potters because they can no longer perform child care and household responsibilities along with making pots. Ceramic production then becomes predominantly a male activity.

Demand is another relationship between ceramics and culture which affects pottery production and involves the reasons why people desire and use ceramic vessels. First, ceramics have a number of technological advantages over other kinds of vessels: their refractory properties, their flexibility of form, and the widespread availability of clay compared to certain lithic and metal resources. Second, yearly replacement figures from ethnoarchaeological studies (for example Foster 1960; David and Hennig 1972) suggest that population growth provides limited demand

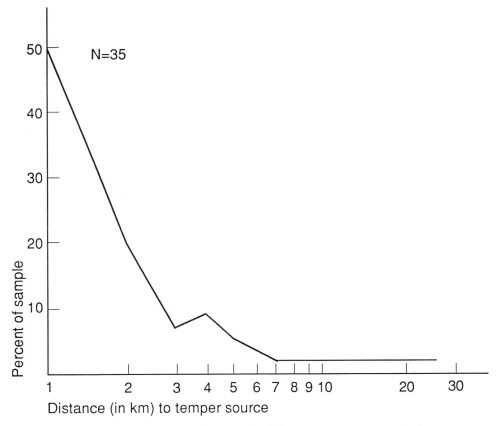

Figure 9.2 Graph showing the percent of the sample of distances to temper sources in the ethnographic literature plotted on a log scale of those distances (from data in Arnold 1985: 39–49; 1988).

for ceramics. Rather, the stimulus for sufficient demand necessary for full-time ceramic specialization can only occur by forging new links between the ceramics and the culture's belief system. This stimulus can occur by using pottery for ritual, for expressing mythical themes or for communicating differences in social structure through creating elite objects for social display (Arnold 1985: 127–167). The use of ceramics for ritual activities and mythological expression can thus create a demand which may help propel ceramic craftsmen into full-time production.

There is also a relationship between pottery making, agricultural land and the population that tills it. Population pressure (by several mediating factors) can cause the expansion of pottery making, and may be one factor responsible for its development into a full-time craft (Arnold 1985: 168–201). Such pressure may cause the demise of agricultural land resulting in erosion and may further spur dependence on pottery production as a full-time activity. Just as erosion destroys agricultural land, it may expose a variety of raw materials for the potter's craft.

Finally, technological innovations mitigate the limiting effects of climate on drying and firing and can also permit the evolution of pottery making into a full-time specialty. These innovations include changes in forming techniques to increase efficiency and the use of drying facilities, ovens and kilns to offset the regulatory effects of weather and climate on ceramic production (Arnold 1985: 201–224).

Applying the processual analogies

The application of these processual analogies to the Ayacucho Valley will focus on the Middle Horizon (approximately A.D. 600–800) when the valley was the center of one of the most extensive pre-Inca states in ancient Peru. Ceramic specialization in the valley reached an apex of development during this time when the valley was the source of a number of ceramic styles which were distributed throughout much of Peru. Several of these styles combined a wide repertoire of colors with motifs from the Altiplano and the south coast of Peru.[13]

The close proximity of the modern potters and the ancient city of Huari suggests that an ecological approach to ceramic production in Quinua may provide some insight into the pottery production in and around the ancient city of Huari. The pottery of Quinua, like that of Huari, is unique in the Ayacucho Valley. The other contemporary pottery-making communities in the Valley (Ayacucho, Ticllas, Huayhuas, and the Luricocha area) produce few vessel shapes in comparison to Quinua and most are undecorated. The few decorated shapes made in those communities have limited plastic or painted decoration. Quinua potters, on the other hand, produce a large repertoire of shapes in three painting schemes. The uniqueness of Quinua pottery thus suggests that the co-occurrence of potters in Quinua and nearby Huari is not merely coincidental, but rests, at least in part, on the ecological potential of an area for specialized ceramic production. This ecological potential was expressed first in the ancient styles of Huari and more recently in the modern ceramics of Quinua. An ecological approach to the ceramic production of Quinua thus provides a number of implications for understanding the ancient ceramic production in the region.

The relationship of climate to the scheduling of pottery production during dry weather suggests that Middle Horizon potters probably lived within the city of Huari. This inference is supported by the fact that excavations at Huari have produced evidence of pottery-making equipment.[14] Furthermore, the technical quality and stylistic complexity of this pottery suggests that the producers were full-time specialists. Huari potters did not face the same climatic constraints on their ceramic production as Quinua potters. Huari lies further down the slope than modern potters within the lower montane thorn steppe and the climate there does not limit the development of full-time specialization as it does where Quinua potters live today (see chapters 2 and 5). Without the environmental limitations on drying and firing, potters in Huari did not need to be part-time farmers and could become full-time specialists. Living and working within the city thus removed the climatic restraints on full-time ceramic production. Huari was thus located in a climatically strategic location for the full-time potters who produced the elaborate polychrome styles of the Middle Horizon.

Besides inferences about the effect of climate on ancient production, an ecological approach can also provide a picture of the ceramic resources available in the area. Such studies can document the amount of variability inherent in local materials and the resource potential for intensive and specialized ceramic production. Chapters 4 and 5 document a diversity of sources and a wide availability of ceramic materials (clays, tempers and paints) that indicate that the Quinua region had a rich array of raw materials available for ancient potters. Suitable clays and tempering materials come from a variety of locations and are abundant. Mineral paints and slips with superior spreading qualities are also found in the area. Contemporary paints have a smaller color repertoire than those used in the Middle Horizon, but they are abundant enough to suggest that additional colors may occur nearby or could have been produced from the existing ones. Large quantities of superior fuel for firing and a material for making a vessel-forming device also occur nearby. Fuel for firing could also have been provided by the many trains of llamas which would have visited the city. The Quinua region thus appears to have a sufficient quantity and diversity of ceramic resources to support highly specialized pottery production which resulted in the many polychrome styles produced in the valley during the Middle Horizon (A.D. 600–800).

Besides the general ecological potential of the Quinua/Huari area for intensive ceramic production, this study has several specific implications for the study of the ancient pottery of the region. First of all, since all of the modern sources of clays and tempers are within the resource catchment distance of 7 kilometers from Huari (tables 9.1 and 9.2), ancient potters could have used the same raw materials as modern potters. Some modern sources are, in fact, within the second threshold distance from Huari of 3 kilometers for temper and 4 kilometers for clay. In addition, several of the paint and slip resources occur within the preferred distance of 10 kilometers and all such sources lie within the third threshold distance of 30 kilometers for these materials (Arnold 1985: 52).

Because modern ceramic raw materials occur within a worldwide catchment area of ceramic resources for Huari potters, a study of these raw materials can provide insight into understanding the characteristics of the ancient ceramic materials and the pastes made from them. Great mineralogical variability occurs in clays and tempers in the area. This variability is related to both natural and cultural factors. First, the geological setting in Quinua is highly variable with clays, volcanic ash and some basalt occurring at various points on a slope which extends over a vertical distance of more than 500 meters. This slope is greatly eroded exposing horizontal strata which include a variety of clay and volcanic ash deposits. Second, the actual sources used by potters for clay, and to a lesser extent temper, are greatly dispersed over this area. These varied sources occur in part because potters' households are widely distributed over the Quinua landscape. Because the energy costs of obtaining raw materials cannot exceed the returns of making pottery (Arnold 1985: 32–57), potters generally exploit their raw materials within the preferred threshold distance of one kilometer from their households. The dispersed settlement pattern of Quinua potters thus plays an important role in the mineralogical variability of ceramic raw materials. Even though the geological variability of the region affects the potential variability of ceramic raw materials, it is the settlement pattern of the potters along with the widely dispersed sources of clay and temper that affect the mineralogical variability of their raw materials.

Because of all of this variability, changes in the source locations of clays and tempers may affect the chemical and mineralogical variability of these materials over time. In 1978, for example, a new source of clay was being exploited just below the village near the grammar school. This source did not exist in 1967 and is about a kilometer from the main clay source used in 1967 (Tantarniuq). A new source for white sand temper was also utilized in 1978 when potters reported that sand was mined in the Hatun Wayqu ravine in the *barrio* of Hanansayuq. This source is outside of the *barrio* in which potters lived and also did not exist in 1967. The changing locations of temper and clay sources over time are further confirmed by the fact that in 1967, there was little evidence of extensive or intensive mining of ceramic raw materials in any one location (see figures 4.7 and 4.8). This lack of evidence thus suggests that there is little time depth for any particular clay pit or temper mine in the area. Since erosion is constantly altering the landscape by revealing new raw material sources and destroying old ones, sources of ceramic materials would be expected to change over time and the raw materials obtained from them would vary in composition.

The complex geological picture of the area also suggests that the composition of ceramic raw materials (such as clays) may change over time even if the same source is utilized. Temper sources are located in areas susceptible to collapse and clay pits are situated on slopes. These locations suggest that new sediments may be added to existing sources through collapse and erosion. Erosion can obliterate the original source by depositing materials with a different composition from elsewhere (Charles Kolb, personal communication).

The religious belief and reticence of landowners to allow clay to be mined on their land also contribute to the mineralogical variability of local raw materials. Given the geology of the region in which clays, tempers and slips occur over a wide area, a variety of cultural factors help randomize procurement. Sacred sites require making an offering to the mountain god before raw materials are procured. Landowners may refuse to allow clay mining on their property because it destroys agricultural land. Furthermore, source locations tend to remain within a restricted area in order to minimize energy costs. Finally, source locations for raw materials can change often and this change can create a highly variable set of clay and temper sources over space and time.

The great mineralogical variability of Quinua ceramic raw materials and the environmental and cultural factors that create this variability mean that ancient ceramic pastes from the area will have a similar range of variability. This mineralogical variability will affect the chemical variability of the pastes such that source areas of ancient pottery made within the Ayacucho Valley cannot be identified precisely using trace element analyses without collecting a large sample of local clays and tempers. Even then, ancient pottery probably can never be assigned to precise clay pits or workshops (see Arnold, Neff and Bishop 1991).

The great mineralogical variability of Quinua ceramic raw materials has other implications for the analysis of the ancient ceramics in the region. First, archaeologists may have difficulty distinguishing between clays and tempers in local pottery. Both contain plastics and non-plastics and have several mineralogical similarities. Nevertheless, tempering materials consist mostly of non-plastics like quartz and volcanic tuff whereas clays consist mostly of the plastic minerals of montmorillonite, illite and kaolinite (or halloysite). The difference between tempers and clays, then, is a relative difference in the proportion of non-plastics present and not an absolute difference between clay minerals (plastics) and non-clay minerals (non-plastics). Temper contains more non-plastics than clay whereas clay contains more plastics than temper.

Since there is a great deal of overlap of the minerals found in the clays and tempers and since plastics and non-plastics occur in all tempers and clays of the Quinua region, how can the archaeologist distinguish pastes that the potter has behaviorally tempered from those he has not tempered? The culturally significant difference between the tempered paste and the untempered paste is the presence of substantial quantities of mica. Mica can be seen in untempered pastes because the mica plates become oriented in a position parallel to the surface of a vessel during the finishing process (Shepard 1956: 162). On the other hand, only very small amounts of mica occur in the clay and temper used for the behaviorally tempered paste. Furthermore, the tempered paste contains abundant amounts of volcanic glass because both the clay and the temper used to make this paste contain it. Little or no volcanic glass occurs in the untempered paste. By applying these distinctions to the ancient pottery of the area, one can make two inferences. First, paste that contains substantial amounts of volcanic glass and very little mica was behaviorally tempered by the potter. Second, paste that contains substantial quantities of mica and no volcanic glass was not tempered by the potter.

The analyses of the Quinua raw materials further suggest that the terminology used to describe ancient ceramics needs to reflect the realities of the local raw materials, on the one hand, and the behavior of the potter, on the other. For example, descriptions of ancient pottery in the valley such as "mica tempered" (MacNeish 1969: 44–45) do not reflect the potters' actual behavior because mica minerals occur naturally in the clays of the region. Rather, "micaceous paste" or "natural mica inclusions" better describe the behavioral preparation of this paste.

Another implication of the ecological approach of this work to the archaeology of the valley involves distinguishing ancient vessel shapes from one another. Potters' perceptions of the differences between the liquid-carrying shapes have correlates in both the absolute mouth and neck sizes and in the ratios of these dimensions to the greatest diameter (see chapter 5). Differences between shapes of the cooking and brewing pottery also appear to be based on the ratio of mouth diameter to greatest diameter.

There are other criteria, however, that can be used to distinguish the different shapes of the cooking pottery. When a potter tried to identify these shapes using sherds from kiln wasters rather than whole vessels, he used fire blackening and sherd thickness as criteria. First, he separated fire-blackened sherds as fragments of cooking pots (*manka*). Then, he sorted the remainder of the sherds by thickness, with the sherds of the *tumin* being thinner than those of the *urpu* and *maqma*. It thus appears that thickness of vessel wall is an important criterion distinguishing different shapes of the cooking ware in addition to the mouth diameter and the ratio of that diameter to the greatest diameter.

The vessel-forming techniques used in Quinua provide some insight into making inferences about the forming technology used for ancient pottery in the region. In modern Quinua, modeling and molding have permitted great variability in vessel shapes. These techniques not only enable the production of a great variety of traditional shapes but this technology facilitates the innovation of new shapes. Because the ancient vessels of the valley were diverse and included shapes that could only be made by molding and/or modeling (for example figures 3.1 and 3.2), it is probable that these same techniques were used to fabricate the ancient vessels made in the valley. Indeed, excavations at the Middle Horizon site of Conchopata have found potters' workshops with molds, pottery turntables and burnishing stones (Pozzi-Escot 1982, 1991) which appear to be similar to those used in modern Quinua.

An ecological approach to ceramic production in Quinua also has implications for the use of color to analyze and classify ancient ceramics in the area. While gross color distinctions of slips and paints distinguish the three painting schemes in Quinua, fine color gradations of paste, slip, or paints do not appear to have behavioral nor cultural significance. Paste color can be affected by several factors. First, it can be affected by firing. The use of the dual-chambered updraft kiln provides some control over firing, but this control is not sufficient to compensate for a second factor that affects paste color: the variability of local ceramic materials. Some local clays are black and have considerable carbonaceous matter in them which may not be oxidized by firing. Fired vessels may thus have a black core or may be partially black after firing. Third, paste color is also affected by the presence of iron minerals in the clays causing paste colors to range from orange to red and brown. Fourth, paints and slips range in color from white through yellow, red and brown. Depending on firing conditions, these iron minerals may cause a "red" slip to become black and a "white" slip to become yellow. Since the raw materials used in Quinua are varied and firing is not well-controlled, one could expect great variability in paste color even in the ceramics of a single potter. Classifications of ancient ceramics utilizing detailed descriptions of paste, paint and slip color should be viewed with caution and should be reformulated in terms of design structure, design symmetry, design content, vessel shape and overall paste composition.

Ceramic production in the Middle Horizon

How did apparently full-time ceramic specialization develop in the valley during the Middle Horizon? One of the ways to answer this question is to propose a model which suggests the relationships between the ancient population and the processual analogies described earlier in this chapter (see Arnold 1985). Before this model is presented, however, three inferences will be made about the prehistoric population in the valley.

The Middle Horizon probably constitutes the peak of population size in the Ayacucho Valley. The largest sites known are urban Middle Horizon sites.[15] Since there are no known urban sites in the valley after this period, the prehistoric population probably declined after Huari was abandoned and apparently did not reach Middle Horizon levels again until historic times.

These data about the prehistoric population in the valley suggest that population growth and pressure may have been significant variables in producing the cultural changes which led to the development of urbanization in the valley and some of the accoutrements of civilization such as full-time ceramic specialization. The assumption, of course, is that population growth was taking place in the valley prior to the development of the Middle Horizon during the Early Intermediate Period.

In order for population growth to result in population pressure, certain constraints must operate upon the population. One such constraint is environmental circumscription. Carneiro (1970) argued that environmental circumscription plus population growth was a necessary condition for the evolution of the state. Environmental circumscription occurs in an area with natural barriers around it which prevent a growing population from expanding into nearby agricultural land. These barriers limit migration out of the area and thus help to create an increase in population density. With increasing density, competing political units increase in size and decrease in number through warfare and conquest until the area is unified under a centralized state.

This scenario could easily apply to the Ayacucho Valley. It is an environmentally circumscribed unit entirely surrounded by mountains and this topography prevents the expansion of the population into nearby agricultural land. Mitchell (1991a) has shown that circumscription and population growth as well as cultural factors help explain the dramatic social and economic changes that have occurred in contemporary Quinua in the last twenty-five years. Population growth combined with inadequate agricultural land and environmental circumscription have favored such non-farm work as migration and the growth of ceramic production. Subsidized prices have depressed the value of peasant farm production and discouraged future production. These factors have subsequently exerted negative forces on the political, religious and social institutions which are tied into agricultural production. The result has been profound cultural changes such as the decline of the fiesta system, the growth of the guerrilla group Sendero Luminoso, and the rise of Protestantism. All of these factors can be linked to the decline of traditional agriculture.

Another constraint that creates population pressure does not involve population growth at all, but rather a decline in the carrying capacity of the agricultural land necessary for subsistence. This decline can be created by climatic change which reduces the amount of, and/or the days with, rainfall. Carrying capacity can also be reduced by a decrease in the number of frost-free days caused by a consistent early frost. These factors, however, affect different crops in different ways because some crops (for example maize) are more affected by a decrease in rainfall and the onset of frost. Other crops (such as the Andean tubers) are not as adversely affected by these factors because they require less rainfall and are more frost resistant.

Another factor creating a decrease in carrying capacity is the destruction of agricultural land through erosion. Agricultural land can be lost through the loss of nutrient-rich top soil. Ultimately, this process creates gullies which make the loss of agricultural land irreversible.

Several factors can thus create population pressure: population growth, circumscription, and decline in carrying capacity through climate change and/or erosion. Some factors are natural while others can be human induced (like erosion). Whatever the cause, however, population pressure can stimulate the intensification of agriculture (Boserup 1965) and help set into motion forces that may result in the development of the state.[16]

Another important inference that one could make about the Middle Horizon in the valley concerns the relationship of ideology, religion and pottery. One of the innovations of the early Middle Horizon period that profoundly affected the rise of full-time ceramic production was the fusion of religious ideology with ceramic technology. The most obvious expression of this fusion was the use of pottery as a vehicle for the expression of mythological themes.[17] Pottery may have been used in ritual in the valley before the Middle Horizon, but the extensive use of pottery as an expression of mythological themes separates Middle Horizon pottery from the local pottery which preceded it during the Early Intermediate Period. Elsewhere in Peru, however, the use of pottery for expressing mythical themes is much older. On the nearby south coast it dates back to the Early Horizon period (1400–400 B.C.). Contact with the south coast prior to the Middle Horizon thus not only brought a new ceramic technology (Isbell 1991) and design to the Ayacucho Valley (see Menzel 1964), but also may have introduced the idea of using pottery as a channel of ideological information.

The use of religious and mythological themes on pottery during the Middle Horizon thus provided a sustained demand for ceramic output both in the capital and in the territory that it controlled. When this innovation was combined with the iconographic themes from the Titicaca Basin, there was a powerful impetus for the demand for religious pottery. This demand may have been amplified by the ritual smashing of large vessels decorated with these religious themes during Epoch I of the Middle Horizon (at Conchopata, see Menzel 1964).

A third inference about the Middle Horizon involves the importance of interregional trade in the development and maintenance of the Huari state. The Ayacucho Valley is one of the largest agricultural areas of relatively low elevation in the entire southern Peruvian Andes (see chapter 3). The valley was in a superior position for the abundant production of maize, which today, at least, is the most highly valued Andean crop. The valley was also a significant transportation corridor during both prehistoric and historic times (see chapter 3) and was thus in a critical location for the trade and exchange of agricultural products (such as maize).

Ancient trade and exchange could also have involved other resources as well. Salt is mined across the valley near the community of San Pedro de Cachi. In 1967, this distinctive purple salt occurred in all of the contemporary markets visited in the valley. It may have been an important commodity in the trade networks in the past as well. The religiously expressive pottery of the Middle Horizon would also have been a source of exchange since it occurs throughout much of the Central Andes during the Middle Horizon.[18] The presence of Cajamarca pottery at Huari, and the presence of Huari pottery near Cajamarca also suggests an extensive pottery trade with populations outside the valley.[19]

Besides the products (salt and ceramics) from within the valley, there were also non-agricultural products traded into the valley from other regions. Analyses of obsidian artifacts from throughout the central Andes indicate that the Huari state may have been involved in the distribution of obsidian from the Quispisisa source in the Department of Huancavelica (northwest of the valley) because the artifacts from this source reached their widest distribution during Middle Horizon times.[20] The fragments of chrysocolla artifacts found at Huari[21] also suggest external trade since no source for this mineral is known within the valley.[22]

Ethnographic evidence suggests that large interregional trading networks existed in the valley in the immediate past as well. Until recently, the *barrio* of Carmen Alto in the city of Ayacucho was known for its muleteers who traveled regularly to the south coast to trade highland products for wine and cane alcohol (Tschopik 1947: 30–31). In addition, the yearly fairs of Chupas and Acuchimay near the city of Ayacucho bring together buyers and sellers from much of southern Peru. People from Quinua have also worked as muleteers, trading such things as maize, cloth, *coca* leaves, guitars, hats, potatoes and ceramics with the coast, jungle and highland areas. Many have traveled throughout Peru since at least the beginning of the twentieth century.[23] Both the annual fairs and the presence of muleteers/traders further underscore the importance of the valley as a transportation corridor in historic and prehistoric times. All of these data suggest that economic contact has existed between the valley and other areas of Peru (particularly the south coast) throughout the last 2,000 years.[24]

A hypothetical developmental model

Given the ethnographic data, the processual analogies described earlier in this chapter and the archaeological inferences just presented, it is possible to build a speculative model concerning the rise of ceramic specialization in the valley based upon paleoclimatic data derived from the Quelccaya Ice Cap, a permanent ice cap located approximately 300 kilometers southeast of the Ayacucho Valley in southern Peru.[25] Unfortunately, inferences from these data are not straightforward because complex factors affect ice cap formation and various interpretations of them can be made. Furthermore, there are questions about the specifics of the relationships between ice-caps and ancient climate (Browman 1991). Finally, the reconstruction of the Andean climate in ten year intervals from the Quelccaya data is not always concordant with other data sets.[26] Nevertheless, the Quelccaya data do provide important paleoclimatic information, but it must be used cautiously. Only future research will be able to adequately test the model proposed here.

After permanent agricultural settlements developed in the region, increased use of irrigation and terracing in the valley during the Early Intermediate Period increased the amount and productivity of agricultural land. This change increased the carrying capacity of the area and stimulated further population growth. This population growth in the circumscribed Ayacucho Valley probably produced population pressure on the better agricultural land. This pressure resulted in the continued agricultural intensification in the form of terracing and irrigation.[27]

The population of the valley at this time was large, becoming urban (at sites such as Ñawim Pukyu) and was sustained by five times as much agricultural land as there is in production today.[28] Huari was already occupied at this time (Isbell 1991) and was also urban, but continued population pressure created the erosion of agricultural land mediated by reduced fallow times and excessive cultivation. These factors marginalized previously arable land, destroying agricultural land for some farmers and forcing others into areas which were too eroded for much agriculture. As a result, there was a net loss in the amount of agricultural land available for cultivation.

Pottery was probably being made in or near Huari because of the availability of ceramic raw materials there, and some farmers who were already part-time potters found their fields in marginal agricultural areas. While erosion destroyed or marginalized agricultural land, it also provided resources for ceramic production. It is possible that some farmer-potters turned to intensified ceramic production by increasing their utilization of nearby ceramic raw materials given the decline in the amount and quality of their land for agriculture. The increasingly marginalized agricultural land for farmer-potters further selected for increased dependence on an alternative means of subsistence besides agriculture such as increased ceramic specialization.

Near the end of the sixth century A.D., an excessively dry period began in the southern Andes.[29] This dry period probably created an agricultural crisis in the Ayacucho Valley because it reduced the amount of land available for agriculture as well as the amount of water for irrigation. With five times as much land under cultivation during this time as there is now (Lumbreras 1974), a successive number of dry years would have greatly reduced the carrying capacity of the agricultural land creating population pressure on the existing land. This increased desiccation may have been at least partly responsible for the subsequent abandonment of the Early Intermediate sites in the valley (like Ñawim Pukyu) after the first phase of the Middle Horizon and the movement of their populations into the city of Huari.[30] Huari had already begun an innovative religious tradition at this time and these innovations may themselves have been a response to the agricultural crisis in the valley brought on by desiccation. This crisis would have created an openness for populations to experiment with new (or revitalized) religious ideas which were expressed in newly constructed temples and ceremonial precincts in the city and symbolically in new media such as pottery.[31] These religious ideas may have been an attempt to mitigate the disastrous effects of the agricultural crisis brought on by drought.

With continued desiccation, farmer-potters living in formerly productive agricultural areas found themselves farming increasingly marginal land and could no longer use agriculture as a complementary activity to ceramic production. These part-time potters had a variety of options. If they chose to intensify their agricultural techniques or shorten the fallow time, they would create even more erosion and more marginal land. Some probably did, and the quality of their land continued to deteriorate. Another option was cultivating land in other zones. The population growth sustained by intensive agricultural practices in the Early Intermediate period, however, and the circumscribed character of the Ayacucho Valley had probably already overcrowded the best agricultural land in the valley. If farmer-potters chose to cultivate the land in the flood plain in the bottom of the valley, they would be faced with difficulties. The alluvial valley probably was over-crowded, but was not conducive to pottery production because of the scheduling conflicts resulting from year-round cultivation supported by irrigation. Movement into agricultural zones at a higher altitude was not feasible because these zones had a restricted crop repertoire, increased amounts of fallow time and therefore overall lower agricultural productivity than the lower zones. Ceramic production in these zones, however, was less viable because of lower temperatures and the limiting factors of local micro-climate. Farmer-potters with increasingly marginal agricultural returns thus could not migrate into other zones which were favorable for agriculture and still make pottery. Farming in other zones selected against continued pottery production.

Although increased desiccation in the valley was devastating to farming, it created better conditions for pottery production and provided deviation amplifying feedback for intensifying the craft. Furthermore, the eroded land around the potters provided an opportunity to intensify their craft by exploiting the ceramic resources that erosion had exposed. Although the dryness selected against agriculture, it selected for increased intensification of ceramic production.

Another option for potters was to move into the city of Huari. The city provided an attractive niche because it was drier and sunnier than zones further up the slope. By moving into the city, potters were largely freed from the seasonal climatic constraints on pottery making. The city was still close to the ceramic resources created by erosion. Fuel for firing was available from the abundant brush that grew in the mountain slopes on the edge of the valley and from the dung left behind from the frequent llama caravans which visited the city. Most of all, residence in Huari provided a ready outlet for potters' finished ceramics and they could devote themselves full-time to making utility, service and ritual pottery for the needs of the city. The city was also attractive because it was close to the rich agricultural land in the alluvial bottom of the valley which was a source of food that could be exchanged for the potters' wares.

Along with the movement of potters into the city of Huari came a greater demand for pottery. The need for utilitarian and service pottery by such a large population created a concentrated demand for this pottery.

Contact with Pucara and Tiahuanaco in the Titicaca Basin had brought a series of additional changes to the valley. Because the increased aridity had created an agricultural crisis, the population was vulnerable and open to new religious ideas which might bring them out of this crisis. Even though the religion of the Ayacucho Valley and Tiahuanaco might not have been that different from its predecessor in the valley (Isbell 1983), the valley may have been the site of a renewal or revitalization movement symbolized by a set of Titicaca iconographic themes. Nevertheless, a new hierarchical religious organization was evident at Huari from the time of the earliest contact with Tiahuanaco (see Isbell 1988 and chapter 3) and this organization apparently became the foundation for the expansion of the Huari state during the Middle Horizon.

The innovation of using ceramics as an expression of mythical themes came after the new architectural developments of the Middle Horizon which linked Huari and Tiahuanaco (Isbell 1991) and probably was the product of experimentation. Techniques such as modeling, modified coiling, and multicolored slipping and painting would have facilitated this experimentation and some of these techniques were introduced during this time from the south coast of Peru. The use of pottery for mythical themes stimulated the demand for pottery and this demand further compensated for the potters' lack of an agricultural subsistence base created by their movement into the city and their loss of agricultural land through desiccation. It was thus the introduction of the religious symbols from the Titicaca Basin and their expression on ceramics that probably created the greatest demand for the products of the potters' craft.

Some of these processes can be illustrated at the site of Conchopata located 8 kilometers south of Huari (see figure 3.4). Recent excavations have revealed quantities of pottery associated with pottery-making implements.[32] Moreover, potters' tools[33] and pottery with firing defects occurred in almost every room excavated (Pozzi-Escot 1991). These data indicate that ceramic production was a dominant economic activity at Conchopata and suggest the site was probably an important center of ceramic production during the early part of the Middle Horizon (Pozzi-Escot 1982, 1991).

Being located in the lower montane thorn steppe, Conchopata was strategically located for both agriculture and pottery production. The area around the site had the potential for agriculture in years that were wetter than it is now, but the site was also close to the valley floor with its excellent agricultural land which, with irrigation, could be cultivated year around. The site, however, is lower in elevation and drier than other nearby Early Intermediate sites (like Ñawim Pukyu) and once the climate became drier, Conchopata probably became marginal for agriculture as it is today. Yet, like Huari, it was located in an ideal position for making pottery because of its dry climate and was close to the agricultural resources in the valley floor which could be exchanged for the potters' wares. Still unknown, however, was its position relative to ceramic resources.

It may be no accident that the first ceramic evidence of the Titicaca Basin religious themes occurred at Conchopata. Being in the lower montane thorn steppe meant that agricultural production outside of the alluvial valley was precarious when the climate became drier. With increased desiccation, the farmer-potters already present at the site could easily intensify their ceramic production. But, without a sufficient agricultural base which provided food in exchange for pots, potters could not be sustained. The new religious themes on pottery at Conchopata and the deliberate breaking of large numbers of these vessels were perhaps desperate attempts to participate in a revitalization movement and therefore to change the local conditions to make agriculture possible again where it had once flourished. These attempts failed, Conchopata was ultimately abandoned, and its inhabitants apparently moved into the city of Huari.

Huari was attractive for potters because of its closeness to abundant ceramic resources. Water, a crucial resource for pottery making and a scarce commodity during drought, was also available a few hundred meters below in the irrigated valley. Water may also have been brought into the city by a canal from above. Given the topography of the land around Huari, such a canal would have to have come through much of rural Quinua from the Huamangura Ravine and/or the Hatun Wayqu Ravine.

Resources like chrysocolla and obsidian were exchanged for salt, pottery, maize, and other goods and this exchange further stimulated the development of full-time ceramic specialization during the Middle Horizon. While population growth and trade at Huari originally created some demand for pottery, it was the demand for religious pottery that had the greatest impact on ceramic production as a deviation amplifying mechanism. It is hard to assess the existence of mythical or religious themes in portable artifacts besides pottery (such as chrysocolla), but it is likely that ceramics were important to the Huari state because of their massive use as a vehicle of religious expression. Without this kind of demand for pottery in urban Huari, the potters could not have exchanged food for their pots and would have needed to rely upon agriculture to make a living.

The years of aridity in the valley were followed by a period of relative wetness in the seventh century A.D.[34] and the Ayacucho Valley increased its agricultural productivity and perhaps experienced population growth. This period probably corresponds to the early part of Epoch 2 of the Middle Horizon when the Huari influence expanded once again. Epoch 2 pottery occurred in the Ayacucho Valley outside of Huari (Azángaro), in the southern highlands (Jincamocco), in the north highlands (Huamachuco), and on the south coast (Nazca and Chincha/Soras valleys) (Knobloch 1991: 256).

But another dry period began later in the seventh century A.D. While the climatic data from the Quelccaya Ice Cap suggest that the lack of precipitation at this time was not as severe as that in the sixth century, this drought was longer.[35] Population levels of the previous wet period probably could not be maintained because of the shrinkage of agricultural land and it was quite possible that Huari was ultimately abandoned during this time.

With the collapse of Huari, potters could no longer support themselves by pottery alone because of the insufficient demand for their wares. With no outlet for the ceramics in the city and in the territory that it once controlled, potters had to return to agriculture to meet their subsistence needs. They thus moved out of the city into an agricultural area where pottery making and agriculture could be undertaken together. Agricultural land above Huari (near modern Quinua) provided an excellent location to combine both agriculture and pottery. The agricultural land was adequate in quality and potters were still very close to their resources. Unfortunately, local agricultural land could support only a small fraction of the former population of Huari and it was probably already occupied. But, the rainfall necessary for agriculture limited ceramic production to the dry season. Ceramic production and agriculture returned as complementary activities particularly where farming was limited by scarcity of water and the amount and quality of arable land.

If the relationship between prolonged desiccation and the beginning of the Middle Horizon is sustained by future research, it is likely that the development of religious architecture noted during the earliest phase of the Middle Horizon at Huari may have been a response to cope with a local agricultural crisis. The use of an old Andean symbol (the staff god) on new media (pottery) with new ceramic technology (from the south coast) suggests a coalescence of ideas and innovations which have the trappings of a revitalization movement. Religious pluralism noted in Huari architecture and its continuing change during the Middle Horizon[36] suggests experimentation in coping with a local crisis. Humans, however, are not attracted to religion because of its pluralism, but because it gives their life-experience meaning. The attractiveness of Huari as a residence location was not just because of its religious pluralism,[37] but also because the inhabitants of the valley were searching for meaning to explain, understand and cope with an agricultural crisis in Huari's immediate hinterland. They needed something to eat.

In summary, the rise of ceramic specialization in the Ayacucho Valley is a complex phenomenon created by several interdependent causes. First, the expansion of agricultural land in the Early Intermediate period probably created a decline in fertility and a shrinkage of arable terrain because of erosion. Second, the prolonged drop in rainfall at the end of the sixth century A.D. reduced the amount of un-irrigated land suitable for agriculture and the amount of water available for irrigation. Both of these factors reduced the carrying capacity of the land (which had previously expanded with terracing and irrigation) and created agriculturally marginal zones in which inhabitants had to utilize non-agricultural resources to compensate for lowered subsistence returns. With a decrease in the carrying capacity of the land, potters ultimately had to move into settlements like Huari and Conchopata, settlements outside of the most productive agricultural zones. Movement into these centers was attractive for potters because they remained close to their resources, but they had access to an outlet for their pottery. Since these centers were located in a dry zone, migration into them removed the seasonal climatic constraints on the drying and firing of pottery which had limited ceramic production in the higher, more agriculturally productive zones. This change of residence permitted year-long production, and yet provided access to food through local and long-distance exchange. Third, the development of full-time specialization was favored by the existence of abundant ceramic resources such as clay, paints, and tempers which were exposed in the erosion of agricultural land.

Finally, increased pottery production and the changes that came with it were also profoundly affected by the innovation of using pottery as an expression of religious symbols. This innovation stimulated a strong demand for ceramic cult items so that as the drought created pressure on agricultural land, people responded to the crisis by appealing to a deity symbolized in ceramic decoration. As the demand for religious pottery became greater, increased ceramic specialization was favored because it provided food to specialists who could not make their living by agriculture.

With the application of the Quinua ethnographic data and the processual analogies to ancient ceramic production in the Ayacucho Valley complete, it is now time to turn to the application of the Quinua data to the central Andes as a whole. The remainder of the chapter will detail the application of the ecological approach developed in this work to the ceramic production in the central Andes both in the present and in the past.

Climate and ceramic specialization in the Peruvian Andes

How does the ecological approach developed here contribute to understanding ceramic production in the central Andes? Just as the climate limits pottery making to the dry season in Quinua, climate also has a profound effect on the seasonality of the craft elsewhere in the Peruvian Andes. In Quinua, this seasonality is further reinforced by the fact that ceramic production conflicts with the labor demands for agricultural activities (such as weeding and harvest) which must be met during the rainy season. These relationships between weather and agriculture have implications for the development of full-time ceramic production throughout the ancient Andes.

The climatic pattern of the central Andes consists of a distinct wet season and a dry season. The wet season extends from November until April with the greatest amount of rainfall occurring between December and March (figure 9.3). Generally, the heavy rains of this period are accompanied by high humidity, persistent heavy cloud cover and little sunshine. The dry season occurs between May and October with June, July and August being the driest months (figure 9.3). These months are characterized by little or no rainfall, lower relative humidity than the wet season, and little, if any, cloud cover. Sunshine is persistent during this period; the hours of sunshine are greater even though the number of daylight hours is the shortest for the entire year. The dry season, however, has the coldest temperatures with night frosts possible in some zones during June and July.[38]

These seasonal climatic patterns are greatly affected by altitude and by the distance from the tropical forest to the east of the Andes. Temperature, of course, varies inversely with altitude, but the intensity of the rainfall and cloud cover decreases as one moves down slope and westward away from the tropical forest. Evapotranspiration increases as one moves down slope so that lower zones are warmer, drier and sunnier than the higher ones (Holdridge 1947; Tosi 1960).

The rainy season of the central Andes thus provides partial regulatory feedback for ceramic production. Since pottery making requires dry weather, the wet months of December to March limit production to a part-time activity (table 9.3). The degree to which regulatory feedback affects ceramic production, however, also depends upon the ecological zone in which potters live. Colder, higher, cloudier and wetter zones limit ceramic production more than warmer, lower, sunnier and drier zones. Each zone has a different potential for ceramic specialization.

The alpine and sub-alpine zones (like the rain tundra and wet paramo) lie immediately below the permanent snow zone and are the highest zones regularly exploited by human populations. Since these zones are characterized by night frosts and low mean annual temperatures, agriculture is not possible here. These zones have a very low population density and serve only as pasture for llamas, alpacas and wild camelids. Generally, this zone is too cold for much ceramic production.

The montane prairie or moist forest lies below the alpine and sub-alpine zones. It covers an area of 62,616 square kilometers in Peru and extends from the Bolivian border to a few kilometers north of Cajamarca. In the central and southern part of this area, the zone occupies the majority of high and open valleys like the Peruvian Altiplano around Lake Titicaca, the flatlands between the upper Urubamba, Apurimac and Vilcanota Rivers and the high riverbeds of the upper Mantaro and Marañon. In the majority of this zone, the topography and climate unite to provide favorable conditions for agriculture and thus a high percentage of the native Andean population lives in this zone (Tosi 1960: 109).[39]

The montane steppe occurs at the same elevation as the montane prairie or moist forest, but it is found mainly in southeastern Peru. It covers 26,900 square kilometers and occupies large sections of the high interior valleys along the upper drainage of the Pampas and Pachachaca Rivers (both tributaries of the Apurimac), and part of the area west of Lake Titicaca. Further north, between 8° and 12° south latitude, the zone is a narrow band located on very steep terrain. This zone receives 250–500 millimeters of precipitation annually, but in reality, the rainfall varies greatly from year to year. As a result, this zone can only sporadically be used for agriculture without irrigation and then only for root crops and small grains like barley. Crop lands require a long fallow time for every one to two years of cultivation, so this zone is used mainly for grazing land. As a result, population densities are very low here (Holdridge 1947; Tosi 1960: 80–86).

The lower montane savannah or dry forest lies below the montane zones and covers an area of 24,946 square kilometers in Peru. It is the most typical zone of the great Andean valleys from the Ecuadorian border to 14° south latitude. This zone has the greatest percentage of the highland population with many small hamlets, secondary population centers, and Andean cities[40] located here (Tosi 1960: 101).

The montane prairie or moist forest and the lower montane savannah or dry forest

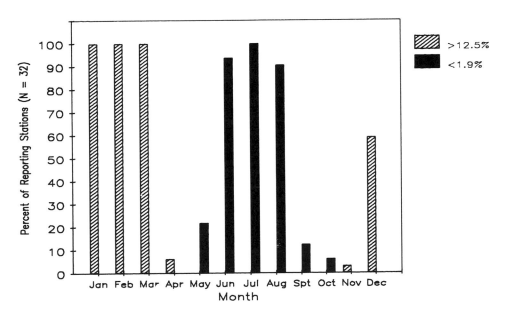

Figure 9.3 The distribution of relative dryness and wetness in the highland region of Peru showing the percent of weather stations (N = 32) reporting monthly precipitation greater than 12.5 percent and less than 1.9 percent of the yearly total (mean precipitation = 724 mm; median precipitation = 742 mm). The data used for this graph were summarized from weather stations in the following departments in highland Peru: Department of Ancash (Paron [Huaron], Ticapampa), Department of Arequipa (Andahua, Cabanconde, Imata, Orcopampa, Pane, Sibayo, Yanque), Department of Cajamarca (Cajamarca, Huacraruco, Sunchubamba), Department of Cerro de Pasco (Cerro de Pasco, Laguna Huaron), Department of Cuzco (Cuzco), Department of Huancavelica (Accnacocha), Department of Junín (Huancayo, Jauja, Pachachuca), Department of Lima (Yauricocha), Department of Puno (Azángaro, Capachica, Cojata, Crucero, Desaguadero, Isla Solo, Juli, Mazo Cruz, Puno, Putina), Department of Tacna (Paucarany, Tacalaya). (Data from Instituto Nacional de Planificación 1969: 139, 135 and summarized in Arnold 1985: 78–79.) Some stations in northern Peru tended to have a longer wet season with more months exceeding 12.5 percent of the yearly rainfall while some reporting stations around Lake Titicaca and near the coast (in the Departments of Arequipa and Tacna) in southern Peru had a longer dry season with more months having rainfall of less than 1.9 percent of the yearly total.

Table 9.3. *The time of the year when pottery is made in some central Andean communities in Peru*

Department (Province)	Community	Source	Pottery made during
Huancavelica (Huancavelica)	Huaylacucho (Totorapampa)	Ravines 1963–64: 92	July–August (dry season)
Huancavelica (Huancavelica)	Ccaccasiri (Acoria)	Ravines 1966: 210	May–October (dry season)
Puno (Lampa)	Pucara	Potter in Calca market	Not in rainy season
		Jorge Flores, personal communication	Mostly in dry season
		Potters in Cuzco railroad station	When pottery will dry
Cuzco (Canchis)	Raqch'i	Visit to community, Dec., 1972	Dry season
		Orlove 1974: 199; K. Chavez 1984–85: 162, 180	Dry season
		Sillar 1988: 47	Dry season (May–November)
Junín (Concepción)	Aco	LaVallée 1967: 104	June–October (dry season)
		David Browman, personal communication	June–October (dry season)
Ayacucho (Huamanga)	Ayacucho (*Barrio* of Santa Ana)	Visit to community, Feb., 1967	After rainy season passes (dry season)
Ayacucho (Huanta)	Luricocha (Pampay)	Visit to community, May, 1967	Dry season; after harvest
Ayacucho (Huamanga)	Ticllas	Informant in Ayacucho (marketing pattern)	Dry season; after harvest
Ayacucho (Huanta)	Huayhuas	Marketing pattern, Feb.–June 1967	Dry season
Ancash (Huarás)	Taricá	Donnan 1971	During harvest beginning March–May (beginning of the dry season)
Cochabamba, Bolivia (Quillacollo)	Calcapirhua	Litto 1976: 57, 61	Dry season; May–October
Cuzco (Cuzco)	Chitapampa	Litto 1976: 21	August (dry season)

Table 9.3 (*cont.*)

Department (Province)	Community	Source	Pottery made during
Chuquisaca Bolivia (Yamparaez)	Villamalecita	Grace Sherman, personal communication	Dry season
	Tarabuco	Grace Sherman, personal communication	Dry season
Cuzco (Quispicanchis)	Machacca	Sillar 1988: 14	Dry season (July–September)
Cuzco (Cuzco)	Seq'ueraccay	Sillar 1988: 23	Dry season (July–September)
Cuzco (Chumbivilcas)	Charamoray/ Urubamba	Sillar 1988: 29	Dry season (July–October)
Cuzco (Paruro)	Araypallpa	Sillar 1988: 40	Dry season (May–October)
Junín (Concepción)	Quicha Grande	Hagstrum 1989: 110, 116	Primarily in the dry season

both constitute the most significant zones for human occupation in the Andes. Both have enough rainfall (500–1,000 millimeters) and warm enough temperatures for agriculture, and thus both constitute the most favorable zones for agriculture in the Andes. Since the montane prairie is higher than the savannah, however, it has a lower mean annual temperature and a somewhat restricted crop repertoire consisting of mostly Andean grains, root crops and barley. The lower montane savannah is warmer and can produce root crops, Andean grains, more Old World grains than the montane zone and, most importantly, maize.

The lowest group of Andean ecological zones consists of the lower montane thorn steppe and the tropical and subtropical zones. These zones occupy intermontane valleys or canyons of relatively low elevation. They are generally dry and frequently lie in a rain shadow except where the valley lies near the eastern slopes. There, the wet/dry climatic pattern is similar to the highland pattern, but with a much greater quantity of rainfall. With the exception of the wetter zones near the eastern slopes, the tropical and subtropical zones are usually too dry for agriculture without irrigation (Tosi 1960).

Since the montane prairie, the lower montane savannah, and the montane steppe are the most favorable zones for agriculture in the Andes and contain most of the highland population (Tosi 1960: 101, 109), one would expect most of the potters to live in these zones as well. This expectation is borne out by the ethnographic data. There are twenty-six communities of potters for which the location was sufficiently precise to pinpoint their position in the ecological zones on Tosi's (1960) map

Table 9.4. *The ecological zones of some Andean pottery-making communities*

Community (District)	Department	Province	Source	Zone
Pucara	Puno	Lampa	Spahni 1966: 53–67	Moist forest
Checca (Pucara)	Puno	Lampa	Spahni 1966: 36–50	Moist forest
Santiago de Pupuja	Puno	Azángaro	Spahni 1966: 53	Moist forest
Qota Ayllu (Chucuito)	Puno	Puno	Tschopik 1950: 205	Moist forest
Palala Ayllu (Chucuito)	Puno	Puno	Tschopik 1950: 205	Moist forest
Q'arukaya (Chucuito)	Puno	Puno	Tschopik 1950: 205	Moist forest or wet paramo
Tinta	Cuzco	Canchis	Map[a] and notes on visit[b]	Moist forest
Raqch'i	Cuzco	Canchis	Map and notes on visit	Moist forest
Machaqmarca	Cuzco	Canchis	Map and notes on visit	Moist forest
Quea	Cuzco	Canchis	Map and notes on visit	Moist forest
Colquemarca	Cuzco	Chumbivilcas	Map	Moist forest
Huayllay estancias	Pasco	Pasco	Tschopik 1947: 52–53	Wet paramo or tundra
Huaychao estancias	Pasco	Pasco	Tschopik 1947: 54	Wet paramo or tundra
Aco	Junín	Concepción	LaVallée 1967: 103–4	Savannah
Mito	Junín	Concepción	Tschopik 1947: 36	Savannah
Orcotuna	Junín	Concepción	Tschopik 1947: 36	Savannah
Muqui	Junín	Jauja	Tschopik 1947: 48	Moist forest
Totorapampa (Huaylacucho)	Huancavelica	Huancavelica	Ravines 1963–64: 92	Moist forest
Ccaccasiri (Acoria)	Huancavelica	Huancavelica	Ravines 1966: 210	Moist forest
Huayhuas	Ayacucho	Huanta	Map	Savannah
Pampay (Luricocha)	Ayacucho	Huanta	Map and notes on visit	Steppe
Ayacucho, *Barrio* of Santa Ana	Ayacucho	Huamanga	Map and notes on visit	Savannah
Ticllas (San Jose de Ticllas)	Ayacucho	Huamanga	Map	Savannah

Table 9.4 (*cont.*)

Community (District)	Department	Province	Source	Zone
Hualcán (Carhuas)	Ancash	Carhuas	Stein 1961: 91–92	Moist forest
Taricá	Ancash	Huarás	Donnan 1971	Moist forest
Quicha Grande	Junín	Concepción	Hagstrum 1989: 116	Moist forest

[a] Indicates the community was located on Tosi's (1960) map as being in a particular zone.
[b] Indicates notes from a visit to the community.

(table 9.4). Of these twenty-six communities, 65 percent (17) occurred in the montane prairie or moist forest, 23 percent (6) in the lower montane savannah or dry forest, 8 percent (2) in the high sub-alpine and alpine zones and 4 percent (1) in a lower and drier zone – the lower montane thorn steppe. Since rain, cold temperatures and fog in these zones limit the drying and firing of ceramics during the rainy season in all but the lower montane thorn steppe, potters in most of the Andes are subject to the same regulatory feedback of weather and climate as occurred in Quinua.

Scheduling conflicts with agriculture also provide regulatory feedback for ceramic production throughout much of the Andes. The timing of agricultural activities varies depending on the onset of rains and the utilization of irrigation. Generally speaking, most agricultural tasks occur from September to April because of the amount of rainfall and the lack of frosts.[41]

The scheduling of labor for planting, weeding and harvesting is critical. If crops are planted too soon, they may not receive sufficient water. If planting is delayed too long after the start of the rains (or irrigation), there will not be enough time for the crops to mature before the onset of frost. If the cultivation of tubers is delayed for lack of manpower, they will rot because of insufficient drainage. If cultivation of tubers is delayed during a dry year, they will not receive enough moisture. Unharvested crops left too long in the field may be stolen, or destroyed by frost or hail (Brown 1987: 227). Once labor has been invested in agriculture, the responsibilities of planting, weeding and harvesting must thus take priority if the farmer wants a successful crop.

The labor requirements of weeding, and the planting and harvest of short season crops during the rainy season are particularly acute and could conflict with ceramic production on those rainless days which might be suitable to make pottery. Since potters generally do not make pottery in the rainy season, and cannot eat the fruit of their ceramic-related labors, agricultural responsibilities must take priority when labor requirements for agriculture conflict with those for making pottery.

In the dry season, however, lack of rain (figure 9.3) and the presence of night frost[42] restrict agricultural activity to harvest, cleaning irrigation ditches and plowing, but provide excellent conditions for making pottery. Pottery production begins after the harvest is over. Planting may be as early as August for irrigated fields and may stretch into November. With irrigation, however, a dry season crop could be grown in highland valleys of lower elevation if there was no frost. In these areas, agricultural activities continue all year round. Those potters with little agricultural land and those with land that did not need to be prepared for planting between August and November would be in a position to make more pottery during this time than other farmer/potters. Pottery making and agriculture in the central Andes thus represent activities which seasonally complement one another and provide a significant adaptation for peasants when agriculture alone is insufficient for subsistence.

Ceramic specialization on the coast of Peru

Since damp weather and climate provide a regulatory feedback for ceramic production, a perpetually warm, dry climate with much sunshine and little or no rainfall provides deviation amplifying feedback for pottery production. This climate thus favors the development of pottery making with the potential for full-time specialization.

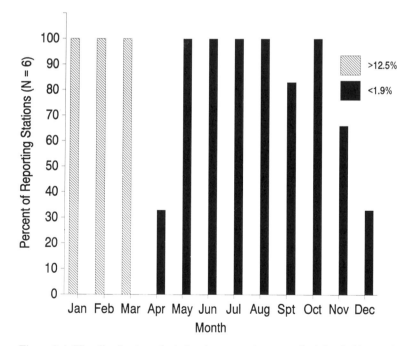

Figure 9.4 The distribution of relative dryness and wetness for inland cities on the south coast of Peru by the percent of reporting stations (N = 6). The graph shows the percent of reporting stations where the monthly total of yearly precipitation (mean precipitation = 39 mm; median values = 7 mm, 22 mm) exceeds 12.5 percent of the yearly total and is less than 1.9 percent of that total. The data used for this graph were summarized from weather stations in the following departments: Department of Ica (Ica), Department of Arequipa (Arequipa, Vitor, Ayo, Pampa Majes), and the Department of Moquegua (Moquegua). (Data compiled from Instituto Nacional de Planificación 1969: 139, 135 and summarized in Arnold 1985: 78–79.)

Parts of the Peruvian coast would provide deviation amplifying feedback for the development of pottery making into a full-time craft. Most of the coast is extremely dry with no rainfall. The little precipitation that does occur averages about 4 centimeters per year across all reporting stations (figures 9.4–9.6). In some parts of the coast, however, periodic heavy fogs and high relative humidity probably limited the development of full-time ceramic specialization. These fogs come at different times in different parts of the coast (figures 9.4–9.6), but they could limit pottery production by inhibiting the drying of pottery as they do at the pottery-making community of Simbilá on the north coast (Litto 1976: 13).[43]

There are no such fogs, however, in the river valleys in the western foothills of the Andes away from the coast. Little rainfall, if any, falls in these valleys and sunshine persists for the entire year. In many of these valleys, agriculture is possible because the moisture necessary for agriculture comes from seasonal flooding and irrigation rather than rainfall. These valleys thus provide ideal conditions for the development of the full-time, year-round ceramic specialization. Climate would not limit the development of full-time ceramic specialization on agricultural land as it did in the highlands or in other areas of the coast.

From an ecological point of view, then, it was no accident that a number of highly

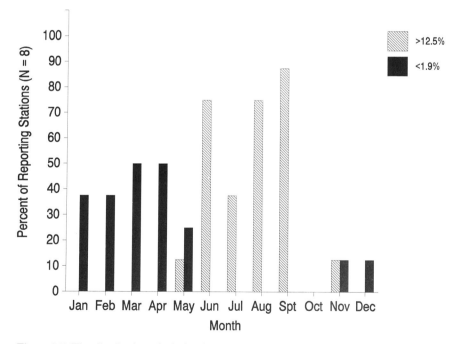

Figure 9.5 The distribution of relative dryness and wetness in the yearly precipitation in the south and central Peruvian coast by percent of reporting stations (N = 8). The graph shows the percent of reporting stations where the monthly total of yearly precipitation (mean precipitation = 41.88 mm; median values = 23 mm, 27 mm) exceeds 12.5 percent of the yearly total and is less than 1.9 percent of that total. The data used for this graph were summarized from weather stations in the following departments: Department of Ica (Pisco, San Juan), Department of Lima (Campo de Marte, La Molina, Cañete, Isla San Martín, Lomas de Lachay), Department of Tacna (Tacna). (Data compiled from Instituto Nacional de Planificación 1969: 139, 135 and summarized in Arnold 1985: 78–79.)

complex ceramic styles (for example Paracas, Nazca, Ica, and certain of the Middle Horizon styles like the Atarco Style) developed along the coast of Peru in the inland river valleys. Ceramic raw materials were probably readily available in the alluvial sediments along the rivers. And, because agriculture was dependent on irrigation rather than rainfall, climate did not limit ceramic production as it did elsewhere on the coast or in the highlands. The perpetually dry weather thus permitted the evolution of specialized, full-time ceramic production without the use of extensive drying sheds and complex kilns which would protect the fragile moisture-sensitive vessels during the pot-making process. Large populations in these valleys probably provided a ready outlet for service and utility wares, but it was the use of pottery in ritual and as an expression of mythical themes (for example, Moche, Nazca, Paracas) that provided the greatest demand for the potter's wares.

Ceramic specialization in the ancient Andes

Given the adverse effect of rainy weather and climate on ceramic production, it is possible to suggest some of the locations of full-time ceramic production in the ancient Andes. If potters lived in the same ecological zones as they do today (that is the lower montane savannah and the montane prairie or moist forest), then pottery production would be restricted to the dry season. Potters would also have to be part-time agriculturalists in order to subsist during the wet season when the weather and climate precluded most pottery production. Conversely, if ancient potters were year-round, full-time specialists, then it would be impossible for them to practice their craft in the same zones as their modern counterparts because of the inclement weather during the wet season.

Full-time ceramic specialization thus could only develop in areas of continual dryness which were contiguous to suitable agricultural land and also contained the necessary ceramic resources. This dry terrain would not be suitable for agriculture except in areas like the active floodplain of the dry highland alluvial valleys where the moisture for agriculture came from irrigation and seasonal flooding rather than from rainfall.

Where then could full-time ceramic specialization take place in the central Andes given the ecological limits on the potter's craft? By examining Tosi's (1960) map of Peru's ecological zones, it is possible to suggest those areas which were ecologically favorable for full-time ceramic specialization. Generally speaking, the most favorable zones are the lower montane thorn steppe and the sub-tropical thorn forest – the two driest zones of the central Andean highlands. Both of these zones receive 250–500 millimeters of rainfall per year, have a mean annual temperature between 12° and 24° Celsius (Tosi 1960: figure 1), and have greater evapotranspiration than the zones above.[44] These combined factors of relatively low rainfall, warm temperatures and probable low relative humidity provide excellent conditions for full-time ceramic specialization.

One cannot assume that such ecologically favorable zones had precisely the same boundaries in the past as they do today. Rather, the dry zones proposed here represent areas presently favorable for full-time ceramic specialization with boundaries subject to fluctuation due to climatic change. The climatic changes that occurred in the southern Andes during the last 2,000 years,[45] for example, undoubtedly modified the boundaries of these zones. Dry periods would expand such favorable zones for ceramic specialization and excessive wet periods would reduce them. These zones are thus only general areas which are climatically favorable, but do not correspond exactly to the boundaries of such zones in the past.

The dry zones favoring full-time ceramic specialization in the Andes consist of the lower montane thorn steppe and sub-tropical zones and occur in highland valleys along the following rivers (figure 9.7): (1) the Santa River in the northern half of the Callejón de Huaylas; (2) the Huallaga River in the vicinity of the city of Huánuco; (3) the Huarpa River in the Ayacucho Basin; (4) the Mantaro River from 12° 45' S to 12° 17' S; (5) the Apurimac River from 13° 35' S to 13° 22' S, including the following tributaries: (a) the lower Pachachaca from 13° 50' S (south of Abancay) and two of its tributaries, the Antabamba and the Chalhuanca, and (b) the Pampas River from 74° 40' W including its tributaries: the Pampamarca, the Chicha, and the lower San Miguel; (6) the area around the city of Tarma; (7) the Marañon from 9° 10' S to 8° 10' S and from 7° 0' S to 6° 40' S including the following tributaries:

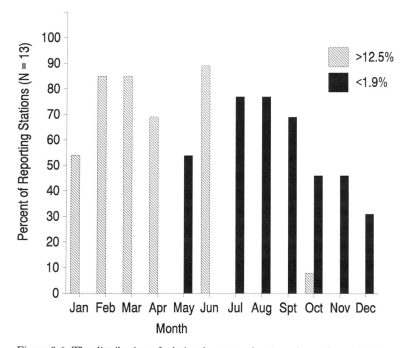

Figure 9.6 The distribution of relative dryness and wetness in yearly precipitation on the north coast of Peru by percent of reporting stations (N = 13). The graph shows the percent of reporting stations where the monthly total of yearly precipitation (mean precipitation = 46 mm; median precipitation = 18 mm) exceeds 12.5 percent of the yearly total and is less than 1.9 percent of that total. The data used for this graph were summarized from weather stations on the coastal regions in the following departments: Department of Piura (Piura, Represa San Lorenzo, Talara, El Alto), Department of Lambayeque (Lambayeque, Chiclayo, Cayalti), Department of La Libertad (Puerto Chicama, Casa Grande, Trujillo, Cartavio), and Department of Ancash (Chimbote, San Jacinto). (Data compiled from Instituto Nacional de Planificación 1969: 139, 135 and summarized in Arnold 1985: 78–79.)

(a) the lower Chasgón from 7° 40' S, (b) the Puccha from 9° 20' S, (c) the lower Chotano from 6° 15' S, and (d) between Cajamarca and Huamachuco along the Condebamba from 7° 40' S downward along the Criquegas to the Marañon (the Condebamba Basin); (8) other tributaries of the Marañon where these zones exist are: (a) the Huancabamba River south of the city of Huancabamba and along its lower tributaries to the Chamaya, and (b) the upper Anaolla in a small area in the vicinity of 5° 20' S and 79° 10' W east of Huancabamba.

The only other region outside of these zones where full-time ceramic specialization might have been possible is the montane steppe in the high plains west of Lake Titicaca and along the upper Pampas and Pachachaca drainage. Like the lower montane thorn steppe and the sub-tropical forest, this zone receives 250–500 millimeters of rainfall annually, but its mean annual temperature (6° to 12° Celsius) and evapotranspiration potential are lower than the lower montane and sub-tropical zones. The montane steppe, however, might have been too cold for much ceramic production.

In order to remove the climatic constraints on ceramic production, minimize the regulatory feedback of weather and climate and thus create deviation amplifying feedback for the craft, one or more of the following "kicks" would have to occur: (1) a climatic change towards desiccation; (2) movement of potters into a drier area where climate did not limit the craft; (3) the development of kilns, ovens and drying facilities. The initiation of any of these changes alone, however, would not necessarily bring about the development of a full-time craft.

Full-time ceramic specialization must also depend upon sufficient demand and adequate methods of distribution and exchange so that potters can exchange their wares for food. Full-time potters thus could only pursue their craft in areas with large populations where there was great demand for their wares through trade and exchange. Significant demand could also be created by using pottery as an expression of mythical and religious themes. Without cities and extensive exchange systems, however, the demand for pottery would not be great enough to support full-time potters, and potters would have to support themselves in part by agriculture. Therefore, without a series of processes which forced potters out of the agricultural land into urban settlements and into nearby dry areas, full-time ceramic specialization could not develop in much of the central Andes, except in the active floodplains of the dry valleys.

The high probability that full-time ceramic specialization was limited to the dry areas of the Andes has great implications for the study of Andean culture history as it is currently understood. Most interpretations of central Andean archaeology rest upon distributions of various ceramic styles which are assumed to reflect the culture history of the region. If it is true that large quantities of complex ceramics were produced by full-time potters in relatively few climatically favorable locations in the central Andes, then it is possible that reliance on ceramics alone for reconstructions of culture history may give a distorted picture of central Andean prehistory.

Ecological factors may influence the location of pottery production centers and thus affect the distribution of ceramic styles. Favorable climate for year-round

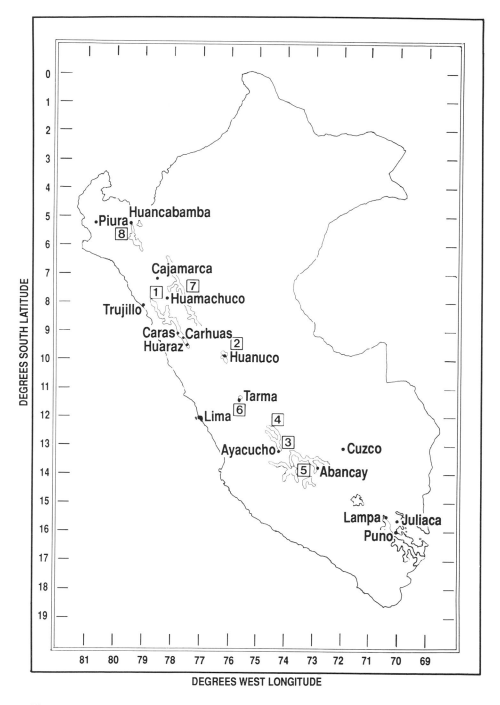

Figure 9.7 Location and distribution of the driest ecological zones in highland Peru. These zones (the lower montane thorn steppe and the sub-tropical thorn forest) have the most favorable climate for full-time ceramic specialization (data from Tosi 1960) and are the sources of at least some of the complex ceramics made in the Andes in the past. The numbers on the map correspond to numbers in the list of ecologically favorable areas mentioned in the text. Cities are shown on the map for reference and to show their relationship to the dry areas.

full-time ceramic specialization thus exists in relatively few areas of the central Andes. Complex highland ceramic styles such as Huari, Cajamarca, and Recuay occur in or near areas climatically favorable for full-time ceramic production. All of these areas[46] include the lower montane thorn steppe zone, a zone favorable for full-time ceramic specialization. It is reasonable to infer that such favorable zones also existed within these areas in the past and that full-time potters could have worked there. If these dry zones expanded in the past because of desiccation as the data from the Quelccaya Ice Cap suggest, the potential for full-time ceramic specialization would increase. Conversely, if these zones decreased in the past, because of a wetter climate, the potential for full-time ceramic production would be much more limited in these areas.

Although climatically favorable, these dry zones would not necessarily be suitable for the development of full-time ceramic specialization for other reasons. Some may be excessively steep, with non-existent valley floors. Furthermore, suitable ceramic resources may not be present. It is now clear, however, that good quality ceramic resources do exist in the Ayacucho Basin (chapters 4 and 5). Such resources also occur in the northern highlands in the southern Condebamba/Cajamarca Basin (near Huamachuco) where kaolin clays are readily available.[47] These clays were used to produce white wares during the Early Intermediate Period and the Middle Horizon (Czwarno 1985). Finally, full-time specialization would need a sizeable demand and market for pottery to support full-time potters. So, without cities, the linkage of religious symbols with pottery and extensive mechanisms of tribute, trade or exchange, climatically favorable areas would not be suitable for full-time ceramic production.

Because inter-zonal economic exchange was very important in the pre-Columbian Andes, pottery produced in areas ecologically favorable for full-time specialization could have a wide distribution without significant culture-historical contact. Huari, the capital of a Middle Horizon Empire, is a case in point. Huari is located in an area of favorable climate for full-time ceramic production and lies near excellent ceramic resources. These factors, plus the use of pottery as a channel of mythological and religious information played an important role in accounting for its wide distribution throughout the central Andes during the Middle Horizon. Huari also had a large population which together with a long-distance network of trade and exchange could have supported full-time potters.

Have other Andean states escaped our notice because they did not lie in such ecologically favorable areas for pottery production? The highland cultures which inhabit the comparatively few climatically favorable areas for full-time ceramic production and have access to ceramic resources may have more archaeological visibility than those which did not occur in such favorable areas. Furthermore, these not-so-favorable areas may not have had a pottery that expressed mythological themes. The abundance of ceramics produced in ecologically favorable areas may thus not reveal an accurate picture of a culture's importance in Andean prehistory. The study of ancient ceramics has provided important chronological controls, but do ceramics reflect culture history?

In summary, there are relatively few areas of the central Andes where climatic conditions favor the development of full-time ceramic specialization. If other environmental and cultural factors are taken into consideration and critically examined, the list of suitable locations would probably be shorter. Nevertheless, the ecological and ethnographic data suggest that full-time ceramic specialization is not possible everywhere in the Andes and those complex ceramic styles of highland origin which are assumed to be products of full-time specialists were probably made in a few locations and widely distributed. From the archaeologically best known areas in the central Andes and the list of climatically favorable areas for full-time ceramic specialization, it is reasonable to suggest that full-time potters could have worked in the Ayacucho Basin, in the region around Huánuco, in the Cajamarca–Huamachuco area, in the northern half of the Callejón de Huaylas and in parts of the Titicaca Basin. The Ayacucho region is already recognized as the source area of some Middle Horizon styles[48] and this region also has the ceramic resource potential, favorable climate and large population during the Middle Horizon to support full-time potters. Inferring the existence of full-time potters in other dry areas of the Andes will have to await the results of further archaeological research.

Conclusion

In general, then, how does an ecological approach to Quinua ceramic production inform the study of central Andean archaeology? Ceramic specialization develops in a region that is climatically favorable for ceramic production. Full-time production almost certainly developed out of part-time production where potters were also agriculturalists. The conditions that favor agriculture, however, may not always be favorable for pottery making. Pottery making requires clear, dry weather. If, however, the moisture necessary for agriculture comes from rainfall rather than irrigation, and there is no provision for shelters for drying and firing pottery, the potter's craft may be limited to a part-time activity. Therefore, in areas where a dry climate is broken by a substantial rainy season, full-time potters can develop from farmer-potters only if there is sufficient environmental diversity in the region to contain an agricultural niche and a niche of relative dryness year-round. Movement into these dry areas means the lifting of climatic limitations on the potter's craft.

Full-time ceramic specialization also requires diverse and abundant ceramic resources. Such an area, however, may not necessarily be favorable for agriculture. The terrain which exposes mineral materials for clays, tempers, and paints may be highly eroded. Since erosion continually destroys agricultural plots and removes topsoil, eroded land is marginal for agricultural use. Good quality agricultural land and land which exposes a diversity and abundance of ceramic resources would not be expected to co-occur.

Increase in population size and density will produce an increased demand for pottery and may cause potters to move out of agricultural zones into drier areas where they can become full-time specialists. Potters may also be forced into such dry areas by a reduction in the carrying capacity of the land through an extended period of dryness. In these drier areas, they no longer need to rely on agriculture to subsist, but will need to have access to agricultural products in order to exchange their pots for food. In areas where moisture for agriculture is supplied by irrigation or seasonal flooding rather than rainfall, however, the varied environment is not necessary. Climate may not limit full-time ceramic specialization, and potters can become full-time specialists without moving away from agricultural land. Finally, demand for pottery may also be stimulated by using pottery as a vehicle of mythological and ritual expression.

10

Conclusion

This book has applied an ecological approach to the study of ceramic production. It has focused on a single community and examined the relationships of its ceramic production to its environment and its sociocultural patterns of behavior. The work argues that understanding ceramic production more broadly as the product of the interaction of a population of potters with its environmental and cultural context can help understand ancient ceramic production of an area even though there may be no evidence for a direct historical link between a modern community and an ancient one. The population of potters was used as the unit of analysis and description and it was traced through its relationship to the environment, its production process, the distribution of its products and the relationships of these products to the consumers in the community. The design correlates of the population were then derived and some explanations for those correlates were explored. Finally, in the last chapter, the results of the ecological approach were applied to the archaeology of the Ayacucho Valley and that of Peru as a whole showing the kinds of inferences that can be made about the ancient ceramic production in those areas. Now, it is time to discuss the implications of this ecological approach to archaeology in general.

The community of potters
In harmony with ecological studies, this work suggests that the basic unit of ceramic analysis should be the local ceramic-producing community. This community is defined by two criteria: its members should be able to interact often and regularly and it should be geographically localized. Potters may be spread out over a territory in a dispersed settlement pattern, but there should be a geographical limit of such a population so that different communities of potters are spatially discrete.

The ecological approach views ceramic production as the result of the inter-relationships of a population of potters with the environment and the cultural and social patterns of a community. The environment may provide the resources necessary to support production, but potters must input energy to extract, transport and utilize these materials. Because pre-industrial pottery production is dependent upon the air drying of raw materials and finished vessels, local climate may limit production. Cold, wet and rainy weather can also prevent successful firing. When production is successful, finished ceramics serve as channels of matter and energy which flow from the environment to humans in order to meet their nutritional and caloric needs. Ceramics may also serve as channels of religious and/or social structural information between members of a society.

When potters are part-time and depend upon agriculture for part of their subsistence, production may be limited by the rainy weather necessary for growing crops and by scheduling conflicts with agriculture. In such a wet/dry cycle, a combination of agriculture and pottery production are mutually complementary activities with each being undertaken during a different season of the year. Successful use of the potter's craft to supplement subsistence, however, depends upon sufficient demand for ceramic products, which is the product of a large population and/or a location accessible to extensive transportation routes. Intensive demand for pottery can develop when ceramic vessels are used to express mythical and religious themes, are used in ritual, or to communicate social structural information. Such demand can help stimulate the development of full-time specialists.

If the community of potters is such an important analytical unit in the study of ceramic production, it should have tangible correlates in its ceramic products. One of these correlates consists of the raw materials used to make the pottery. Each community has access to a limited set of raw materials which it classifies, selects and uses in community-defined ways. Although the range of raw materials used by potters worldwide may be highly variable, those clays and tempers used by any given population are generally limited to those within a 7 kilometer radius of the potters' households. Since most communities of potters use these materials within a 1 kilometer radius, and few obtain their raw materials beyond 7 kilometers, the most probable radius of the "resource area" for ancient potters would be 1 kilometer with a maximum radius of 7 kilometers. This "resource area" will be likely to contain raw materials compositionally different than those in the resource areas of other communities. Since communities of potters are spatially discrete and geographically separate, the classification, selection and use of raw materials would be expected to produce pastes in one community which are compositionally distinct from those produced in other communities. Ancient populations of potters with inter-community distances of more than 7 kilometers would be easiest to identify by compositional analyses, while pottery-making populations with overlapping resource areas would be more difficult to recognize.[1]

The relationship of vessel shapes to particular communities of potters is more complex than the relationship of raw materials to these communities. Vessel shapes may be shared between discrete populations of potters. Nevertheless, each population would be expected to produce vessels with local raw materials which are different than those of other communities of potters. This proposition could easily be tested by analyzing the trace elements and mineralogical constituents of a large sample of ethnographic vessels of known provenance from an area (see Arnold, Neff and Bishop 1991). If the sample size was large enough, the same procedure could also be used to analyze archaeological vessels of an area.

Finally, each community of potters decorates its pots in community-defined ways and this decoration is different from that used in other communities. Although some design attributes (like slip and paint combinations, motifs, elements and symmetry patterns) may occur over a larger area, a particular community of potters shares similarities in design behavior not found in other communities. These similarities are reflected in the design in several ways. First, since any portion of a vessel can be selected for decoration, each community defines the size and location of the field of decoration in its own way. Second, since the design field can be arbitrarily subdivided into design zones, each community subdivides this field in a way which will be uniquely appropriate for that community. Third, while there may be any number of motifs that potters can place in the design zones, potters in each community utilize those motifs which they define as acceptable and appropriate for each zone. Finally, although a wide variety of repetitive motions (symmetry patterns) can produce motifs, bands and surface patterns on pottery, each community tends to use relatively few such motions with any frequency. To summarize, while all of these design attributes could produce an almost infinite array of variations of design fields, design zones, and motif and symmetry patterns, any one community of potters utilizes only a very limited number of these possibilities which will not be shared with other communities.

Community-defined decorative patterns are thus complex and must be understood on each of several different levels. The first level is the vessel shape. Vessel shapes are the most obvious behavioral category to both the ethnographer and the archaeologist, and ceramic design tends to be organized differently on different shapes. Second, ceramic design must be understood relative to the location of decorative space on each shape and how that space is subdivided into smaller units. Third, the design must be understood relative to consistent, high frequency use of particular motions of repetition (symmetry) for the formation of motif and band patterns. Finally, one must understand the relationships of these levels to one another. Do symmetry classes, for example, tend to co-occur with certain shapes and design zones?

Relative consistency of the design in a community is maintained through inter-generational transmission, interpersonal interaction, and by a process of selection which labels inappropriate decoration as "ugly." Ceramic production is stimulated when potters produce vessels which conform to the aesthetic standards of the consumers. These consumers may be local or they may be external to the community.

While there are patterns of production and design which are correlates of a community of potters, there is also a great deal of variability in these patterns. The kind and amount of design variability produced by a community of potters is greatly affected by the vessel shape, layout type and design zones. Some vessel shapes have more variability in types of layouts and design zones than others. Similarly, some design layouts have more variation in motifs and symmetry patterns than others. Finally, some design zones have little variation in motif vocabulary and symmetry classes whereas other zones have much greater variation.

Not only is design variability affected by the structure of the design itself, but it is produced by multiple sources. Such variability is not only multivariate, but it is also multicausal. Some variability is the result of individual creativity, but it appears to occur within the design structures that are characteristic of the community. Potters express their creativity in community-defined ways only on vessels and in zones which appear to allow that creativity. Other kinds of variability (such as the choice of design organization and motifs) appear to have their source in social groups below the level of the community. Still other kinds of variability (such as innovative shapes) occur as the result of culture change.

Production of pottery for the tourist/artisan market is the most significant example of the effect of culture change on variability. The demand for most of this artisan pottery comes from outside of the valley and acts as a selective force on the vessels produced and sold. This selective force can be an instrument of change because purchasers may use a set of aesthetic values for selection of the vessels that are different than those of the traditional producers and consumers of the vessels. Although traditional vessels may also be selected by tourists and merchants, this selective force from outside the community has the potential to change shapes and design away from traditional vessels. Pottery made for the tourist/artisan market may thus favor individual creativity to produce innovative vessels and designs. This market for pottery could increase the variability of vessels in the community by increasing the frequency of creative, experimental, and unsold products which outsiders would not purchase.

Ceramic ecology: climate and paste

An ecological approach to ceramic production provides a conceptual understanding of the relationships of ceramic production to the environment and the society. By understanding the environment around an ancient archaeological site at a particular point in time, one can make inferences about ceramic production at that site in antiquity. In the Andes, for example, it is possible to understand the potential for ceramic specialization in the region by the study of the ancient climate. Without drying facilities and kilns, full-time ceramic production is not possible everywhere in the Andes. In areas with cool temperatures, high humidity and little sunshine, weather and climate provide regulatory feedback for ceramic production. This observation has implications for the interpretation of central Andean archaeology based on pottery and has been elaborated in a previous chapter.

The technological information encoded in the ceramics provides little help in making social inferences about an ancient community of potters. Little, if any, social and economic information is encoded in ceramic pastes and great variability may exist in the composition of the paste because of the multicausal factors affecting raw material procurement. Paste analysis largely provides information on the geographical (and geological) location where the pottery was produced. Using paste to infer other aspects of the society has very limited utility although compositionally varied pastes may suggest that the producers were living in a highly dispersed settlement pattern and were using diverse sources of raw materials.

Paste color does not clearly reflect behavioral patterns. A black paste, for example, can occur for many reasons; none of these reasons have much cultural or social meaning. Furthermore, since iron minerals create color changes in pastes and slips, a community of potters using variable raw materials with various iron minerals could be expected to produce highly variable paste and slip colors.

Ceramic design

This study also has general implications for the analysis of ceramic design. Design analysis should use units of description such as the vessel shape, design field, design zone, and the motions of repetition (symmetry). The patterning of these units relative to one another should also be taken into account. Symmetry may also vary relative to the design zone in which it occurs. It may vary greatly in some zones, but may be relatively consistent in others. One would also expect the patterning of different design features within the same vessel category, and some of these patterns may also occur across the entire sample of vessels from a community.

This study also suggests that the community of potters has definite behavioral correlates in ceramic design that can be ascertained apart from potters' statements about the meaning of the designs. These correlates consist of the design structure which potters collectively use to decorate their pottery. This structure includes the organization and the subdivision of design space for a particular shape, the use of certain repetitive motions (symmetry), and the use of particular zones and motifs within those zones. In Quinua, these correlates are unique to the community and are different, or non-existent, in other pottery-making communities in the Ayacucho Valley.

One of the problems of inferring social information from ceramic design is that there is no way to specify the precise nature of the local ceramic-producing group. What kind of social unit is reflected in the ceramic design? Is the unit an ethnic group, lineage, clan, *barrio*, or community? In this study, this problem has been approached differently by beginning with an ecological approach to the potter's craft and specifying the unit of production in advance. This unit was considered to be the unit of adaptation, defined as the local community of potters, and was then used as the unit of design analysis. This approach has now shown that when one analyzes the design made by a local community of potters, one can find specific and unique design correlates of that community which are different from that of other communities of potters in an area. The local population of potters thus has a tangible material expression in the design. As a unit of analysis, the unit of adaptation may be a more universal social correlate of stylistic patterns than other kinds of social units (such as the ethnic group) that vary greatly in size and degree of interaction.

By controlling the variable of space and time in an archaeological context, it is possible to analyze ancient ceramics using the approach presented here. If one finds particular vessel shapes associated with high frequencies of specific slip and paint combinations, types of design layout, use of specific designs in specific zones and consistent symmetry types, one could infer that a particular community of potters produced these vessels. In other words, a community of potters will paint a particular vessel shape with a specific paint and slip combination in a particular design layout. Certain designs will repeatedly occur in certain zones, and each shape will share common patterns of symmetry in particular design zones. Because different communities of potters use different sets of raw materials, this approach could be easily tested by utilizing compositional analysis to analyze both the minerals and the trace elements in the paste and comparing these results with the design analysis advocated here.

The design patterns of the community of potters vary according to vessel shape and not all shapes reveal the community design correlates to the same degree. The analysis of the design on a single vessel shape may thus provide erroneous results. The *plato*, for example, has more variability than other vessels and simply may not reveal community patterns of design. Similarly, infrequent layouts or design zones contain the most variability in designs and symmetry types. Most of this variability, however, occurs within the community-defined decorative space on the vessels and may reflect individual creativity or sub-groups below the level of the community rather than community patterns of design. These conclusions thus suggest that decorative and spatial units that cross-cut vessel shapes (whether sherds, wares or types) may produce analyses which are behaviorally spurious.

The Quinua data suggest that the use of pottery design to identify ancient communities of potters must be done within the behavioral domain of particular vessel shapes, layout types and design zones. Sherds, of course, represent only random and arbitrary subdivisions of vessel shapes, and do not represent discrete units of cultural behavior. They should not be used as *ad hoc* boundaries for defining units of design analysis. This, of course, is an old problem highlighted long ago by many, including Anna Shepard (Canouts 1991: 299).

Nevertheless, sherds are all that most archaeologists have. A great deal of design information can still be obtained from sherds by analyzing the design on them with reference to the organization of design space on the vessel shapes represented by the sherds. This approach thus views design with reference to the actual behavioral units in a culture (such as vessel shapes) rather than as arbitrary entities defined by sherds.

Standardization

This study also has implications for the recent discussions about the development of specialization (see Rice 1981, 1987, 1991). The essential assumption of specialization is that as pottery production becomes more specialized, variability is reduced and the pottery becomes more standardized. In paste preparation, this means that more specialized potters will presumably select more restricted raw materials (perhaps raw materials from a single mine or pit) and produce a paste that is more uniform. The problem with this notion is that it suggests that the process of technological evolution expresses itself in the ceramic products such that increased specialization monocausally decreases paste variability. In Quinua, however, the factors that affect paste variability are multiple: great geological variability, multiple raw material sources, great mineralogical variability, variable distances to resources, dispersed settlement patterns, religious beliefs, land tenure patterns and the potter's own definition of "suitable" clay. With all of these factors affecting paste variability, it is not likely that potters would restrict themselves to a single source over time. Furthermore, great paste uniformity would not be expected under any circumstances. The composition of Quinua paste types may be able to be uniquely characterized relative to other pastes produced outside of its resource area, but one probably could never rely upon paste uniformity as an index of highly specialized potters in the Quinua area.

Even with highly specialized potters at Huari during the Middle Horizon, one would not expect to find a highly standardized paste type across the entire population of potters. Consistent procurement of raw materials from a particular location may produce paste uniformity within workshops for a period of time. But, the raw materials of the region are simply too abundant and too variable and the cultural factors affecting selection are simply too complex to suppose that reduced paste variability could exist in the past and that it is simply caused by increased specialization. Furthermore, there is little evidence of intensive mining of raw materials in the area. Even if pottery temper from a particular bed of volcanic ash was uniform within the resource area,[2] and potters were using ash from many locations, the potter's behavior could not be said to be standardized. This lack of compositional variability may look like the standardization of tempering behavior, but it would not be. Rather, potters were, in reality, procuring the ash temper from many locations. The explanation for compositional uniformity in this case would be environmental, not technological. If archaeologists want to use paste to infer anything about ancient societies, it must be understood relative to the local materials available in the resource area of an ancient site.

The present and the past

More than anything, this work returns to a point made in the introduction that an approach to ceramic production should be holistic and synthetic. One of the problems of studying ceramics is that the process of analysis destroys the potential of developing links to other cultural phenomena. If ceramics are ever going to provide archaeologists with information about ancient social and cultural behavior, then they must be studied holistically and ethnographically. Such approaches are essential for building a theory for relating ceramics to socio-cultural behavior. Such understanding cannot come from the study of the ceramic technology itself, as important as it is, but rather must come from a theory derived from an ethnographic understanding of the relationships of that technology to adaptive, social and ideological factors in many societies.

At least some processes of cultural evolution are common to the present as well as to the past. The present is not a special case of cultural evolution irrelevant to the past, but rather it is the extension of some of the same processes acting on ancient societies. In this book, it was argued that climate, resources, lack of scheduling conflicts, religion and population were all important factors that accounted for the development of full-time ceramic specialization in the Ayacucho Valley in antiquity. It is not accidental that these same factors are still at work in Quinua and producing parallel outcomes to those seen in antiquity. In the last twenty-five years, population growth, limited ecological potential, and the guerrilla movement have created pressures which have eroded traditional beliefs and practices. Quinua's location near a department capital and its proximity to transportation routes has facilitated increased contact with the tourist and artisan market. This has created a demand for vessels of "folk art" which are seen as symbols of the simple rural life, uncontaminated by the urban and industrialized world. This secular ideology has appeared to replace the traditional folk catholic beliefs which linked ceramic products to sociopolitical structures of irrigation control, fiesta sponsorship and cooperative work efforts. In the present as in the past, ideology still provides a stimulus for ceramic production, but the content of the ideology itself has changed.

As a result of all of these factors, Quinua ceramic production has dramatically increased with approximately twenty-five times as many potters in Quinua in the late 1980s as there were in 1967. Potters from Quinua also work in Lima making ceramics in private households and in some twenty other workshops using raw materials transported from Quinua (Mitchell 1991a). What is so remarkable about these changes is that they appear to be the result of the same kinds of processes that led to the development of the ceramic specialization in Huari some 1,400 years ago. While the ceramic production of Quinua appears to have changed greatly since 1967, the underlying processes that maintain ceramic production and stimulate it to evolve have not changed.

Unless the ceramics are understood with reference to the processes that produce them in cultures other than our own, interpretations of the past will be limited. Without the development of ethnoarchaeological theories that relate ceramics, behavior and society, understanding of archaeological ceramics will be limited in application to the unique circumstances in a particular time and place. One task of the ceramic ethnoarchaeologist, then, is to develop theories of ceramic production and search for the continuities, processes and commonalities of the present and the past,[3] and test them cross-culturally. If one wants to interpret the past more precisely, the development of such a ceramic theory is essential to understanding ancient ceramic production and its relative relationship to an ancient society.

NOTES

Preface

1 Arnold 1967a, 1967b, 1971a, see also Arnold and Bohor 1975, 1976.
2 Mitchell 1972, 1973, 1974, 1976a, 1976b, 1977, 1979, 1987, 1991a, 1991b, in press a, in press b.
3 The 26 days with rain in February turned out to be 32 percent higher than the mean of 20 days for February while the 29 days with rain in March were 48 percent higher than the mean of 20 days for that month (Rivera 1971: 41).
4 The amount of rainfall for February, 1967 (131.5 mm) was 23 percent above the mean of 107.1 mm for this month while the precipitation total for March (194.3 mm) was 86 percent more than the mean of 104.3 mm for that month (Rivera 1971: 43).
5 France Presse 1984; UPI 1986; Reuters 1987; Bonner 1988; Riding 1988a, 1988b, 1988c; McClintock 1989; Lama 1989.
6 See Mitchell 1987: 43; Mitchell 1991a: 10–13.
7 *MTW Network* 1984; Overseas Crusades 1985; see also McClintock 1989: 89–91.
8 See Mitchell 1987: 43; Bonner 1988; Riding 1988a.
9 For example Oswalt and VanStone 1967; Oswalt 1974.

1 Introduction

1 See Oswalt and VanStone 1967; Oswalt 1974: 5.
2 Called "ceramic ethnoarchaeology" by Kramer 1985.
3 For example Kramer 1985; Rice 1987; Arnold 1985; Kolb 1988, 1989a, 1989b, 1989c; Sinopoli 1991; Longacre 1991; Rice and Saffer 1982; Longacre and Stark 1991; Peacock 1982; Lackey 1982; Dietler and Herbich 1989; P. Arnold 1991.
4 Sabloff, Binford and McAnany 1987; Killion 1990; P. Arnold 1991.
5 Harris 1979; Price 1982; Lett 1987.
6 To some, the cultural ecological approach may imply a strong causative priority for the role of the environment and technology determining the social structure and ideology. A more reasonable viewpoint (and the interpretation of cultural ecology preferred here) sees the environment and the technology as selective forces for social organization and ideology. Adaptation not only involves the processes of adjustment to the physical and biological environment, but also to the environment changed by humans and to the social environment as well. Combining a systems approach with cultural ecology, however, mitigates the deterministic and materialistic tendencies of cultural ecology by acknowledging that the factors that affect cultural behavior are multicausal, and include beliefs and social structure as well as technology and environment.
7 See Kolb 1976, 1989a, 1991.
8 Arnold 1975a; Kolb 1976; Rice 1977; Howard 1981; Annis 1983, 1985; Annis and Jacobs 1987; see Kolb 1989a, 1989b for a review.
9 Matson 1965a, 1965b; Van der Leeuw 1976; Rice 1983a; Van der Leeuw and Pritchard 1984; Arnold 1985; Rice 1987; Kolb 1988, 1989c; Kolb and Lackey 1988.
10 Kolb 1976, 1989a, 1991.

11 Miller, Galanter and Primbaum 1960: 42.
12 Maruyama 1963: 178. Too much emphasis on deviation counteracting feedback creates a closed rather than an open system. Human cultures, however, are open systems. This discussion is concerned with the nature of interrelationships within a human/ environmental system. These interrelationships can be described as both deviation counteracting and deviation amplifying feedback.
13 Stebbins 1982: 7–8; Dobzhansky, Ayala, Stebbins and Valentine 1977: 31.
14 See Sabloff, Binford and McAnany 1987: 208.
15 Communities of potters use raw materials in unique ways in Yucatan (see Arnold 1971a) and among the Luo (see Dietler and Herbich 1989: 150).
16 As in the valley of Guatemala, see Arnold 1978b, 1978c; Arnold, Neff and Bishop 1991.
17 See Arnold 1978b, 1978c; Dietler and Herbich 1989: 150.
18 For example, Rice 1981, 1983b, 1991; Van der Leeuw and Pritchard 1984; Krause 1984, 1985; Dietler and Herbich 1989.
19 See Benco 1987; Pritchard and Van der Leeuw 1984.
20 See Hodder 1989: 273; 1991: 10–13.
21 Machacca, Seq'ueraccay, Charamoray and Urubamba, Araypallpa, and Raqch'i.
22 Mitchell 1972, 1973, 1976a, 1976b, 1977, 1991a, 1991b, in press a, in press b.
23 Spahni 1966; Litto 1976; Stastny 1981; Curatola 1983: 80.
24 Arnold 1970, 1972a, 1972b, 1975a, 1978a, 1979, 1983, 1984.
25 Spahni 1966; Mitchell 1991a.

2 The community: its physical environment and adaptation
1 Specifically, the village of Quinua is located at 13° 3' South latitude and 74° 8' 30" West longitude.
2 Dirección Nacional de Estadística y Censos 1966: 4171.
3 *Ibid.*, p. 345.
4 Geological Society of America 1964; Rivera 1971: 16.
5 Precise weather data were not available for Quinua, but were drawn from the weather station in the city of Ayacucho which lies 15 kilometers across the valley to the southwest (Rivera 1967, 1971).
6 The temperatures were interpolated from the Ayacucho temperatures. The village of Quinua is about 650 m higher than Ayacucho, but most of the population in the district is dispersed over an area between the altitude of the village (3,280 m) and the elevation of Ayacucho (2,761 m). Because the temperature drops 0.6° Celsius for every 100 m of elevation (Rivera 1967: 15), the temperatures in the village are 3.9° C lower than Ayacucho (figure 2.6).
7 For a different interpretation of the ecological zones of the valley, see MacNeish 1969: fig. 2; MacNeish, Nelken-Turner and Cook 1970: fig. 2; Flannery, Marcus and Reynolds 1989.
8 Tosi 1960: 121–123; see Flannery, Marcus and Reynolds 1989.
9 *Oxalis tuberosa.*
10 *Tropaeolum tuberosum.*
11 *Ullucus tuberosus.*
12 Mitchell 1991a: 41, in press a; see also Flannery, Marcus and Reynolds 1989.
13 Mitchell in press a.
14 *Chenopodium quinoa.*
15 Mitchell 1991a: 41, in press a.
16 Tosi 1960: 101–108; see the footnote for table 2.1.
17 *Schinus molle* L. called *molle* in Spanish (Benavides 1984: 156).
18 *Opuntia ficus-indica* or *nopal* in Spanish (Benavides 1984: 156).

19 Mitchell 1991a; Flannery, Marcus and Reynolds 1989.
20 Murra 1972, 1985; Webster 1971; Brush 1977; B. Isbell 1978; Bastien 1978.
21 Zuidema and Quispe 1968; B. Isbell 1978; Bastien 1978.
22 Mitchell 1972: 174–206, 1991a: 149–155.
23 Mitchell 1976b: 195, 1977: 50, 1991a: 149–155.
24 Mitchell 1979, in press a.
25 Wagley 1968: 166–167; Mitchell 1979, 1991a: 8, in press a.
26 Mitchell 1972: 75–127, 1979, 1991a: 8, in press b.
27 Kin related through the male line.
28 Kin related to both one's mother and one's father.

3 The environment and culture history

1 Southern Peru was wetter at certain periods during the last 2,000 years than it is today (see Thompson, Mosley-Thompson, Bolzan, and Koci 1985). One of these wetter periods probably occurred during part of the Early Intermediate Period when at least five times as much land was cultivated in the Ayacucho Valley than is being cultivated today (Lumbreras 1974).
2 MacNeish, Berger and Protsch 1970; MacNeish 1971.
3 Isbell and Schreiber 1978; Bragayrac and Gonzalez Carre 1982; Isbell, Brewster-Wray and Spickard 1991: 24, 51.
4 Knobloch 1991: 248–249; Menzel 1964: 67.
5 Isbell, Brewster-Wray and Spickard 1991: 45.
6 *Ibid.*; Menzel 1964: 69; Isbell 1988: 181; Cook 1984–85; Isbell 1984–85; Isbell 1991: 309.
7 Cook 1983; Menzel 1964; Cook 1984–85; Isbell 1984–85; Knobloch 1991.
8 Isbell 1983; see also K. Chavez 1988: 19, 24.
9 Isbell, Brewster-Wray and Spickard 1991: 48; Spickard 1983; Menzel 1964: 69.
10 McEwan 1987, 1991; Sanders 1973; T. Topic 1984: 58; J. Topic 1991; Isbell 1991: 310; Isbell and Schreiber 1978; Schreiber 1987, 1991.
11 Isbell, Brewster-Wray and Spickard 1991: 51.
12 *Ibid.*, pp. 48–49.
13 Menzel 1964: 69; Anders 1989, 1991.
14 Betanzos [1551], Cieza de León [1553], Sarmiento de Gamboa [1572], Garcilaso de la Vega [1609], Santa Cruz Pachecuti Yamqui [1613], and Guaman Poma de Ayala [1615].
15 Cieza de León [1553, chapter 90] 1959: 130–133; Sarmiento [1572, chapter 26] 1947: 162–163; Garcilaso [1609, Part I, Book 5, chapter 18] 1966: 279–281.
16 Cieza de León [1880, Part II, chapter 44–45] 1959: 222–227; Sarmiento [1572, chapter 26] 1947: 162–163; Santa Cruz Pachecuti Yamqui [1613] 1926: 178; Betanzos [1551, chapter 6] 1987: 23–26.
17 Sarmiento [1572, chapter 26] 1907: 88–89; Rowe 1963: 204.
18 *Ibid.*
19 Sarmiento [1572, chapter 26] 1947: 162–163; Cieza de León [1880, chapters 44–45] 1959: 224–227; Rowe 1963: 204.
20 Sarmiento [1572, chapter 28] 1907: 94–96.
21 Sarmiento [1572, chapters 29, 37–38] 1907: 97, 111–119; Rowe 1963: 204.
22 Cieza [1552, chapter 90] 1959: 130–133.
23 Sarmiento [chapter 26] 1947: 162–163.
24 Guaman Poma [1615] 1956 (Part I): 63, 330–331.
25 Descripción de la provincia de los Angaraes [n.d.] 1965: 203; Dillon 1983: 269.
26 Lumbreras 1974: 198; Zuidema, personal communication.
27 Lumbreras 1959a, 1959b, 1974: 198–200.

28 Zuidema 1966; see, for example, Descripción de la provincia de los Angaraes [n.d.] 1965: 203.
29 *Incas de Privilegio*, see Guaman Poma [1615] 1956 (Part I): 63; Bauer 1990: 33–50.
30 Guaman Poma [1615] 1956 (Part I): 266–269, 497–8; Bauer 1990: 166.
31 Sarmiento de Gamboa [1572, chapter 35] 1947: 185–186; translation mine.
32 Cieza de León [1553, chapter 85] 1959: 119.
33 *Ibid.*: Descripción de la provincia de los Angaraes [n.d.] 1965: 203.
34 Cieza [1553, chapter 85] 1959: 119.
35 Archivo Nacional de Perú 1632; Archivo Nacional de Perú 1702.
36 Zuidema 1966: 71; Sarmiento de Gamboa [1572, chapter 35] 1947: 186.
37 Ladrón de Guevara 1959: 247–248. Not to be confused with an Early Intermediate Period site of the same name on the valley floor.
38 Cieza [1553, chapter 86] 1959: 121–122; Stern 1982: 28.
39 Guaman Poma [1615] 1956: 413; Rivera Serna [1539–1547] 1966: 7, 8, 33; Cieza [1553, chapter 87] 1959: 123. Some writers say that the settlement was founded as early as January 9 (Cieza [1553, chapter 87] 1959: 124) and others say that it was founded as late as March 7 (Rivera and Chaves y de Guevara [1586] 1881: 106).
40 Rivera and Chaves y de Guevara [1586] 1881: 106; Rivera Serna [1539–1547] 1966: 9, 29–30.
41 Rivera Serna [1539–1547] 1966: 33; Rivera and Chavez y de Guevara [1586] 1881: 106.
42 Guaman Poma [1615] 1956: 413; Damian de la Bandera [1557] 1881; Stern 1982: 28.
43 Cieza [1553, chapter 87] 1959: 123.
44 Rivera Serna [1539–1547] 1966: 10; Rivera and Chaves y de Guevara [1586] 1881: 107.
45 Rivera Serna [1539–1547] 1966: 10.

4 Ecological interrelationships of the community of potters
1 About forty households were making pottery in 1967. This number represents approximately one percent of the population of 5,348 inhabitants counted for the District of Quinua in the census of 1961 (Dirección Nacional de Estadística y Censos 1966: 345).
2 William P. Mitchell, personal communication.
3 *Ibid.*
4 Peacock 1982: 9; Van der Leeuw 1976.
5 Spahni 1966: 87–88; Mitchell 1991a.
6 William P. Mitchell, personal communication.
7 *Ibid.*
8 Mitchell 1991a: 26, 77, 85–87.
9 Dirección Nacional de Estadística y Censos 1966 (vol. 1): 345; Mitchell 1991a: 85.
10 These data were summarized from Mitchell 1991a: 85–86.
11 Cited by Mitchell 1991a: 55.
12 Mitchell 1991a: 87–118.
13 William P. Mitchell, personal communication.
14 Mitchell, personal communication; 1991a: 71.
15 See Arnold 1985: 211–212.
16 Mitchell 1973: 18, 23; 1991a: 61.
17 Mitchell 1991a: 72; personal communication.
18 The single exception to this generalization is the *pago* of Muya, which lies near the beginning of the Lurinsayuq irrigation system. Since the Muya canal branches off the main canal first, it is the first *pago* of the barrio of Lurinsayuq to receive irrigation water (Mitchell 1976a). Nevertheless, Muya potters plant the dry season cycle, but at least some of the Muya potters are in the lower savannah.
19 William P. Mitchell, personal communication.

20 Mitchell 1976a: 36–37; 1991a: 144–149.
21 Mitchell in press a.
22 In Larampampa, Aquqata, Tantarniuq, Sururuyuq, and Wayuniuq in the *pago* of Lurinsayuq; and in other hamlets in the *pago* of Muya.
23 William P. Mitchell, personal communication.
24 *Ibid.*
25 *Ibid.*
26 Arnold 1985: 38–50, 1988.
27 *Ibid.*
28 *Ibid.*
29 Arnold 1975a, 1985: 37.

5 Ceramic production in Quinua

1 Smith 1962; Van der Leeuw and Pritchard 1984; Pritchard and Van der Leeuw 1984; Krause 1984, 1985.
2 See Shepard 1956; Steponaitis 1983: 17–45; Bronitsky 1986, 1989; Cuomo de Caprio 1985; Rice 1987; Sinopoli 1991.
3 See Shepard 1956; Rice 1987; Arnold, Neff and Bishop 1991.
4 Bronitsky 1984, 1986; Pinto, Schiffer, Smith and Skibo 1987; Skibo and Schiffer 1987.
5 Clays occur in the hamlets of Aquqata, Larampampa, Tantarniuq, Sururuyuq, Pakaqaqa, Añaqata, the pampa of Ayacucho, Lurinsayuq Pampa and Wayuniuq in the *pago* of Lurinsayuq and in various hamlets in the *pago* of Muya.
6 Wallace and Viana 1982: 8–9; Wallace 1989: 39.
7 William P. Mitchell, personal communication.
8 Mitchell in press a.
9 These vessels are called *porongos* in Spanish.
10 This paint is called *zapolina* "red ocher" in Spanish.
11 Bruce Bohor, personal communication; Rice 1987: 49.
12 The motifs on the red-on-white painting scheme are often floral motifs which potters identify as palms, flowers, maize or eucalyptus.
13 Probably *Baccharis* sp. (Towle 1961: 95; Soukup 1970: 36–37, 111) such as *B. latifolia* (R & D) Persoon (Michael Dillon, personal communication).
14 Probably *Baccharis* sp. (Soukup 1970: 36–37, 337), or *Parastrephia lepidophylla* (Wedd.) Cabrera (Michael Dillon, personal communication).
15 For example see Rye 1981: 96–100, 105; Arnold 1978b: 352–354, 356.
16 Spahni 1966; Wiesse 1982; Ravines 1963–64, 1966; Christensen 1955; Tschopik 1950; Litto 1976; K. Chavez 1984–85.
17 Black clay occurs in Larampampa, Aquqata and Añaqata.
18 See Arnold 1985: 24–25; Rye 1976: 117.
19 For an opposing view, see Eggert 1976: 514–515.
20 Arnold 1975a, 1985; Kolb 1988, 1989a, 1989b, 1989c.

6 Ceramic products and society

1 This is a weaker definition of "toxin" than is commonly used, but it is a definition advocated by Liener (1980a: 4) in *Toxic constituents of plant foodstuffs.*
2 William P. Mitchell, personal communication.
3 A third type of *chicha* is not made from maize at all, but is produced by fermenting the small fruits of the pepper tree (*molle* [*Schinus molle* L., see Benavides 1984: 156]).
4 See Spier 1967: 97–98; Arnold 1985: 147ff.
5 See Reina and Hill 1978: 238–242.
6 See Hagstrum 1988: 130, 1989: 148–150.

7 Such as the fiesta of the Virgin of Cocharcas in September.

8 Such as the Day of Pentecost (*Día del Espíritu Santo*).

9 The *chunchu* is a symbol of the jungle in highland Ecuador (see Salomon 1981: 203).

10 William P. Mitchell, personal communication.

11 *Ibid.*

12 The *yarqa aspiy*, see Mitchell 1991a: 148.

13 Mitchell 1991a, personal communication.

14 William P. Mitchell, personal communication.

15 *Ibid.*

16 *Ibid.*

17 Clymer's of Buck's County, New Hampshire.

18 Carson, Pirie Scott and Company 1977: 27–30.

19 David Browman, personal communication.

20 *Ibid.*

21 *Platos*, *yukupuynus*, *tachus* and cooking pots (*mankas*).

22 Rudolfo Vizcardo, personal communication.

23 Karen Chavez, personal communication; see Wrigley 1919: 71; Fioravanti-Molinié 1982: 221; Sallnow 1987: 257.

24 That is 20 centavos; 100 centavos = 1 sol; in 1967, 1 sol = U.S.$0.043.

25 This includes the market in nearby Acos Vinchos (figure 3.4) which was not visited.

26 That is, the *puna* or *sallqa*, see also Tschopik 1947: 33.

27 William P. Mitchell, personal communication.

28 *Ibid.*

29 This hacienda was located between the archaeological sites of Ñawim Pukyu and Acuchimay in figure 3.4.

30 Mitchell 1991a: 191–196.

7 Design correlates of the community

1 For a complete list of the vessels analyzed and the variations of each see the appendices in Arnold 1970.

2 See Shepard 1948: 217, 1956: 268; Washburn 1977a, 1977b; Zaslow 1977; Zaslow and Dittert 1977; Crowe and Washburn 1987; Washburn and Crowe 1988.

3 To facilitate comprehension of this analysis, layout types and design zones use consistent conventions throughout this presentation. Layouts and zones referred to as "A" are the most frequent patterns on each shape in the sample. Those designated as "B" have a lower frequency than "A." Other patterns which have lower frequencies than "A," are given a designation of "C" and "D" for convenience.

4 Washburn 1977a, 1977b, 1990; Crowe and Washburn 1987; Zaslow 1977; Canouts 1991: 296.

5 Crowe and Washburn 1987; Washburn and Crowe 1988.

6 Shepard 1948: 217, 1956: 268–269; Washburn and Crowe 1987.

7 Shepard (1948, 1956) originally used the categories of "rotation," "radial" and "bifold rotation." Radial symmetry combines rotational symmetry and bilateral reflection while bifold rotation is two-fold rotation.

8 Shepard 1948: 217–226, 1956: 268–269; Crowe and Washburn 1987.

9 Shepard 1956: 167; Crowe and Washburn 1987; Canouts 1991.

10 Zaslow 1977; Zaslow and Dittert 1977.

11 For example, Washburn 1977a, 1977b; Washburn and Crowe 1988; Crowe and Washburn 1987.

12 Such as Zaslow 1977; Zaslow and Dittert 1977.

13 63.4 percent or 26/41.

14 80.5 percent or 33/41.
15 24.4 percent or 10/41.
16 39.0 percent or 16/41.
17 39.0 percent or 16/41.
18 4.9 percent or 2/41.
19 9.9 percent or 4/41.
20 See also Limaco 1961: 24; O'Neale 1977.
21 Literally "place with earth or clay" (Soto Ruiz 1976: 140).
22 *Tinaqas*, pitchers (*puynus*), cooking pottery (*mankas*), beer-brewing vessels (*maqma* and *urpu*) and liquid-transport vessels (*tumins*).
23 Cooking pots from another hamlet in the Luricocha area had a kind of lug attached, consisting of a small clay cylinder (1.5 cm in diameter) placed at right angles to the handles.
24 Such as water-carrying jars (*tumin*), *chicha*-brewing vessels (*maqma*), cooking pots (*manka*).
25 Such as cooking pots (*manka*), beer-brewing vessels (*maqma, urpu*) and certain liquid transport vessels (*tumin, tinaqa*).

8 Design and society

1 Sackett 1985, 1986, 1990; Wiessner 1983, 1984; Conkey 1990; Conkey and Hastorf 1990a, 1990b.
2 Deetz 1965; Longacre 1970; Hill 1970.
3 Stanislawski 1977, 1978; Stanislawski and Stanislawski 1978.
4 Bunzel 1929; Friedrich 1970; Hayden and Cannon 1984; DeBoer 1990.
5 Bunzel 1929; Friedrich 1970; see also Conkey 1990; Wiessner 1990 for summaries of various views of style.
6 Wobst 1977; see also Conkey 1990; Wiessner 1990.
7 Wobst 1977; Sampson 1988; Shennan 1989.
8 This lack of data about the meaning of ceramic designs in Quinua places the data set analyzed here in the same position as an archaeological assemblage. Informants cannot be asked about their designs and there are no empirical data that can relate the designs to the communication of social information without making unsupported assumptions.

9 Archaeological implications: the Ayacucho Valley

1 For example, vessels like those illustrated in Lister and Lister 1976, 1982: 45–79, 1987.
2 Shapes for cooking, carrying water, brewing beer and for storage.
3 Damian de la Bandera [1557] 1881: 97.
4 Damian de la Bandera [1557] 1881: 97.
5 For example, in areas further to the southeast between Acos Vinchos and Acocro, see figure 3.4.
6 See Bauer 1990; Bauer and Stanish (1990) for descriptions of Killke and Killke-related styles.
7 The two similar motifs are the "lollipop" motif (motif 1, figure 7.15(a)) and the fern motif (motif 13, figure 7.15(c)).
8 See Rowe 1944: 48; Pardo 1957: 541–546.
9 Benavides 1984: plates X–XXI.
10 For example Benavides 1984: plates XIg, XIIa, XVi, XXIIIe.
11 For example Ponce 1971: 21–22, 1972: 210, 211, 223, 227.
12 The use of canoes, domestic animals, and modern transportation complicates this model, and does not apply to those few hunting and gathering societies which make pottery, see Arnold 1985: 32–60.

13 Cook 1984–85; Isbell 1984–85; Menzel 1964; Isbell 1991; Knobloch 1991.

14 Gary Vescelius, personal communication.

15 Menzel 1964; Isbell and Schreiber 1978.

16 Harner 1970; Boserup 1965; Dumond 1965, 1972; Sanders and Price 1968.

17 For example Menzel 1964; Cook 1984–85.

18 From the Cajamarca/Huamachuco area in the north to Cuzco in the south (T. Topic 1984: 52–57; S. Chavez 1984–85, 1985; Knobloch 1991: 253–255).

19 Menzel 1964: 35, 67, 70–72; T. Topic 1984: 52–57; J. Topic 1991: 159, 161; Knobloch 1991: 254–255.

20 Burger and Asaro 1977: 300, 308–310.

21 See Benavides 1984: 186; Bennett 1953.

22 Bennett (1953) called the material "turquoise" which is easily confused with chrysocolla (Pough 1957: 277).

23 Mitchell 1991a; personal communication.

24 See Menzel 1964: 3–5, 9–10, 67, 71; Paulsen 1983.

25 Thompson, Mosley-Thompson, Bolzan and Koci 1985.

26 The Thompson, Mosley-Thompson, Bolzan and Koci reconstruction (1985) is plotted in 10 year intervals (see Browman 1991, personal communication).

27 For example, at Raqay Pampa in Chupas, and at the site of Lagunillas near Pacaycasa (see Lumbreras 1974: 135).

28 Lumbreras 1974: 135; Isbell, Brewster-Wray and Spickard 1991.

29 Thompson, Mosley-Thompson, Bolzan and Koci 1985.

30 Isbell, Brewster-Wray and Spickard 1991: 51.

31 See Isbell, Brewster-Wray and Spickard (1991) for a discussion of the religious innovations at Huari.

32 Sherd scrapers, basalt burnishing stones, ceramic molds, potter's work tables.

33 Circular pottery supports, press molds, sherd scrapers, containers of red pigments, burnishing stones, and slate tools.

34 Thompson, Mosley-Thompson, Bolzan and Koci 1985.

35 *Ibid.*

36 Isbell, Brewster-Wray and Spickard 1991.

37 *Ibid.*

38 Instituto Nacional de Planificación 1969: 131, 135; Olivera 1971; Rivera 1967, 1971.

39 The cities of Cuzco, Puno, Sicuani, Huancavelica, Jauja and Recuay are located in this zone.

40 Such as Cajamarca, Huaraz, Chanchapoyas, Huancayo, Ayacucho, Andahuaylas, Abancay, Urubamba, and Paucartambo.

41 Adams 1959: 122; Stein 1961: 22–23; Mishkin 1946: 416–417; Tschopik 1946: 513; Mitchell 1991a.

42 Instituto Nacional de Planificación 1969: 131, 135; Rivera 1967, 1971; Olivera 1971.

43 Relative humidity can also impede the drying of pottery and is high year around with monthly means from 74–95 percent at the weather stations in the Fortaleza, Pativilca, Supe, Moche and Viru Valleys on the north coast (ONERN 1972, vol. 2: 15–16, 20; 1972, vol. 3: 9, 14, 33, 36).

44 The amount of evapotranspiration is probably not as great as that indicated by Holdridge (1947) and Tosi (1960). See Mitchell (1991a: 37) and table 2.1.

45 See Thompson, Mosley-Thompson, Bolzan and Koci 1985.

46 The Ayacucho Basin (the Huari Styles), the Cajamarca Basin (the Cajamarca Style; see also Czwarno 1985), and the Callejón de Huaylas (the Recuay Style, Lumbreras 1974: 111–115).

47 Kaolin clays are white clays which are relatively free of iron minerals (Czwarno 1983, 1985: 67, 74–75, 77; T. Topic 1984; John Thatcher, John Topic, Teresa Topic, Michael Czwarno, personal communication).

48 Bennett 1953; Isbell 1983, 1984–85, 1988; Cook 1984–85; Benavides 1984; Anders 1989; Menzel 1964, 1968; Knobloch 1991.

10 Conclusion

1 Communities with overlapping "resource areas" would consist of populations of potters separated by less than two radii of 7 km (for example see Arnold, Neff and Bishop 1991).

2 The thick beds of volcanic ash in the northern valley of Guatemala appear to be compositionally uniform (see Arnold, Neff and Bishop 1991).

3 See Sabloff, Binford and McAnany 1987; Killion 1990.

Adams, Richard N. 1959. *A community in the Andes: problems and progress in Muquiyauyo.* Monographs of the American Ethnological Society, no. 31. Seattle, University of Washington Press.

Allen, William L. and James B. Richardson III. 1971. The reconstruction of kinship from archaeological data: the concepts, the methods, and the feasibility, *American Antiquity,* 36: 41–53.

Anders, Martha B. 1989. Wamanga pottery: symbolic resistance and subversion in Middle Horizon Epoch 2 ceramics from the planned Wari site of Azángaro (Ayacucho, Peru). In Diana Claire Tkaczuk and Brian C. Vivian (eds.), *Cultures in conflict: current archaeological perspectives,* pp. 7–18. Calgary, Alberta, University of Calgary, Department of Archaeology.

   1991. Structure and function at the planned site of Azángaro: cautionary notes for the model of Huari as a centralized secular state. In William H. Isbell and Gordon F. McEwan (eds.), *Huari administrative structure: Prehistoric monumental architecture and state government,* pp. 165–197. Washington, D.C., Dumbarton Oaks Research Library and Collection.

Anderson, A. 1984. *Interpreting pottery.* London, Batsford.

Annis, Beatrice M. 1983. Potters from Sardinia: an interim report, March 1982, *Newsletter: Department of Pottery Technology,* 1: 13–26. University of Leiden, The Netherlands.

   1985. Ethnoarchaeological research: water vessels in Sardinia, *Newsletter: Department of Pottery Technology,* 3: 3–94. University of Leiden, The Netherlands.

Annis, Beatrice M. and L. Jacobs. 1986. Ethnoarchaeological research – pottery production in Oristano (Sardinia): relations between raw materials, manufacturing techniques and artifacts, *Newsletter: Department of Pottery Technology,* 4: 56–85. University of Leiden, The Netherlands.

Archivo Nacional de Perú. 1632. Títulos de propiedad. Legajo no. 13, Cuaderno no. 354. Lima.

Archivo Nacional de Perú. 1702. Derecho indígena y encomiendas. Legajo no. 8, Cuaderno no. 186. Lima.

Arnold, Dean E. 1967a. Maya Blue: A new perspective, M.A. Thesis in Anthropology, University of Illinois, Urbana.

   1967b. Sak lu'um in Maya culture: and its possible relationship to Maya Blue, *University of Illinois Department of Anthropology Research Reports,* no. 2.

   1970. *The emics of pottery design from Quinua, Peru.* Unpublished Ph.D. dissertation, Department of Anthropology, University of Illinois, Urbana.

   1971a. Ethnomineralogy of Ticul, Yucatan potters: etics and emics, *American Antiquity,* 36: 20–40.

   1971b. Inter-community ceramic differences among the central Pokoman, Guatemala. Paper presented at the American Anthropological Association, New York City, November 19.

1972a. Mineralogical analyses of ceramic materials from Quinua, Department of Ayacucho, Peru, *Archaeometry*, 14: 93–101.

1972b. Native pottery making in Quinua, Peru, *Anthropos*, 67: 858–872.

1975a. Ceramic ecology in the Ayacucho Basin, Peru: implications for prehistory, *Current Anthropology*, 16: 185–203.

1975b. Discussion and criticism: reply to Haaland and Browman, *Current Anthropology*, 16: 637–640.

1975c. Principles of paste analysis: a preliminary formulation, *Journal of the Steward Anthropological Society*, 6 (1): 33–47 (Fall, 1974).

1978a. The ceramic ecology of the Andes. Paper presented at the Institute of Andean Studies, Berkeley, January 7.

1978b. The ethnography of pottery making in the Valley of Guatemala. In Ronald K. Wetherington (ed.), *The Ceramics of Kaminaljuyu*, pp. 327–400. University Park, Pennsylvania State University Press.

1978c. Ceramic variability, environment and culture history among the Pokom in the Valley of Guatemala. In Ian Hodder (ed.), *Spatial organization of culture*, pp. 39–59. London, Duckworth.

1979. Style without time: community-wide stylistic correlates of Quinua potters. Paper presented at Institute of Andean Studies meetings, University of California, Berkeley, January 6.

1983. Design structure and community organization in Quinua, Peru. In Dorothy K. Washburn (ed.), *Structure and cognition in art*, pp. 56–74. Cambridge, Cambridge University Press.

1984. Social interaction and ceramic design: community-wide correlates in Quinua, Peru. In Prudence M. Rice (ed.), *Pots and potters: current approaches in ceramic archaeology*, pp. 133–161. Monograph XXIV, Institute of Archaeology, University of California, Los Angeles.

1985. *Ceramic theory and cultural process.* Cambridge, Cambridge University Press.

1988. "A Universal Catchment Area for Ceramic Resources: Update" in Symposium "Ceramic Ecology Revisited: Current Research on Ceramic Materials," American Anthropological Association, November 16, Phoenix.

1989. Patterns of learning, residence and descent among potters in Ticul, Yucatan, Mexico. In S. J. Shennan (ed.), *Archaeological approaches to cultural identity*, pp. 174–184. London, Unwin Hyman.

Arnold, Dean E. and B. F. Bohor. 1975. Attapulgite and Maya blue: an ancient mine comes to light, *Archaeology*, 28: 23–29.

1976. An ancient attapulgite mine in Yucatan, *Katunob*, 8 (4): 25–34 (June, 1974).

Arnold, Dean E., Hector N. Neff, and Ronald L. Bishop. 1991. Compositional analysis and "sources" of pottery: an ethnoarchaeological approach, *American Anthropologist*, 93: 70–90.

Arnold, Phillip J. 1991. *Domestic ceramic production and spatial organization: a Mexican case study in ethnoarchaeology.* Cambridge, Cambridge University Press.

Bankes, George. 1985. The manufacture and circulation of paddle and anvil pottery on the north coast of Peru, *World Archaeology*, 17: 269–276.

Bastien, Joseph W. 1978. *Mountain of the condor: metaphor and ritual in Andean ayllu.* American Ethnological Society Monograph no. 64. St Paul, Minn., West Publishing.

Bauer, Brian S. 1990. State development in the Cusco region: archaeological research on the Incas in the Province of Paruro. Ph.D. Dissertation, Department of Anthropology, University of Chicago.

Bauer, Brian S. and Charles Stanish. 1990. Killke and Killke-related pottery from Cuzco,

Peru, in the Field Museum of Natural History, *Fieldiana: Anthropology*, n.s., 15. Chicago, Field Museum of Natural history.

Benavides, Mario. 1984. *Carácter del estado Huari*. Ayacucho, Perú, Universidad Nacional de San Cristóbal de Huamanga.

Benco, Nancy L. 1987. *The early medieval pottery industry at al-Basra, Morocco*. BAR International Series 341. Oxford, British Archaeological Reports.

Bennett, Wendell C. 1953. Excavations at Wari, Ayacucho, Peru, *Yale University Publications in Anthropology*, no. 49. New Haven.

Betanzos, Juan de. 1987. *Suma y narración de los Incas* [1551]. Translated with notes and introduction by Maria del Carmen, Martin Rubio. Madrid, Ediciones Atlas.

Bonner, Raymond. 1988. A reporter at large: Peru's war, *The New Yorker*, Jan. 4, pp. 32–58.

Boserup, Ester. 1965. *The conditions of agricultural growth: the economics of agrarian change under population pressure*. Chicago, Aldine.

Boulanger, G. R. 1969. Prologue: what is cybernetics? In J. Rose (ed.), *Survey of cybernetics*, pp. 3–9. New York, Gordon and Breach.

Bragayrac, Enrique and Enrique Gonzalez Carre. 1982. Investigaciones en Wari, *Gaceta Arqueológica Andina: Informativo Bimenstral Instituto Andino de Estudios Arqueológicos*, 1 (4–5): 8.

Bronitsky, Gordon. 1984. The potential of material science approaches in the study of Virginia ceramics: An overview, *Southeastern Archaeological Conference Newsletter*, 26 (2): 15–20.

1986. The use of materials science techniques in the study of pottery construction and use, *Advances in archaeological method and theory*, 9: 209–276.

(ed.) 1989. *Pottery technology: ideas and approaches*. Boulder, Colo., Westview Press.

Browman, D. L. 1981a. Prehistoric nutrition and medicine in the Lake Titicaca Basin. In J. W. Bastien and J. M. Donahue (eds.), *Health in the Andes*, pp. 103–118. Special Publication of the American Anthropological Association, no. 12.

1981b. New light on Andean Tiwanaku, *American Scientist*, 69: 408–419.

1991. The dynamics of Chiripa Polity. Paper presented at the 47th International Congress of Americanists, July 11, 1991, New Orleans, Louisiana.

Brown, Paul F. 1987. Population growth and the disappearance of reciprocal labor in a highland Peruvian community, *Research in Economic Anthropology*, 8: 225–245.

Brush, Stephen R. 1977. *Mountain, field and family*. Philadelphia, University of Pennsylvania Press.

Bunzel, Ruth L. 1929. *The Pueblo potter: a study of creative imagination in primitive art*. New York, Columbia University Press.

Burger, Richard and Frank Asaro. 1977. Analysis de rasgos significados en la obsidiana de los Andes Centrales, *Revista del Museo Nacional*, 43: 281–325. Lima.

Canouts, Veletta. 1991. A formal approach to design: symmetry and beyond. In R. L. Bishop and F. W. Lange (eds.), *The ceramic legacy of Anna O. Shepard*, pp. 280–320. Boulder, University Press of Colorado.

Carneiro, R. L. 1970. A theory of the origin of the state, *Science*, 1969: 733–738.

Carson, Pirie Scott and Company. 1977. Mid-year linen and home sale catalog. Chicago, Carson, Pirie Scott and Company.

Chavez, Karen M. 1984–85. Traditional pottery of Raqch'i, Cuzco, Peru: A preliminary study of its production, distribution and consumption, *Ñawpa Pacha*, 22–23: 161–210.

1988. The significance of Chiripa in Lake Titicaca Basin developments, *Expedition*, 30 (3): 17–26.

Chavez, Sergio Jorge. 1984–85. Funerary offerings from a Middle Horizon context in Pomacanchi, Cuzco, *Ñawpa Pacha*, 22–23: 1–48.

1985. Ofrendas funerarias dentro de los límites meridionales del territorio Huari en el Departamento del Cuzco, *Diálogo Andino*, 4: 179–202. Departamento de Historia y Geografía, Universidad de Tarapacá, Arica, Chile.

Christensen, R. T. 1955. A modern ceramic industry at Simbila near Piura, Peru, *Chimor, Boletín de Museo de Arqueología de la Universidad Nacional de Trujillo*, Año 3, pp. 10–20.

Cieza de Leon, Pedro. 1959. *The Incas* [*Crónica del Perú* 1553 (Part I), 1880 (Part II)]. Translated by Harriet de Onis and edited with an introduction by Victor Wolfgang von Hagen. Norman, University of Oklahoma Press.

Collier, D. 1959. Pottery stamping and molding on the north coast of Peru, *Actas del XXXIII Congreso Internacional de Americanistas*, 2: 421–431. San Jose, Costa Rica, Editorial Antonio Lehman.

Conkey, M. 1990. Experimenting with style in archaeology: some historical and theoretical issues. In M. Conkey and C. Hastorf (eds.), *The uses of style in archaeology*, pp. 5–17. Cambridge, Cambridge University Press.

Conkey, M. and C. Hastorf (eds.). 1990a. *The uses of style in archaeology*. Cambridge, Cambridge University Press.

Conkey, M. and C. Hastorf. 1990b. Introduction. In M. Conkey and C. Hastorf (eds.), *The uses of style in archaeology*, pp. 1–4. Cambridge, Cambridge University Press.

Cook, Anita G. 1983. Aspects of state ideology in Huari and Tiwanaku iconography: the central deity and the sacrificer. In Daniel H. Sandweiss (ed.), *Investigations of the Andean past: papers from the first annual Northeast Conference on Andean archaeology and ethnohistory*, pp. 161–185. Ithaca, N.Y., Cornell University Latin American Studies Program.

1984–85. The Middle Horizon ceramic offerings from Conchopata, *Ñawpa Pacha*, 22–23: 49–90.

Cortazar, Pedro Felipe, Director General. 1967. *Departamento de Ayacucho. Documental del Perú*, V. Lima.

Crowe, Donald W. and Dorothy K. Washburn. 1987. Flow charts as an aid to the symmetry classification of patterned design. In Barrie Reynolds and Margaret A. Stott (eds.), *Material anthropology: contemporary approaches to material culture*, pp. 69–101. New York, University Press of America.

Cuomo di Caprio, Ninina. 1985. *La ceramica in archeologia: Antiche tecniche di lavorazione e moderni methdi d'indagine*. Rome, L'erma di Bretschneider.

Curatola, Marco. 1983. *La regione Andina*. Novara, Italy, Istituto Geografico de Agostini.

Czwarno, R. Michael. 1983. Ceramic indications of cultural interaction: evidence from northern Peru. M.A. Thesis, Department of Anthropology, Trent University.

1985. Trace elements and interaction: Three cases from northern Peru. In Marc Thompson, Maria Teresa Garcia and François J. Kense (eds.), *Status, structure and stratification: current archaeological reconstructions: Proceedings of the Sixteenth Annual Conference, The Archaeological Association of the University of Calgary*, pp. 67–85. Calgary, Alberta, University of Calgary Department of Archaeology.

Damian de la Bandera. 1881. Relación general de la disposición y calidad de la Provincia de Guamanga, llamada San Joan de la Frontera, y de la vivienda y costumbres de los naturales della. – año de 1557. In *Relaciones Geográficas de Indias*, Perú, I, pp. 96–103. Madrid, Ministerio de Fomento.

David, N. and H. Hennig. 1972. The ethnography of pottery: a Fulani case seen in archaeological perspective, *Addison Wesley Modular Publications*, no. 21, pp. 1–29. Reading, Mass., Addison Wesley.

DeBoer, Warren. 1990. Interaction, imitation and communication as expressed in style. In M. Conkey and C. Hastorf (eds.), *The uses of style in archaeology*, pp. 82–104. Cambridge, Cambridge University Press.

Deetz, James. 1965. *The dynamics of stylistic change in Arikara ceramics*. Urbana, University of Illinois Press.

Descripción de la provincia de los Angaraes [n.d.] 1965. In *Relaciones Geográficas de Indias-Perú*, por M. Jiménez de la Espada, edición y estudio preliminar por J. U. Martínez Carreras, I, pp. 201–204. *Biblioteca de Autores Españoles desde la Formación de Lenguaje Hasta Nuestros Dias*, vol. 183. Madrid, Atlas.

Dietler, M. and I. Herbich. 1989. *Tich Matek*: the technology of Luo pottery production and the definition of ceramic style, *World Archaeology*, 21: 149–164.

Dillon, Paul H. 1983. The Chancas of Angaraes: 1459(?)–1765. In Daniel H. Sandweiss (ed.), *Investigations of the Andean past: papers from the first annual Northeast Conference on Andean archaeology and ethnohistory*, pp. 268–290. Ithaca, N.Y., Cornell University Latin American Studies Program.

Dirección Nacional de Estadística y Censos. 1966. *Sexto Censo Nacional de Población de 2 de julio de 1961*, I. Lima, Peru.

Dobzhansky, Theodosius, Francisco J. Ayala, G. Ledyard Stebbins and James W. Valentine. 1977. *Evolution*. San Francisco, Freeman.

Donnan, C. B. 1971. Ancient Peruvian potters' marks and their interpretation through ethnographic analogy, *American Antiquity*, 36: 460–466.

Dumond, D. E. 1965. Population growth and cultural change, *Southwestern Journal of Anthropology*, 21: 302–324.

1972. Population growth and political centralization. In Brian Spooner (ed.), *Population growth: anthropological implications*, pp. 286–310. Cambridge, Mass., M.I.T. Press.

Eggert, Manfred K. H. 1976. Prehistoric archaeology and cognitive anthropology: a review, *Anthropos*, 71: 508–524.

Fioravanti-Molinié, Antoinette. 1982. Multi-levelled Andean society and market exchange: The case of Yucay (Peru). In David Lehmann (ed.), *Ecology and exchange in the Andes*, pp. 211–230. Cambridge, Cambridge University Press.

Flannery, K., J. Marcus, and R. G. Reynolds. 1989. *Flocks of the Wamani: A study of llama herders on the punas of Ayacucho, Peru*. San Diego, Academic Press.

Foster, G. M. 1960. Life expectancy of utilitarian pottery in Tzintzuntzan, Michoacan, Mexico, *American Antiquity*, 25: 606–609.

France Presse. 1984. Consternación en Perú por la matanza de 50 personas. *Diario de Yucatán*, Mérida, Yucatán, Mexico, Aug. 28, 1984, p. 4.

Frère, M., J. Q. Rijks and J. Rea. 1975. *Estudio agroclimatológico de la zona andina (informe técnico)*. Rome, Organización de Las Naciones Unidas para La Alimentación y La Agricultura (Proyecto Interinstitucional FAO/UNESCO/OMM en Agroclimatología).

Friedrich, Margaret Hardin. 1970. Design structure and social interaction: archaeological implications of an ethnographic analysis, *American Antiquity*, 35: 332–343.

Garcilaso de la Vega, El Inca. 1966. *Royal commentaries of the Incas and general history of Peru* [1609]. Translated with an introduction by Harold V. Livermore. Austin, University of Texas Press.

Geological Society of America. 1964. *Geological map of South America*. Boulder, Colo., Geological Society of America.

Ghersi, Humberto. 1959. Acomayo: informe antropológico. Mimeographed. Cuzco, Perú.

Gould, Richard A. 1980. *Ethnoarchaeology*. Cambridge, Cambridge University Press.

1983. Review of *Advances in archaeological method and theory*, VI, *American Antiquity*, 49: 875–876.

Guamán Poma de Ayala, Felipe. 1956. *La nueva crónica y buen gobierno* [1615]. Interpretada por Luis Bustíos Gálvez (3 vols.). Lima, Editorial de Cultura, Arqueología e Historia del Ministerio de Educación Pública del Perú.

Hagstrum, Melissa B. 1988. Ceramic production in the Central Andes, Peru: An archaeological and ethnographic comparison. In Charles C. Kolb and Louana M. Lackey (eds.) with Muriel Kirkpatrick, general editor, *A pot for all reasons: ceramic ecology revisited*, pp. 127–145. Philadelphia, Temple University, Laboratory of Anthropology.

1989. Technological continuity and change: ceramic ethnoarchaeology in the Peruvian Andes. Ph.D. dissertation in Anthropology, University of California, Los Angeles.

Hanson, N. R. 1958. *Patterns of discovery: an inquiry into the conceptual foundations of science.* Cambridge, Cambridge University Press.

Harner, M. J. 1970. Population pressure and the social evolution of agriculturalists, *Southwestern Journal of Anthropology*, 29: 67–86.

Harris, M. 1979. *Cultural materialism: the struggle for a science of culture.* New York, Random House.

Hayden, B. and A. Cannon. 1984. Interaction inferences in archaeology and learning frameworks of the Maya, *Journal of Anthropological Archaeology*, 3: 325–367.

Henrickson, E. and M. McDonald. 1983. Ceramic form and function: an ethnographic search and an archaeological application, *American Anthropologist*, 85: 630–643.

Hill, James N. 1970. Broken K Pueblo: prehistoric social organization in American Southwest, *Anthropological Papers of the University of Arizona*, no. 18. Tucson, University of Arizona Press.

Hodder, Ian. 1982a. *Symbols in action: ethnoarchaeological studies of material culture.* Cambridge: Cambridge University Press.

(ed.) 1982b. *Symbolic and structural archaeology.* Cambridge, Cambridge University Press.

1989. Writing archaeology: site reports in context, *Antiquity*, 63: 268–274.

1991. Interpretive archaeology and its role, *American Antiquity*, 56: 7–18.

Holdridge, L. R. 1947. Determination of world plant formations from simple climatic data, *Science*, 105: 367–368.

Howard, Hilary. 1981. In the wake of distribution: towards an integrated approach to ceramic studies in prehistoric Britain. In Hilary Howard and Elaine L. Morris (eds.), *Production and distribution: a ceramic viewpoint*, pp. 1–30. BAR International Series 120. Oxford, British Archaeological Reports.

Instituto Nacional de Planificación. 1969. *Atlas historico, geografico y de paisajes Peruanos.* Lima.

Isaacs, Susan L. F. 1991. American Redware as artifact and art object: Mediating the dichotomies. Paper presented at the American Anthropological Association meeting, Chicago, Ill., November 24.

Isbell, Billie Jean. 1978. *To defend ourselves: ecology and ritual in an Andean village.* Austin, University of Texas Press.

Isbell, William H. 1983. Shared ideology and parallel political development: Huari and Tiwanaku. In Daniel H. Sandweiss (ed.), *Investigations of the Andean past: papers from the first annual Northeast Conference on Andean archaeology and ethnohistory*, pp. 186–208. Ithaca, N.Y., Cornell University Latin American Studies Program.

1984–85. Conchopata, ideological innovator in Middle Horizon 1A, *Ñawpa Pacha*, 22–23: 91–126.

1988. City and state in Middle Horizon Huari. In Richard W. Keatinge (ed.), *Peruvian prehistory*, pp. 164–189. Cambridge, Cambridge University Press.

1991. Huari administration and the orthogonal cellular architecture horizon. In William H. Isbell and Gordon F. McEwan (eds.), *Huari administrative structure: Prehistoric monumental architecture and state government*, pp. 293–315. Washington, D.C., Dumbarton Oaks Research Library and Collection.

Isbell, W. H. and K. J. Schreiber. 1978. Was Huari a state? *American Antiquity*, 43: 372–389.

Isbell, W. H., C. Brewster-Wray and Lynda Spickard. 1991. Architecture and spatial organization at Huari. In William H. Isbell and Gordon F. McEwan (eds.), *Huari administrative structure: Prehistoric monumental architecture and state government*, pp. 19–52. Washington, D.C., Dumbarton Oaks Research Library and Collection.

Jaffé, W. G. 1969. Hemagluttinins. In I. E. Liener (ed.), *Toxic constituents of plant foodstuffs*, pp. 66–101. New York, Academic Press.

   1980. Hemagluttinins. In I. E. Liener (ed.), *Toxic constituents of plant foodstuffs*, 2nd edn., pp. 73–102. New York, Academic Press.

Jenni, D. A. and M. A. Jenni. 1976. Carrying behavior in humans: analysis of sex differences, *Science*, 194: 859–860.

Killion, Thomas W. 1990. Cultivation intensity and residential site structure: An ethnoarchaeological examination of peasant agriculture in the Sierra de los Tuxtlas, Veracruz, Mexico, *Latin American Antiquity*, 1: 191–215.

Knapp, Gregory W. 1988. *Ecología cultural pre-hispanico del Ecuador*, pp. 28–29. Quito, Bibliografía de Geografía Ecuatoriana 3, Banco Central del Ecuador.

Knobloch, Patricia 1991. Stylistic date of ceramics from the Huari centers. In William H. Isbell and Gordon F. McEwan (eds.), *Huari administrative structure: Prehistoric monumental architecture and state government*, pp. 247–258. Washington, D.C., Dumbarton Oaks Research Library and Collection.

Kolata, A. L. 1982. Tiwanaku: portrait of an Andean civilization, *Field Museum of Natural History Bulletin*, 53 (8): 13–28.

Kolb, Charles C. 1976. The methodology of Latin American ceramic ecology, *El Dorado: Newsletter-Bulletin on South American Anthropology*, 1 (2): 44–82.

   (ed.) 1988. *Ceramic ecology revisited 1987: the technology and socioeconomics of pottery*. BAR International Series 436. Oxford, British Archaeological Reports.

   1989a. Ceramic ecology in retrospect: a critical review of methodology and results. In Charles C. Kolb (ed.), *Ceramic ecology, 1988: current research in ceramic materials*, pp. 261–375. BAR International Series 513. Oxford, British Archaeological Reports.

   1989b. The current status of ceramic studies. In Charles C. Kolb (ed.), *Ceramic ecology, 1988: current research in ceramic materials*, pp. 377–421. BAR International Series 513. Oxford, British Archaeological Reports.

   (ed.) 1989c. *Ceramic ecology, 1988: current research in ceramic materials*. BAR International Series 513. Oxford, British Archaeological Reports.

   1991. Holistic ceramic ecology. Unpublished paper presented in the Symposium, "Ceramic Ecology '91: Current Research on Ceramics" at the American Anthropological Association Annual Meeting, Chicago, Ill., November 24.

Kolb, Charles C. and Louana M. Lackey (eds.), with Muriel Kirkpatrick, general editor. Special publication of *Cerámica de la Cultura Maya*. Philadelphia, Temple University, Laboratory of Anthropology.

Kramer, C. 1985. Ceramic ethnoarchaeology, *Annual Review of Anthropology*, 14: 77–102.

Krause, R. A. 1984. Modelling the making of pots: An ethnoarchaeological approach. In S. E. Van der Leeuw and A. C. Pritchard (eds.), *The many dimensions of pottery: Ceramics in archaeology and anthropology*, pp. 615–698. Albert Egges van Giffen Instituut voor Prae- en Protohistorie, VII. Amsterdam, University of Amsterdam.

   1985. *The clay sleeps: an ethnoarchaeological study of three African potters*. Alabama, University of Alabama Press.

Kuhn, T. S. 1962. *The structure of scientific revolutions*. Chicago, University of Chicago Press.

Lackey, L. M. 1982. *The pottery of Acatlán: a changing Mexican tradition*. Norman, University of Oklahoma Press.

Ladrón de Guevara, Carlos Guzman. 1959. Algunos establecimentos Incas en la sierra central, hoyas del Mantaro y del Pampas, *Actos and Trabajos de II Congreso Nacional de Historia de Perú*, I, pp. 243–252. Lima.

Lama, George de. 1989. "More war will bring peace," say Peru's Maoists after 15,000 die, *Chicago Tribune*, Sunday, July 9, Section 1, p. 14.

LaVallée, D. 1967. La poterie de Aco (Andes Centrales du Pérou), *Objets et Mondes*, 7 (2): 103–120.

Lett, James. 1987. *The human enterprise: a critical introduction to anthropological theory*. Boulder, Colorado, Westview Press.

Liener, I. E. 1969. Miscellaneous toxic factors. In I. E. Liener (ed.), *Toxic constituents of plant foodstuffs*, pp. 409–448. New York, Academic Press.

1980a. Introduction. In I. E. Liener (ed.), *Toxic constituents of plant foodstuffs*, 2nd edn., pp. 1–5. New York, Academic Press.

1980b. Miscellaneous toxic factors. In I. E. Liener (ed.), *Toxic constituents of plant foodstuffs*, pp. 429–467. New York, Academic Press.

Liener, I. E. and M. L. Kakade. 1969. Protease inhibitors. In I. E. Liener (ed.), *Toxic constituents of plant foodstuffs*, pp. 8–68. New York, Academic Press.

1980. Protease inhibitors. In I. E. Liener (ed.), *Toxic constituents of plant foodstuffs*, 2nd edn., pp. 7–71. New York, Academic Press.

Limaco, César Augusto. 1961. *La ciudad de Ayacucho: guía para turistas*. Ayacucho, Peru, Imprenta "González".

Lister, F. C. and R. H. Lister. 1976. *A descriptive dictionary for 500 years of Spanish-tradition ceramics [13th through 18th centuries]*. Special Publication Series, no. 1, The Society for Historical Archaeology.

1982. Sixteenth-century maiolica pottery in the Valley of Mexico, *Anthropological Papers of the University of Arizona*, no. 39. Tucson, University of Arizona Press.

1987. *Andalusian ceramics in Spain and New Spain: A cultural register from the third century B.C. to 1700*. Tucson, University of Arizona Press.

Litto, Gertrude. 1976. *South American folk pottery: traditional techniques from Peru, Ecuador, Bolivia, Venezuela, Chile and Colombia*. New York, Watson Guptill.

Longacre, William A. 1964. Sociological implications of the ceramic analysis. In P. S. Martin et al., *Chapters in the prehistory of eastern Arizona*, II, *Fieldiana: Anthropology*, 55: 155–170.

1970. Archaeology as anthropology: a case study. *Anthropological Papers of the University of Arizona*, no. 17. Tucson, University of Arizona Press.

(ed.) 1991. *Ceramic ethnoarchaeology*. Tucson, University of Arizona Press.

Longacre, William A. and Miriam Stark. 1991. References cited and a ceramic ethnoarchaeology bibliography. In William A. Longacre (ed.), *Ceramic ethnoarchaeology*. Tucson, University of Arizona Press.

Lopez, Laura. 1988. Behind Bars with the Senderistas, *Time Magazine*, p. 57, May 9, 1988.

Lumbreras, Luis G. 1959a. Esquema arqueológica de la sierra central del Perú, *Revista del Museo Nacional*, 28: 63–116. Lima.

1959b. Sobre los Chancas, *Actas y Trabajos de II Congreso Nacional de Historia de Perú – Epoca Pre-Hispánica*, I, pp. 21–24. Lima.

1974. *The peoples and cultures of ancient Peru*. Translated by Betty J. Meggers. Washington, Smithsonian Institution Press.

MacNeish, R. S. 1969. *First annual report of the Ayacucho Archaeological-Botanical Project*. Andover, Mass., Phillips Academy.

1971. Early Man in the Andes, *Scientific American*, 224 (4): 36–46.

MacNeish, R. S., A. Nelken-Turner, and A. G. Cook. 1970. *Second annual report of the Ayacucho Archaeological-Botanical Project*. Andover, Mass., Phillips Academy.

MacNeish, R. S., R. Berger and R. Protsch. 1970. Megafauna and man from Ayacucho, Highland Peru, *Science*, 168: 975–977.

Maruyama, M. 1963. The second cybernetics: deviation-amplifying mutual causal processes, *American Scientist*, 51 (2): 164–179.

Matson, F. R. 1965a. Ceramic ecology: an approach to the study of the early cultures of the Near East. In F. R. Matson (ed.), *Ceramics and man*, pp. 202–217. Chicago, Aldine.
(ed.) 1965b. *Ceramics and man*. Chicago, Aldine.

McClintock, Cynthia. 1989. Peru's *Sendero Luminoso* rebellion: origins and trajectory. In Susan Eckstein (ed.), *Power and popular protest: Latin American social movements*, pp. 61–101. Berkeley, University of California Press.

McEwan, Gordon F. 1987. *The Middle Horizon in the Valley of Cuzco, Peru: The impact of the Wari occupation of the Lucre Basin*. BAR International Series 372. Oxford, British Archaeological Reports.
1991. Investigations at the Pikillacta site: a provincial Huari center in the Valley of Cuzco. In William H. Isbell and Gordon F. McEwan (eds.), *Huari administrative structure: prehistoric monumental architecture and state government*, pp. 93–119. Washington, D.C., Dumbarton Oaks Research Library and Collection.

Menzel, Dorothy. 1964. Style and time in the Middle Horizon, *Ñawpa Pacha*, 2: 1–105.
1968. New data on the Huari Empire in Middle Horizon Epoch 2A, *Ñawpa Pacha*, 6: 47–114.

Miller, G. A., E. Galanter and K. H. Primbaum. 1960. *Plans and the structure of behavior*. New York, Henry Holt.

Mishkin, Bernard. 1946. The contemporary Quechua. In Julian H. Steward (ed.), *Handbook of South American Indians, Volume 2: The Andean Civilizations*, pp. 411–470. *Smithsonian Institution Bureau of American Ethnology Bulletin*, no. 143. Washington, D.C.

Mitchell, William P. 1972. The system of power in Quinua: a community of the Central Peruvian Highlands. Unpublished Ph.D. Dissertation, Department of Anthropology, University of Pittsburgh.
1973. A preliminary report on irrigation and community of the Central Peruvian Highlands. Paper presented at the Symposium on Irrigation and Communal Organization, 72nd annual meeting of the American Anthropological Association, New Orleans, La.
1974. Status inconsistency and dimensions of rank in the central Peruvian highlands. Paper presented at the Symposium on Social Stratification in the Andes, 41st International Congress of Americanists, Mexico, D.F., September.
1976a. Irrigation and community in the central Peruvian highlands, *American Anthropologist*, 78: 25–44.
1976b. Social adaptation to the mountain environment of an Andean village. In J. Luchop, J. D. Cawthon and M. J. Breslin (eds.), *Hill lands: proceedings of an international symposium*, pp. 187–98. Morgantown, University of West Virginia Press.
1977. Irrigation farming in the Andes: evolutionary implications. In Rhoda Halperin and James Dow (eds.), *Peasant livelihood: studies in economic anthropology and cultural ecology*, pp. 36–59. New York, St. Martin's Press.
1979. Inconsistencia de estatus social y dimensiones de rango en los Andes Centrales del Perú, *Estudios Andinos*, 15: 21–31.
1987. The myth of the isolated native community: a case study. In Judy Himes (ed.), *Global interdependence in the curriculum: case studies for the social sciences*, pp. 35–49. Princeton, N.J., Woodrow Wilson National Fellowship Foundation.
1991a. *Peasants on the edge: crop, cult and crisis in the Andes*. Austin, University of Texas Press.

1991b. Some are more equal than others: labor supply, reciprocity, and redistribution in the Andes, *Research in Economic Anthropology*, 13: 191–219.

In press a. Multi-zone agriculture in an Andean village. In Richard S. MacNeish (ed.), *Ayacucho archaeological-botanical project*, I. Ann Arbor, University of Michigan Press.

In press b. Dam the water: The ecology and political economy of irrigation in the Ayacucho Valley, Peru. In David Guillet and William P. Mitchell (eds.), *Irrigation at high altitudes: The social organization of water control systems in the Andes*. Washington, D.C., American Anthropological Association, publication series of the Society for Latin American Anthropology.

Montgomery, R. D. 1969. Cyanogens. In I. E. Liener (ed.), *Toxic constituents of plant foodstuffs*, pp. 143–157. New York, Academic Press.

1980. Cyanogens. In I. E. Liener (ed.), *Toxic constituents of plant foodstuffs*, 2nd edn., pp. 143–160. New York, Academic Press.

Moran, Emilio F. 1982. *Human adaptability: an introduction to ecological anthropology*. Boulder, Colo., Westview Press.

MTW Network. 1984. Terrorist activity stops MTW mission work. Winter. Atlanta, Ga., Presbyterian Church in America.

Murra, John V. 1972. "El Control vertical" de un máximo de pisos ecológicos en la economía de las sociedades Andinas. In *Visita de la Provincia de Leon de Húanuco en 1562*, Iñigo Ortiz de Zuñiga, visitador, Documentos para la Historia y Etnología de Húanuco y la selva central, II, pp. 427–76. Húanuco, Peru, Universidad Nacional Hermilio Valdizán.

1973. Rite and crop in the Inca state. In Daniel R. Gross (ed.), *Peoples and cultures of native South America*, pp. 377–389. Garden City, N.Y., The Natural History Press.

1985. "El archipiélago vertical" revisited. In Shozo Masuda, Izumi Shimada, and Craig Morris (eds.), *Andean ecology and civilization: an interdisciplinary perspective on Andean ecological complementarity*, pp. 3–13. Tokyo, University of Tokyo Press.

O'Brien, Michael J. and Thomas D. Holland. 1990. Variation, selection and the archaeological record. In Michael B. Schiffer (ed.), *Archaeological method and theory*, II, pp. 31–79. Tucson, University of Arizona Press.

1992. The role of adaptation in archaeological explanation, *American Antiquity*, 57: 36–59.

Olivera, L. O., Jefe. 1971. *Boletín del servicio de meteorología Año 1971*. Cuzco, Perú, Universidad Nacional del Cuzco, Programa Academico de Ciencias Biologicas.

O'Neale, Lila M. 1977. Notes on pottery making in highland Peru, *Ñawpa Pacha*, 14: 41–60.

ONERN (Oficina Nacional de Evaluación de Recursos Naturales). 1972. *Inventario, evaluación y uso racional de los recursos naturales de la costa*, 3 vols. Lima.

Onuki, Y. 1967. Ecological backgrounds of the Formative, Classic and Post-Classic Periods of the Central Andes, *Latin American Studies* (Anthropological and Geographical Studies of the Central Andes), 71–100, Tokyo.

Orlove, B. S. 1974. Urban and rural artisans in southern Peru, *International Journal of Comparative Sociology*, 15 (3–4): 193–211.

Oswalt, Wendell H. 1974. Monograph IV, Archaeological Survey. In C. B. Donnan and C. W. Clewlow, Jr. (eds.), *Ethnoarchaeology*, pp. 3–11, Institute of Archaeology, University of California, Los Angeles.

Oswalt, W. H. and J. W. VanStone. 1967. *The ethnoarchaeology of Crow village, Alaska. Smithsonian Institution Bureau of American Ethnology Bulletin*, no. 199. Washington, D.C.

Overseas Crusades. Lost and Found. 1985. "Peru," 4: 4–5.

Pardo, Luis G. 1957. *Historia y arqueología del Cuzco*, 2 vols. Cuzco.

Parker, Gary. 1965. *Gramática del Quechua Ayacuchano*. Lima, Universidad Mayor de San Marcos.

Paulsen, Allison C. 1983. Huaca del Loro revisited: The Nasca–Huarpa connection. In Daniel H. Sandweiss (ed.), *Investigations of the Andean past: papers from the first annual Northeast Conference on Andean archaeology and ethnohistory*, pp. 98–121. Ithaca, N.Y., Cornell University Latin American Studies Program.

Peacock, D. P. S. 1982. *Pottery in the Roman world: An ethnoarchaeological approach*. London, Longman.

Pinto, Inês Vaz, Michael B. Schiffer, Susan Smith and James M. Skibo. 1987. Effects of temper on ceramic abrasion resistance: a preliminary investigation, *Archaeomaterials*, 1: 119–134.

Ponce Sangines, Carlos. 1971. La cerámica de la epoca I de Tiwanaku, *Pumapunku* (Revista Oficial del Instituto de Cultura Aymara, H. Municipalidad de La Paz, Bolivia), 2: 7–28.

1972. *Tiwanaku: espacio, tiempo y cultura*. La Paz, Academia Nacional de Ciencias de Bolivia, Publicación no. 30.

Pough, Frederick H. 1957. *A field guide to rocks and minerals*, 2nd edn. Boston, Houghton Mifflin Company.

Pozzi-Escot, Denise. 1982. Excavaciones en Conchopata, *Gaceta Arqueológica Andina* (Informativo Bimensal, Instituto Andino de Estudios arqueológicos), 1 (4–5): 9.

1991. Conchopata: A community of potters. In William H. Isbell and Gordon F. McEwan (eds.), *Huari administrative structure: Prehistoric monumental architecture and state government*, pp. 81–92. Washington, D.C., Dumbarton Oaks Research Library and Collection.

Price, B. J. 1982. Cultural materialism: a theoretical review, *American Antiquity*, 47: 709–741.

Pritchard, A. C. and S. E. Van der Leeuw. 1984. Introduction: The many dimensions of pottery. In S. E. Van der Leeuw and A. C. Pritchard (eds.), *The many dimensions of pottery: ceramics in archaeology and anthropology*, pp. 1–23. Amsterdam, Albert Egges van Giffen Instituut voor Prae- en Protohistorie, Cingvla VII, University of Amsterdam.

Ravines, Roger H. 1963–64. Alfarería domestica de Huaylacucho, Departamento de Huancavelica, *Folklore Americano*, Año 11–12, no. 11–12, pp. 92–96. Lima.

1966. Ccaccasiri-pi Rurani Mankata, *Folklore Americano*, Año 14, no. 14, pp. 210–222. Lima.

Ravines, Roger and Fernando Villiger (eds.) 1989. *La cerámica tradicional del Perú*. Lima, Editorial Los Pinos.

Reina, Ruben E. and Robert M. Hill. 1978. *The traditional pottery of Guatemala*. Austin, University of Texas Press.

Reuters. 1987. Peruvian rebels leave threats for candidates, *Chicago Tribune*, Monday, November 9, 1987, Section 1, p. 5.

Rice, Prudence M. 1977. Whiteware pottery production in the Valley of Guatemala: specialization and resource utilization, *Journal of Field Archaeology*, 4: 221–223.

1981. Evolution of specialized pottery production: a trial model, *Current Anthropology*, 22: 219–240.

(ed.) 1983a. *Pots and potters: current approaches in ceramic archaeology*. Monograph XXIV, Institute of Archaeology, University of California, Los Angeles.

1983b. The archaeological study of specialized pottery production: some aspects of method and theory. In Prudence M. Rice (ed.), *Pots and potters: current approaches in ceramic archaeology*, pp. 45–54. Monograph XXIV, Institute of Archaeology, University of California, Los Angeles.

1987. *Pottery analysis: a sourcebook*. Chicago, University of Chicago Press.

1991. Specialization, standardization and diversity: a retrospective. In Ronald L. Bishop (ed.), *The legacy of Anna O. Shepard*, pp. 257–279. Boulder, University Press of Colorado.

Rice, Prudence M. and Marian E. Saffer. 1982. Annotated bibliography of ceramic studies, Part 1: analysis: technical and ethnographic approaches to pottery production and use. *Ceramic notes. Occasional publications of the ceramic technology laboratory, Florida State Museum*, no. 1, University of Florida.

Riding, Alan. 1988a. Peruvian guerrillas emerge as an urban political force, *The New York Times*, July 17, 1988, Section 1, pp. 1, 12.

1988b. Human rights group criticizes Peru, *The New York Times*, Nov. 3, 1988, Section 1, p. 3.

1988c. Death gang linked to Peru's rulers: murders and bombings tied to militants in the party, some politicians say, *The New York Times*, Dec. 4, 1988, Section 1, p. 15.

Rivera, Jaime. 1967. El clima de Ayacucho, *Universidad: Organo de Extensión Cultural de la Universidad de San Cristóbal de Huamanga*, Año 3, no. 9, pp. 15–16. Ayacucho, Peru.

1971. *Geografía general de Ayacucho*. Ayacucho, Peru, Universidad Nacional de San Cristóbal de Huamanga, Dirección Universitaria de Investigación.

Rivera, Pedro de and Antonio de Chaves y de Guevara. 1881. Relación de la ciudad de Guamanga y sus términos – año de 1586. In *Relaciones Geográficas de Indias*, Perú, I, pp. 105–139. Madrid, Ministerio de Fomento.

Rivera Serna, Raul. 1966. *Libro de cabildo de la Ciudad San Juan de la Frontera de Huamanga 1539–1547. Documentos regionales de la etnología y etnohistoria andinas*, no. 3. Lima.

Rowe, John H. 1944. An introduction to the archaeology of Cuzco. *Papers of the Peabody Museum of American Archaeology and Ethnology*, Harvard University, vol. 27, no. 2. Cambridge, Mass.

1963. Inca Culture at the time of the Spanish Conquest. In Julian H. Steward (ed.), *Handbook of South American Indians, volume 2: The Andean civilizations*, pp. 183–330. New York, Cooper Square Publishers (Reprint of 1946 edition by *Smithsonian Institution, Bureau of American Ethnology Bulletin*, no. 143).

Rye, O. S. 1976. Keeping your temper under control: materials and the manufacture of Papuan pottery, *Archaeology and Physical Anthropology in Oceania*, 11: 106–137.

1981. *Pottery technology: principles and reconstruction*. Washington, D.C., Taraxacum.

Rye, O. S. and Clifford Evans. 1976. *Traditional pottery techniques of Pakistan: field and laboratory studies*. Washington, D.C., Smithsonian Contributions to Anthropology, no. 21.

Sabloff, J. A., L. R. Binford and P. A. McAnany. 1987. Understanding the archaeological record, *Antiquity*, 61: 203–209.

Sackett, James R. 1985. Style and ethnicity in the Kalahari: A reply to Wiessner, *American Antiquity*, 50: 154–159.

1986. Isochrestism and style: a clarification, *Journal of Anthropological Archaeology*, 5: 266–277.

1990. Style and ethnicity in archaeology: the case for isochrestism. In M. Conkey and C. Hastorf (eds.), *The uses of style in archaeology*, pp. 32–43. Cambridge, Cambridge University Press.

Sallnow, Michael J. 1987. *Pilgrims of the Andes: Regional cults in Cuzco*. Washington, D.C., Smithsonian Institution Press.

Salomon, Frank. 1981. Killing the Yumbo: A ritual drama of northern Quito. In Norman E. Whitten, Jr. (ed.), *Cultural transformation and ethnicity in modern Ecuador*, pp. 161–208. Urbana, University of Illinois Press.

Sampson, C. Garth. 1988. *Stylistic boundaries among mobile hunter-foragers*. Washington, D.C., Smithsonian Institution Press.

Sanders, William T. 1973. The significance of Pikillakta in Andean culture history, *Occasional Papers in Anthropology*, 8: 381–428. Department of Anthropology, The Pennsylvania State University, University Park, Pa.

Sanders, W. T. and Barbara Price. 1968. *Mesoamerica: the evolution of a civilization*. New York, Random House.

Santa Cruz Pachecuti Yamqui Sakamaygua. 1926. Relación de antigüedades deste reyno del Perú [1613]. In *Colección de libros y documentos referentes a las historia del Perú*, 2nd ser. IX, pp. 125–135. Lima.

Sarmiento de Gamboa, Pedro. 1907. *History of the Incas* (1572). Translated and edited with notes by Clements Markham, The Hakluyt Society Publications, 2nd ser., 22. Cambridge.

    1947. *Historia de los Incas* (1572), 3rd edn., edición y nota preliminar de Angel Rosenblat. Buenos Aires, Emecé Editores.

Schiffer, M. 1976. *Behavioral archaeology*. New York, Academic Press.

Schreiber, Katharina J. 1987. From state to empire: the expansion of Wari outside the Ayacucho Basin. In Jonathan Haas, Sheila Pozorski and Thomas Pozorski (eds.), *The origins and development of the Andean state*, pp. 91–96. Cambridge, Cambridge University Press.

    1991. Jincamocco: A Huari administrative center in the south central highlands of Peru. In William H. Isbell and Gordon F. McEwan (eds.), *Huari administrative structure: Prehistoric monumental architecture and state government*, pp. 199–213. Washington, D.C., Dumbarton Oaks Research Library and Collection.

Sharp, L. 1952. Steel axes for stone age Australians, *Human Organization*, 11: 17–22.

Shennan, Stephen J. (ed.). 1989. *Archaeological approaches to cultural identity*. Winchester, Mass., Unwin Hyman.

Shepard, Anna O. 1948. The symmetry of abstract design with special reference to ceramic decoration, *Contributions to American Anthropology and History*, no. 47, Carnegie Institute of Washington.

    1956. *Ceramics for the archaeologist*. Carnegie Institution of Washington, publication 609.

Sillar, W. J. M. 1988. Mud and firewater: making pots in Peru. M.Sc. Thesis, University of London, Institute of Archaeology, Department of Prehistory.

Sinopoli, Carla M. 1991. *Approaches to archaeological ceramics*. New York, Plenum Press.

Skibo, James M. and Michael B. Schiffer. 1987. The effects of water on processes of ceramic abrasion, *Journal of Archaeological Science*, 14: 83–96.

Smith, Watson. 1962. Schools, pots and potters, *American Anthropologist*, 64: 1165–1178.

Soto Ruiz, Clodoaldo. 1976. *Gramática Quechua: Ayacucho-Chanca*. Lima, Ministerio de Educación.

Soukup, Jaroslav. 1970. *Vocabulario de los nombres vulgares de la flora Peruana*. Lima, Colegio Salesiano.

Spahni, Jean-Christian. 1966. *La cerámica popular del Perú*. Lima, Peruano Suiza, S.A.

Spickard, Lynda E. 1983. The development of Huari administrative architecture. In Daniel H. Sandweiss (ed.), *Investigations of the Andean past: papers from the first annual Northeast Conference on Andean archaeology and ethnohistory*, pp. 136–160. Ithaca, N.Y., Cornell University Latin American Studies Program.

Spier, R. F. G. 1967. Work habits, postures and fixtures. In C. L. Riley and W. W. Taylor (eds.), *American historical anthropology: essays in honor of Leslie Spier*, pp. 197–220. Carbondale, Ill., Southern Illinois University Press.

Stanislawski, Michael B. 1977. Ethnoarchaeology of Hopi and Hopi-Tewa pottery making: styles of learning. In Daniell Ingersoll, John E. Yellen and William MacDonald (eds.), *Experimental archaeology*, pp. 378–408. New York, Columbia University Press.

 1978. If pots were mortal. In Richard A. Gould (ed.), *Explorations in ethnoarchaeology*, pp. 201–227. Albuquerque, University of New Mexico Press.

Stanislawski, Michael B. and Barbara B. Stanislawski. 1978. Hopi and Hopi-Tewa ceramic tradition networks. In Ian Hodder (ed.), *The spatial organization of culture*, pp. 61–76. London, Duckworth.

Stastny, Francisco. 1981. *Las artes populares del Perú*. Madrid, Ediciones Edubanco Fundación del Banco Continental para el Fomento de la Educación y la Cultura (EDUBANCO).

Stebbins, G. L. 1982. *Darwin to DNA, molecules to humanity*. San Francisco, Freeman.

Stein, William W. 1961. *Hualcán: life in the highlands of Peru*. Ithaca, Cornell University Press.

Steponaitis, Vincas P. 1983. *Ceramics, chronology, and community patterns: an archaeological study at Moundville*. New York, Academic Press.

Stern, Steve J. 1982. *Peru's indian peoples and the challenge of Spanish Conquest: Huamanga to 1640*. Madison, University of Wisconsin Press.

Steward, Julian H. 1955. *Theory of culture change*. Urbana, University of Illinois Press.

Thompson, L. G., E. Mosley-Thompson, J. R. Bolzan, B. R. Koci. 1985. A 1500-year record of tropical precipitation in ice cores from the Quelccaya ice cap, Peru, *Science*, 229: 971–973.

Topic, John L. 1991. Huari and Huamachuco. In William H. Isbell and Gordon F. McEwan (eds.), *Huari administrative structure: Prehistoric monumental architecture and state government*, pp. 141–164. Washington, D.C., Dumbarton Oaks Research Library and Collection.

Topic, R. L. 1984. Huamachuco Archaeological Project: preliminary report on the third session, June–August 1983, *Trent University Occasional Papers in Anthropology, no. 1*. Peterborough, Ontario: Trent University Department of Anthropology.

Tosi, J. A. 1960. *Zonas de vida natural en el Perú*. Instituto Interamericano de Ciencias Agrícolas de la OEA Zona Andina, Boletín Técnico 5. Lima, Organización de Estados Americanos.

Towle, Margret A. 1961. Ethnobotany of Pre-Columbian Peru, *Viking Fund Publications in Anthropology*, no. 30.

Tschopik, Harry Jr. 1946. The Aymara. In Julian H. Steward (ed.), *Handbook of South American Indians, volume 2: The Andean Civilizations*, pp. 501–573, *Smithsonian Institution Bureau of American Ethnology Bulletin*, no. 143. Washington, D.C.

 1947. *Highland communities of central Peru: A regional survey*. Smithsonian Institute of Social Anthropology, publication 5.

 1950. An Andean ceramic tradition in historical perspective, *American Antiquity*, 15: 196–218.

UPI. 1986. Two cities in Peru shaken by bombings. *The New York Times*, October 5, 1986, p. 45.

Van der Leeuw, S. E. 1976. *Studies in the technology of ancient pottery*, 2 vols. Amsterdam, University of Amsterdam.

Van der Leeuw, S. E. and A. C. Pritchard (eds.). 1984. *The many dimensions of pottery: ceramics in archaeology and anthropology*. Albert Egges van Giffen Instituut vor Prae- en Protohistorie, VII, Amsterdam, University of Amsterdam.

Wagley, Charles. 1968. *The Latin American tradition*. New York, Columbia University Press.

Wallace, Dwight. 1989. Functional factors of burnished and micaceous ceramics. In Gordon Bronitsky (ed.), *Pottery technology: ideas and approaches*, pp. 33–39. Boulder, Colo., Westview Press.

Wallace, Dwight and Carlos Viana. 1982. Functional factors of burnished and micaceous ceramics. Paper presented at Annual Meeting American Anthropological Association, Washington, D.C.

Washburn, Dorothy. 1977a. A symmetry classification of Pueblo ceramic designs. In Paul Grebinger (ed.), *Discovering past behavior: experiments in the archaeology of the American Southwest*, pp. 101–121. New York, Gordon and Breach.

   1977b. A symmetry analysis of upper Gila area ceramic design, *Papers of the Peabody Museum of Archaeology and Ethnology*, Harvard University, vol. 68. Cambridge, Mass.

   1990. Style, classification and ethnicity: design categories on Bakuba raffia cloth, *Transactions of the American Philosophical Society*, vol. 80, Part 3. Philadelphia.

Washburn, Dorothy and D. Crowe. 1988. *Symmetries of culture*. Seattle, University of Washington Press.

Webster, Steven S. 1971. An indigenous Quechua community in exploitation of multiple ecological zones, *Actas y Memorias del 39 Congreso Internacional de Americanistas Actas y Memorias*, vol. 3, pp. 174–183. [*Revista del Museo Nacional* [Lima], vol. 37.]

Wiesse, Jose R. Sabogal. 1982. *La cerámica de Piura*, 2 vols. Lima, Instituto Andino de Artes Populares.

Wiessner, Polly. 1983. Style and social information in Kalahari San projectile points, *American Antiquity*, 49 (2): 253–276.

   1984. Reconsidering the behavioral basis of style: a case study among the Kalahari San, *Journal of Anthropological Archaeology*, 3: 190–234.

   1990. Is there a unity to style? in M. Conkey and C. Hastorf (eds.), *The uses of style in archaeology*, pp. 105–112. Cambridge, Cambridge University Press.

Wobst, H. M. 1977. Stylistic behavior and information exchange. In Charles E. Cleland (ed.), *For the Director: Research essays in honor of James B. Griffin*, Museum of Anthropology Anthropological Paper 61, pp. 317–342. Ann Arbor, Museum of Anthropology, University of Michigan.

Wrigley, G. M. 1919. Fairs of the Central Andes, *Geographical Review*, 7: 65–80.

Zaslow, Bert. 1977. A guide to analyzing prehistoric ceramic decorations by symmetry and pattern mathematics. In G. A. Clark (ed.), *Pattern mathematics and archaeology*, Arizona State University Anthropological Research Papers, no. 2.

Zaslow, Bert and Alfred E. Dittert, Jr. 1977. The pattern technology of the Hohokam, in G. A. Clark (ed.), *Pattern mathematics and archaeology*, Arizona State University Anthropological Research Papers, no. 2.

Zuidema, R. T. 1966. Algunos problemas etnohistóricos del Departamento de Ayacucho, *Wamani: Organo de la Asociación Peruana de Antropólogos. Filial-Ayacucho*, 1: 68–75.

   1967. El origen del Imperio Inca, *Universidad*, Año 3, no. III, Ayacucho, Peru, Universidad de San Cristóbal de Huamanga.

Zuidema, R. T. and U. Quispe. 1968. A visit to god, *Bijdragen*, 124: 22–39.

INDEX